Water for
Western Agriculture

Water for Western Agriculture

Kenneth D. Frederick
with James C. Hanson

RESOURCES FOR THE FUTURE / WASHINGTON, D.C.

Resources for the Future is a nonprofit organization for research and education in the development, conservation, and use of natural resources and on the quality of the environment. It was established in 1952 with the cooperation of the Ford Foundation. Grants for research are accepted from government and private sources only on the condition that RFF shall be solely responsible for the conduct of the research and free to make its results available to the public. Most of the work of Resources for the Future is carried out by its resident staff; part is supported by grants to universities and other nonprofit organizations. Unless otherwise stated, interpretations and conclusions in RFF publications are those of the authors; the organization takes responsibility for the selection of significant subjects for study, the competence of the researchers, and their freedom of inquiry.

Research Papers are studies and conference reports published by Resources for the Future from the authors' typescripts. The accuracy of the material is the responsibility of the authors and the material is not given the usual editorial review by RFF. The Research Paper series is intended to provide inexpensive and prompt distribution of research that is likely to have a shorter shelf life or to reach a smaller audience than RFF books.

CONTENTS

Tables

vii

viii

Figures

x

PREFACE

Agricultural development has been one of the United States' great economic success stories since World War II. Total crop production has increased markedly even though there has been little change in total cropland use and a sharp decline in farm labor. This performance reflects the impressive gains achieved in total farm productivity. If we could be certain agricultural productivity would continue to rise at an average annual rate of nearly 1.9 percent, there would be little cause for concern as to the nation's ability to meet future crop needs without sharp price increases. Furthermore, continued productivity growth would make the environmental impacts of agricultural expansion more manageable. While rapid productivity increases do not necessarily reduce environmental pressures--indeed, the inputs associated with the new technologies may generate additional pressures--they do increase the options for dealing with these problems.

Unfortunately, the performance of the agricultural sector since the early 1970s has raised concern that past productivity trends will not continue and that meeting future demands for food and fiber will result in higher economic and environmental costs per unit. The annual rates of increase for productivity and yield from 1971 to 1977 were less than one-half the respective rates achieved over the prior twenty-one years. Other sources of concern include rising energy and fertilizer prices; mounting evidence that additions to the cropland base will be less productive, more erodable, or more expensive to develop than the lands previously used; increasing water costs; and a growing belief that the major yield gains from the technologies that have revolutionized U.S. agriculture in recent decades have been achieved.

To improve our understanding of these factors, Resources for the Future (RFF) undertook a research program to study the resource and environmental issues associated with expanding agricultural production in the United States. This research effort includes assessing (1) the quantities of land, water, fertilizers, and pesticides U.S. farmers would demand in response to high demand projections; (2) the economic and environmental costs of mobilizing resources on this scale; (3) the

xi

past and future role of irrigation, taking into account the impacts of rising water costs as well as the technologies available for adapting to higher costs; (4) the costs, productivity, and environmental consequences of alternative tillage, pest management and fertilizer technologies; (5) the social and economic obstacles to the adoption of environmentally beneficial technologies; and (6) the alternative policies and institutions appropriate for minimizing the combined economic and environmental costs of agricultural production.

The following study of irrigation in the West is one of three studies, which comprise the third part of this overall research program. The other two irrigation studies focus on different geographical areas of the country. A paper by James Hanson and James Pagano, "Growth and Prospects for Irrigation in the Eastern United States," describes the past growth of irrigation in the thirty-one eastern states and assesses the prospects for increased irrigation in two farm production regions, the Lake States and the Southeast. A study by Robert N. Shulstad, Ralph D. May, Billy E. Herrington, and Jon M. Erstine, "The Economic Potential for the Expansion of Irrigation in the Mississippi Delta Region" employs a cost-benefit analysis to determine the potential for irrigation in the Mississippi Delta region. This latter study was done at the University of Arkansas with financial support from Resources for the Future. These irrigation studies are included in "Summary of Trends in U.S. Irrigation: Three Regional Studies" (EPA Report, June 1981), a project directed by Pierre Crosson.

The study by Pierre Crosson and Sterling Brubaker, "Resource and Environmental Impacts of Trends in Agriculture in the United States," culminates several years of research on the overall resource and environmental issues associated with expanding U.S. agriculture. This capstone study will be published as an RFF Research Paper in 1982.

Kenneth D. Frederick, Director
Renewable Resources Division
Resources for the Future

Washington, D.C.
March 1982

ACKNOWLEDGMENTS

RFF's program of research on resource and environmental factors in agricultural expansion has been supported by the Environmental Protection Agency's Environmental Research Laboratory in Athens, Georgia (George W. Bailey, project officer), the Rockefeller Foundation, the Ford Foundation, and RFF's internal funds. The study of western irrigation is one of several products of that program, and I wish to thank all these institutions for their support.

Many people generously took the time to respond to questions and provide essential research materials. Particularly useful contributions were made by Kenneth Turner and Warren Cole of the Department of Water Resources, State of California; David Aikens, Leon Axthelm, Bruce Johnson, and Raymond Supalla of the University of Nebraska; William Reedy and Bernie Silverman of the Bureau of Reclamation; Jan van Schilfgaarde of the U.S. Salinity Laboratory; and Herbert Grubb of the Texas Water Development Board.

A workshop designed to solicit comments on the research was held in Denver, Colorado, in February 1980. Participants were George Bailey and Arthur Hornsby of the Environmental Protection Agency, Pierre Crosson and James Hanson of Resources for the Future, Ralph May and Robert Shulstad of the University of Arkansas, Gaylord Skogerboe and Robert Young of Colorado State University, Jan van Schilfgaarde of the U.S. Salinity Laboratory, William Martin of the University of Arizona, Gerald Horner of the U.S. Department of Agriculture, Donald Nielsen of the University of California at Davis, Charles Wendt of the Texas Agricultural Experiment Station at Lubbock, and Norman Whittlesey of Washington State University.

Helpful comments on earlier drafts of this manuscript were received from Emery Castle, Pierre Crosson, Jo Hinkel, and Herbert Morton of RFF; Harry Ayer, John Hostetler, and Gordon Sloggett of the Economic

Research Service of the U.S. Department of Agriculture; George Bailey of the Environmental Protection Agency; Gerald Meral of the Department of Water Resources, State of California; and several anonymous reviewers. In addition, Jan van Schilfgaarde commented on chapter 6 and Raymond Didericksen of the Soil Conservation Service commented on appendix 2A.

I am particularly indebted to James Hanson, whose contribution is acknowledged on the title page. Jim helped collect, organize, and analyze much of the data and source materials, and he wrote early drafts of large parts of chapters 4 and 5. His contribution to the project has been a major one. Hanson has not been involved directly with the project since he took a teaching position at the University of Maryland in September 1980, and because there have been major revisions in all components of the study since his departure, it would be inappropriate to hold him responsible for any remaining errors.

James Pagano, who served as research assistant for this study, also merits special thanks. In addition to bringing great diligence and patience to performing some of the more tedious tasks associated with the project, he contributed many useful ideas and insights, especially to chapter 5. Maybelle Frashure has patiently and ably typed the numerous drafts of this manuscript.

RFF's research on resource and environmental factors in agricultural expansion has been supported by the Environmental Protection Agency's Environmental Research Laboratory in Athens, Georgia (George W. Bailey, project officer), the Rockefeller Foundation, the Ford Foundation, and RFF internal funds. This study of western irrigation is one of several products of that support.

K.D.F.

Chapter 1

INTRODUCTION

Irrigation has been an important factor in the impressive performance of U.S. agriculture in recent decades. Irrigated acreage
tripled from 1940 to 1977 and doubled from 1950 to 1977, periods of
great increases in agricultural productivity but virtually no change in
total cropland use. Average yields are greater on irrigated than on
nonirrigated farms, and within the arid and semiarid areas technological change has been higher on irrigated farms.[1] Thus, while
irrigated land currently accounts for only one-seventh of the nation's
cropland, it accounts for more than one-fourth of the value of the
nation's crops.[2]

Western Irrigation in Transition

Since rainfall in much of the West is either insufficient or too
unreliable to support a highly productive agriculture, irrigation is
more important to agriculture in the West than it is in the rest of the
country. About 83 percent of the nation's irrigated acreage is in the
seventeen western states, where irrigation accounts for nearly one-
fourth of the cropland and more than one-half of the crop value. The

---

1. Economic Research Service, U.S. Department of Agriculture, Measuring
the Effect of Irrigation on the Rate of Technological Change, Agricultural Economic Report no. 125, November 1967, p. iv.

2. Data differentiating between the value of production on irrigated
and nonirrigated lands are not available for 1977. Dallas Lea, using a
combination of data from the 1969 Census of Agriculture and 1971-73
estimates of the Statistical Reporting Service, estimated that 27
percent of the value of U.S. crop production was produced on irrigated
lands. (See Lea, "Irrigated Agriculture: Past Trends, Present State,
and Problems of Future Expansion," second review draft, August 1977,
table 2.) Lea is with the Economic Research Service of the U.S.
Department of Agriculture.

future course of western irrigation is the subject of some doubt, however, since it is in a state of transition stemming largely from
changes in the availability and cost of water. These changes in water
supply conditions are altering the pace and nature of irrigation
investments, and the resulting changes in the growth of western irrigation could have important implications for the overall performance of
U.S. agriculture. Accordingly, this study focuses on these seventeen
states: Arizona, California, Colorado, Idaho, Kansas, Montana,
Nebraska, Nevada, New Mexico, North Dakota, Oklahoma, Oregon, South
Dakota, Texas, Utah, Washington, and Wyoming.

The availability of relatively inexpensive water spurred the
growth of irrigated agriculture in the West. Water was initially
treated as a free good; the original users not only were allowed to use
the water without charge but were granted the rights to use similar
quantities in perpetuity. The only costs to the users were those
associated with capturing and transporting water from its source to
point of use. Until recently low energy prices helped keep down the
costs of transporting water, and farmers accounting for about one-
fifth of the West's irrigated acreage continue to benefit from large
federal subsidies on irrigation projects.

Even though the last several decades have provided evidence of
water's increasing scarcity and value in much of the West, water
continues to be treated essentially as a free good. In the absence of
market allocations, current demands on western surface waters commonly
exceed available supplies. Indeed, in at least one important case, the
rights that have been granted for use of western waters exceed the
long-term expected supply. Furthermore, extensive groundwater mining
(that is, withdrawing groundwater faster than it is replenished) has
placed current users in conflict with potential future users. In many
areas these "future" impacts already are being felt by farmers.

Western water use and development have become issues of growing
national concern and debate--often pitting one region of the country
against another, or western farmers, conservationists, and developers
against each other. Development of western energy resources, expansion
of western urban and rural areas, preservation of the West's natural
resources, continuation of federal subsidies for western water develop-

ment, Indian water rights, as well as the role of western irrigation in U.S. agriculture, are at issue in the resolution of these conflicts.

Irrigation is the activity most acutely affected by the rising cost of water in the West. Agriculture, which accounts for about 88 percent of western water consumption, is not only the largest but also the marginal user of western water. That is, irrigators would be least able to compete for scarce supplies if water were allocated through a market mechanism. The prospect of sharply higher water costs not only threatens expansion but also endangers the viability of many current irrigators.

On the other hand, the forces affecting the role of irrigated agriculture in the West are not all negative. Developments which will tend to counter the impact of rising water costs include more efficient irrigation systems, new crop varieties requiring less water, and improved knowledge of the relation between plant growth and water stress. Such developments will enable less water to be applied with little or no decline in yields. Furthermore, most water is not allocated through markets, and farmers who have been irrigating with surface water enjoy a very favorable position in the future allocation of western surface waters. Irrigators possess most of the senior rights to these waters, many are insulated from the pressures pushing up water costs, and in most states a myriad of laws and institutions make it difficult to transfer these rights to nonagricultural uses.

The transition under way in the factors affecting western irrigation clearly will have major impacts on western development. Also it seems likely that the performance of western irrigated agriculture will have significant implications for the nation's ability to meet future demands for food and fiber. But on this latter point there is considerable uncertainty stemming from widely differing views as to both irrigation's importance to the nation's agriculture and the impacts of the transition on western irrigation. This study is an attempt to narrow these sources of uncertainty.

Less may be known about the impact of irrigation on the overall performance of U.S. agriculture than is known about the impact of any of the other principal inputs. Studies and models taking an overall view of U.S. agriculture either ignore differences between irrigated and dryland production or make limited analyses of past, current, and future impacts of irrigation.[3] On the other hand, there is no lack of detailed micro-oriented studies examining irrigation and the forces affecting its growth. But taken alone these studies also are of limited use for analyzing the overall role of irrigation on U.S. agriculture since they focus on farms or localities.

There is a wide divergence of views on irrigation's importance to U.S. agriculture and the implications of a major reduction in irrigated acreage. On one extreme, research done at Iowa State University in the 1970s downplays the importance of irrigation. For example, projections to the year 2000 suggest that if "allowed to be distributed in terms of competitive conditions and interregional comparative advantage (no supply control), the nation's domestic and export food demands could be met more economically by using less water in agriculture and by a wide redistribution of crop acreage."[4]

Not surprisingly, this view is not shared by many, especially,

---

3. For example, consider the shortcomings of the two principal models of U.S. agriculture from the perspective of analyzing the role of irrigation. Irrigation was not a principal concern in developing the National-Interregional Agricultural Projections (NIRAP) system although the model does provide estimates of irrigated crop production. Its insights into the role of irrigation are limited by reliance on data grossly understating recent irrigation and by the absence of any analysis of the factors likely to affect future levels. The other major model, developed at Iowa State University, is designed to analyze least-cost methods of producing alternative levels of output. Both current and future levels of irrigation projected by the model are well below recent actual levels. There is some controversy as to whether these results indicate that irrigation has been inappropriately handled in the model or that many irrigators are high-cost producers who would be eliminated under any socially efficient allocation of farm re-sources. But in either case, the model does not provide a good means for analyzing current or future irrigation levels. (Chapter 7 examines in more detail the limitations of these models for analyzing irriga-tion. The discussion of these models indicates their shortcomings as tools for fulfilling the objectives of this study; the comments should not be interpreted as general criticisms of the modeling efforts which have different objectives than those of this study.)

4. Earl O. Heady, "U.S. Supply Situation for Food and Fiber and the Role of Irrigated Agriculture," paper presented at Texas A&M Conference, March 25-26, 1976, College Station, Texas.

those whose livelihood depends on the output of irrigated lands. For instance, great national and global benefits in the form of abundant and cheap food and fiber have been attributed to the spread of irrigation within the High Plains; dire warnings have been raised as to the consequences of allowing that area to revert to dryland farming.[5] Self-interest undoubtedly underlies some of the concern for the national implications of having irrigated acreage decline in areas where groundwater stocks are being depleted. But the disparity of views persists in part because of the inconsistency among the data describing the extent of irrigation, the lack of reliable data describing the impact of irrigation on yields and production, and the absence of analysis differentiating between the roles of irrigated and dryland farming.

Plan of the Book

This study, as indicated above, examines the importance of western irrigation to U.S. agriculture and the impacts of the changing water supply situation on the development of western irrigation. Past trends, water supply conditions, water institutions, economic forces, technological alternatives, and environmental factors are examined for their impacts on the course of western irrigation over the next two to three decades. The influence of these institutions and economic forces on resource use and the environment also are considered along with the broad policy implications of the analysis.

The analysis is primarily a synthesis of work done elsewhere, supplemented and updated by interviews with agricultural and water experts in the West. But original research was undertaken when the literature was inadequate for the purposes of this study. This approach in part was necessitated by the broad scope of the research and the limited resources available to it. But, in the author's judgment, a synthesis

---

5. For example, see A. L. Black, "High Plains Ogallala Study" in Frank C. Baird, editor, The Multi-Faceted Water Crisis of West Texas, Proceedings of a symposium held November 8-9, 1978, Lubbock, Texas (Texas Tech University, n.d.) p. 147.

also offers the most promising way of assessing the role of irrigation and its future course. Although no effort has been made to generate original data, major inconsistencies among the various sources of irrigation data have been identified and analyzed. This examination involved both a comparison of alternative sources as well as an investigation of the methods used to collect the data.

By focusing on the overall role of western irrigation, variations among and within different regions often are obscured. Countless factors--such as soil type; the cost, availability, and quality of water; the availability and cost of energy; climate; and management capability--are crucial determinants of what crops are grown, what irrigation techniques are used, and what physical and monetary returns are achieved. While the impacts of many of these factors on irrigation are examined, there is nothing in the analysis to suggest how an individual farmer will fare or how the combination of these factors determine the potential of irrigation in a region. On the other hand, an effort is made to isolate and analyze the principal factors affecting the overall level and nature of western irrigation. And for some purposes the analysis is regionalized to farm production regions or more homogeneous irrigation areas. But no systematic attempt has been made to describe either the conditions affecting irrigation in any one region or the full range of conditions affecting western irrigation.

Each of the next five chapters analyzes in some detail one of the principal factors affecting the growth and performance of irrigated agriculture in the West. Chapter 2 examines the current role of western irrigation--that is, the acreage irrigated and its location, the crops grown, the yields, and the importance of this acreage to the national production of major crops--and how it has been achieved. Past trends and the changes in those trends, as well as the impacts of irrigation on past changes in the production and yields of corn, sorghum, wheat, and cotton are analyzed. As noted above, determining current and past levels of irrigation proved to be much more difficult than had been anticipated, and it was necessary to analyze the data sources. A detailed discussion of the data can be found in appendix 2-A at the end of chapter 2.

Chapter 3 considers the supply and demand for western water. The sources of water for the past expansion of irrigation, the adequacy of ground and surface water supplies for maintaining and expanding irrigation, the growing competition for western water, and the possibilities for augmenting supplies all are considered.

Chapter 4 looks at the institutions including the laws and water organizations affecting the allocation of western water. Institutional constraints on transferring water among alternative uses and impacts on farmer's incentives to use water efficiently are examined.

Chapter 5 examines the impacts of rising energy costs and water scarcity on the profitability of irrigation under a variety of circumstances. The possibilities for reducing water costs through alternative irrigation technologies and water management practices and the impacts of higher water and energy costs and alternative crop prices on the relative profitability of irrigated and dryland farming in the semiarid West are assessed.

Chapter 6 focuses on the environmental impacts of irrigated agriculture. First, the nature and extent of the environmental impacts are described and then alternative ways to manage these problems, federal efforts to control irrigation runoff, and several other approaches to managing the environmental impacts of irrigation are examined.

Chapter 7 summarizes the principal conclusions of the previous five chapters. This summary is followed by an evaluation of projections of irrigated acreage which have been made as parts of several major water or agricultural studies. Then drawing on the prior analysis, alternative projections of irrigated acreage and anticipated changes in the nature of irrigated agriculture are presented. Finally, policy implications of the overall study are considered.

Chapter 2

THE ROLE OF IRRIGATION

Current Irrigation Levels

By 1977 irrigation extended to over 60 million acres in the United States and accounted for nearly 14 percent of the nation's total cropland use and 11 percent of combined cropland and pasture use (see table 2-1). More than 50 million of these irrigated acres were in the seventeen western states, where 23 percent of the cropland use and 20 percent of the combined cropland and pasture use was irrigated. Within the West, dependence on irrigation was highest in the more arid areas. In the Pacific and Mountain regions, for example, irrigation accounted for 51 and 36 percent, respectively, of cropland use. In the Southern and Northern Plains, which have extensive areas favorable for dryland agriculture, only 20 and 11 percent of the respective cropland was irrigated.[1]

Table 2-2 indicates the irrigated and dryland acreage planted to five crop categories within each of the western farm production regions.[2] One-half of the 46.4 million irrigated cropland acres in the West were in row crops, principally corn, sorghum, and cotton. Close-grown crops, primarily wheat and other small grains, accounted for 20 percent, various forms of hay and pasture for 9 percent, and orchards, vineyards, and bush fruit for 5 percent of the irrigated cropland. Yet, irrigated exceeded dryland acreage only for the category of orchards, vineyards, and bush fruit. Only 41 percent of

---

1. The U.S. Department of Agriculture's farm production regions are identified in the notes to table 2-1.

2. Total irrigated acreage is the sum of irrigated cropland, which includes rotation hay and pasture, and irrigated pasture.

Table 2-1. Irrigated and Dryland Agricultural Land Use by Farm Production Region, 1977

(millions of acres)

Farm production region[a]	Irrigated land			Dryland			Total		
	Cropland	Pasture	Total	Cropland	Pasture	Total	Cropland	Pasture	Total
Northern Plains	10.6	0.1	10.7	83.9	9.4	93.3	94.6	9.5	104.1
Southern Plains	8.6	0.4	9.0	33.6	27.1	60.7	42.2	27.5	69.7
Mountain	15.2	2.0	17.2	27.1	5.5	32.6	42.2	7.4	49.6
Pacific	11.9	1.4	13.3	11.2	2.8	14.0	23.2	4.1	27.3
Total: 17 Western states	46.4	3.9	50.2	155.8	44.7	200.5	202.2	48.5	250.7
Northeast	0.4	0	0.4	16.5	5.8	22.3	16.9	5.8	22.7
Appalachian	0.4	0	0.4	20.4	18.5	38.9	20.8	18.5	39.3
Corn Belt	1.1	0	1.1	88.8	25.2	114.0	89.9	25.2	115.1
Lake States	1.0	0	1.0	43.2	6.9	50.1	44.1	6.9	51.0
Southeast	2.4	1.0	3.4	15.1	13.1	28.2	17.5	14.1	31.6
Delta States	4.0	0.1	4.1	17.2	12.6	29.8	21.2	12.7	33.9
Total: 31 Eastern states	9.3	1.1	10.4	201.2	82.1	283.3	210.4	83.2	293.6
National total	55.7	5.0	60.7	357.2	127.8	486.1	412.9	132.7	546.9

Note: Minor differences in totals are due to rounding.

Source: U.S. Department of Agriculture, Soil Conservation Service, "Basic Statistics: 1977 National Resources Inventory (NRI)," Revised February 1980, tables 3a, 4a.

[a]These are the U.S. Department of Agriculture's farm production regions. The four western regions are defined as follows: Northern Plains includes Kansas, Nebraska, North Dakota, and South Dakota; Southern Plains includes Texas and Oklahoma; Mountain includes Arizona, Colorado, Idaho, Montana, Nevada, New Mexico, Utah, and Wyoming; Pacific includes California, Oregon, and Washington. The six eastern regions are: Northeast includes Maine, New Hampshire, Vermont, Massachusetts, Rhode Island, Connecticut, New York, New Jersey, Pennsylvania, Delaware, and Maryland; Appalachian includes Virginia, West Virginia, North Carolina, Kentucky, and Tennessee; Corn Belt includes Ohio, Indiana, Illinois, Iowa, and Missouri; Lake States includes Michigan, Wisconsin, and Minnesota; Southeast includes South Carolina, Georgia, Alabama, and Florida; Delta States includes Mississippi, Louisiana, and Arkansas.

Table 2-2. Western Irrigated and Dryland Cropland Use by Crop Group and Farm Production Region, 1977

(thousands of acres)

Region and cropland type	Row crops	Close-grown crops	Rotation hay and pasture	Native hay and occasionally improved hay	Orchards, vine-yards and bush fruit	Total cropland
Northern Plains						
Irrigated	8,651	925	692	362	0	10,630
Dryland	18,059	40,013	5,387	6,375	15	83,944
Total	26,710	40,938	6,079	6,737	15	94,574
Southern Plains						
Irrigated	5,936	2,352	33	286	32	8,639
Dryland	13,906	15,784	802	1,127	152	33,583
Total	19,842	18,136	835	1,413	184	42,222
Mountain						
Irrigated	4,114	3,313	2,300	5,287	147	15,161
Dryland	964	14,026	383	1,595	0	27,063
Total	5,078	17,339	2,683	6,882	147	42,224
Pacific						
Irrigated	4,467	2,750	1,120	1,358	2,239	11,934
Dryland	134	5,558	499	506	184	11,238
Total	4,601	8,308	1,619	1,864	2,423	23,172
Western States						
Irrigated	23,168	9,340	4,145	7,293	2,418	46,364
Dryland	33,063	75,381	7,071	9,603	351	155,828
Total	56,231	84,721	11,216	16,896	2,769	202,192

Source: U.S. Department of Agriculture, Soil Conservation Service, "Basic Statistics: 1977 National Resources Inventory (NRI)," Revised February 1980, table 3.

the row crops, 11 percent of the close grown crops, and 41 percent of the various forms of hay and cropland pasture were irrigated.

There were large variations in the relative importance of the crop groups among the farm production regions. Row crops occupied more than 80 percent of the irrigated cropland in the Northern Plains, 69 percent in the Southern Plains, and between 27 and 37 percent in the other two regions. Hay and pasture occupied 50 percent of the irrigated cropland in the Mountain region and 21 percent in the Pacific region but were relatively unimportant in the other two regions. Orchards, vineyards, and bush fruit were important only in the Pacific region where they accounted for 19 percent of irrigated cropland.

Data Problems

The role attributed to irrigation in U.S. agriculture varies depending on the data sources utilized. For example, the 1974 Census of Agriculture shows only 41.2 million irrigated acres in the fifty states, including 36.6 million in the seventeen western states. In contrast, the 1977 National Resources Inventory (NRI) estimates irrigated acreage at 60.7 million in the fifty states, including 50.2 million in the seventeen western states. As explained in appendix 2-A neither definitional differences nor the three years separating the census and the NRI can explain away all or even most of these differences. Yet, the agricultural censuses and the NRI (which is the latest in the series of inventories prepared by the Soil Conservation Service (SCS) are the two principal sources of primary data providing estimates of irrigated acreage in every state. In view of these problems, a detailed analysis of the irrigation data was necessary before we could attempt to describe current and historic irrigation levels. The appendix presents the analysis of the data; this section summarizes the conclusions of that analysis and indicates how the data are used in this study.

Principal conclusions of the examination of the census, NRI, and other sources of irrigation data included in appendix 2-A of this study are that (1) the 1974 and 1969 agricultural censuses grossly understate the level of irrigation; and (2) the statistical techniques combined with the reliance on trained personnel to gather and independently verify the data suggest that 1977 NRI and 1967 Conservation Needs Inventory (CNI) estimates, especially on the national and regional levels, are the most reliable irrigation data available for all states. Comparisons of these primary data sources with independently gathered irrigation data available for a few states support these conclusions.

Unfortunately, there are some major shortcomings with the SCS survey data for assessing current levels of, and past changes in, irrigation. The surveys were designed for identifying cropping patterns with soil types and related conservation problems; irrigation was not a primary concern. Since irrigated acreage is defined in the 1977 NRI survey to include lands where water is supplied as part of a cropping system as well as the acreage actually irrigated, the estimates overstate acreage irrigated in the survey years. For example, the 1977 NRI survey includes lands irrigated in the survey year or in two of the previous four years. The resulting overestimation probably is not large in the western states, and in view of the alternatives, this shortcoming was not important enough to alter the conclusion that the NRI data offer the most reliable source of recent western irrigation levels. But the usefulness of the SCS irrigation estimates also is limited by data for only two years (1967 and 1977) and the absence of data by crop or for regions divided along non-state boundaries. The only crop disaggregation available in the NRI data are for groups such as row or close-grown crops, and in view of the sampling techniques employed, these data are more reliable when aggregated by farm production region than they are at the state level.

In view of the data deficiencies, estimates from a number of sources have been used to analyze current and historic irrigation levels. The 1977 NRI data are used to examine recent irrigated acreage by state and farm production region. Where greater regional detail or data for individual crops or longer time periods are required, SCS survey data are supplemented with data from the agricultural censuses, state surveys, or other sources. In such cases the biases introduced by use of the various data sources and the manipulations made upon them are examined.

Past Growth of Irrigated Acreage

From 1967 to 1977

Western irrigation expanded by nearly 9 million acres, or 21 percent, from 1967 to 1977, according to SCS survey data (see table 2-3).
Nearly two-thirds of the expansion was in the Northern Plains where
irrigation more than doubled over the decade. The expansion was
concentrated in Nebraska (up 3.7 million acres) and Kansas (up 1.6
million acres) which together accounted for 61 percent of the total
increase in western irrigation.

Irrigation in the rest of the West grew only 0.9 percent annually
over this decade. In the Southern Plains and Mountain regions, which
combined accounted for 60 percent of western irrigation in 1967, irrigated acreage rose only 4 percent over the decade. Growth in the Pacific region was close to the average rate for the West, but underlying
the 21 percent regional increase was a 39 percent rise for Washington
and Oregon combined and only a 9 percent rise in California. Thus, the
Northern Plains and the Pacific Northwest, which together accounted for
less than 20 percent of 1967 western irrigation, contributed 79 percent
of the growth during the subsequent decade.

The expansion of western irrigation is particularly striking when
contrasted with the change in nonirrigated cropland (see table 2-4).
The decline in dryland acreage exceeded the rise in irrigated cropland
from 1967 to 1977 in each of the western farm production regions. For
the West as a whole, total cropland use declined 4.5 percent or nearly
9.5 million acres over the decade. As a result of these trends, the
proportion of cropland under irrigation rose significantly in all four
of the West's farm production regions, even in the Southern Plains
which experienced a slight decline in irrigated acreage. For the
seventeen western states as a whole, irrigated cropland rose from 18 to
23 percent of total cropland.

From 1945 to 1974

A longer-term view of the expansion of irrigation using agricultural census data is presented in table 2-5. These data indicate a

Table 2-3. Irrigated 1967 Acreage and the Growth of Irrigated Acreage
from 1967 to 1977, by Farm Production Region

Region	Acres irrigated in 1967 (thousands)	Change in acres irrigated, 1967–77 (thousands)	(percentages)	Regional increase in irrigation as a percentage of the increase in the West, 1967–77
Northern Plains	5,088	5,665	111	65
Southern Plains	9,138	- 99	- 1	- 1
Mountain	15,916	1,200	8	14
Pacific	11,346	1,982	17	23
17 Western states	41,488	8,748	21	100

Source: Calculated from data in U.S. Department of Agriculture, Soil Conservation Service, "Basic Statistics: 1977 National Resources Inventory (NRI)," Revised February 1980; and U.S. Department of Agriculture, Basic Statistics – National Inventory of Soil and Water Conservation Needs, 1967, Statistical Bulletin no. 461 (Washington, D.C., GPO, January 1971).

Table 2-4. Comparison of Changes in Irrigated and Nonirrigated Cropland
Use by Farm Production Region from 1967 to 1977

Region	Changes between use 1967–77 (millions of acres)		Irrigated cropland as a percentage of total cropland	
	Irrigated	Dryland	1967	1977
Northern Plains	5.5	-6.7	5	11
Southern Plains	-0.2	-6.2	18	20
Mountain	1.5	-1.9	32	36
Pacific	1.0	-2.5	44	51
Western states	7.9	-17.3	18	23

Sources: Calculated from data in U.S. Department of Agriculture, Soil Conservation Service, "Basic Statistics: 1977 National Resources Inventory (NRI)," Revised February 1980; and U.S. Department of Agriculture, Basic Statistics-National Inventory of Soil and Water Conservation Needs, 1967, Statistical Bulletin no. 461 (Washington, D.C., GPO, January 1971).

Table 2-5. Growth of Irrigated Acreage in the West, 1945-74

Year	Millions of acres irrigated	Change in acres irrigated (millions)	Change in acres irrigated (%)	Average annual growth of acres irrigated (%)
1945	19.4			
		4.8	25	4.5
1950	24.3			
		2.7	11	2.7
1954	27.0			
		3.9	14	2.7
1959	30.7			
		2.5	8	1.6
1964	33.2			
		1.6	5	0.9
1969	34.8			
		1.9	5	1.1
1974	36.6			

Note: The last three columns indicate the changes between 1945-50, 1950-54, 1954-59, and so forth. Minor inconsistencies are due to rounding.

Source: U.S. Bureau of the Census, Census of Agriculture, various years (Washington, D.C., GPO).

Table 2-6. Changes in Total Acres Irrigated by Farm Production Region

(thousands of acres)

Region	1945-54	1954-64	1964-74	1945-74
Northern Plains	827	1,723	2,846	5,396
Southern Plains	3,493	1,872	422	5,787
Mountain	506	1,602	-91	2,017
Pacific	2,715	1,041	262	4,018
17 Western states	7,541	6,238	3,439	17,218

Source: U.S. Bureau of the Census, Census of Agriculture, various years (Washington, D.C., GPO).

nearly continuous decline in both the annual rate of growth as well as the absolute growth in the number of acres irrigated in the West from 1945 to 1974. For example, the 4.5 percent annual growth of irrigated acreage and the average annual addition of nearly 1 million irrigated acres achieved from 1945 to 1950 were considerably higher than the growth achieved in any subsequent period. In contrast, irrigation grew only 1.1 percent annually for an average of less than 400,000 acres per year from 1969 to 1974, according to census data.

While the rate of growth of irrigated acreage has declined from the rates achieved from 1945 to 1959, the changes implied by the 1967 CNI data and the 1977 NRI data raise questions as to whether the average change in the number of irrigated acres has declined. As noted earlier, the SCS sources show an 8.7 million acre increase or nearly a 2 percent annual growth rate over the ten years in the seventeen western states compared to the 3.4 million acre ten-year expansion implied by the 1964 and 1974 agricultural censuses. For reasons noted above and in appendix 2-A, the higher increase is probably much closer to actual growth.

Irrigation changes from 1945 to 1974 for the various farm production regions are indicated in table 2-6. Over the entire twenty-nine year period, the census data show the Northern and Southern Plains each accounting for about one-third of the overall increase in western irrigation. Although more than half of all the acres irrigated were in the Mountain region in 1945, these states contributed only 12 percent of the West's growth. The remaining 23 percent of the growth was in the Pacific region.

The centers of growth in irrigation have changed markedly over time. From 1945-54 growth was concentrated in the Southern Plains and Pacific regions. Indeed, Texas alone accounted for 45 percent and California for 28 percent of the total growth in irrigation over this period. In contrast, these two states accounted for only 4 and 6 percent respectively of the growth from 1964 to 1974.

In terms of additions to irrigated acres, growth during the 1954-64 decade was more evenly distributed among the four production regions than in other periods. No region accounted for more than 30 percent or less than 17 percent of the growth of western irrigation.

Variations in annual growth rates, however, ranged from 1.1 percent in
the Pacific to 7.5 percent in the Northern Plains, the only region
where irrigation grew at consistently high rates in each decade.
Starting from a low base in 1945 (only 4 percent of western irrigation), the Northern Plains contribution to the growth of irrigation has
increased markedly, and over the 1964-74 decade reached 83 percent
according to census data.

As noted earlier, the SCS survey data show significantly more
acreage irrigated than the census data in all production regions.
Furthermore, the SCS data indicate an increase of 8.7 million acres
irrigated in the West from 1967 to 1977 (see table 2-3) compared to the
3.4 million acre increase between the 1964 and 1974 censuses (see table
2-6). Among the farm production regions, the major difference implied
by these alternative sources is for the Mountain region. The census
data show irrigation in this region increasing at only 0.6 percent per
year from 1945 to 1974 and declining over the last decade of this
period. In contrast, the CNI and NRI show an increase of 1.2 million
irrigated acres in the Mountain region from 1967 to 1977. Nevertheless, both sources support the conclusion that in recent years the
Northern Plains has been the principal region for new irrigation in the
West.

Growth by Irrigation Region

Further insights into past trends and the potential for continued
growth of irrigated agriculture can be gained by focusing on areas
which are more homogeneous than the farm production regions. The West
would have to be divided into scores of regions to provide study areas
which are relatively homogeneous with regard to crops, soils, climate,
and water sources. Fortunately, such detail is not necessary for
achieving the objectives of this study. As a compromise, the West has
been divided into eight irrigation regions and three subregions
(identified both in the notes to table 2-7 and in the map included as
figure 2-1) which provide a better focus on different water supply
situations important for both past and future growth of irrigation.

Since these regions do not conform to state boundaries, county
level data available only in the agricultural censuses are required to

Table 2-7. Growth of Irrigation by Irrigation Region

Irrigation regions	Average annual growth rate of irrigated acres (percent per year)				Contribution to the growth of total irrigated acreage in the West (percent)			
	1945-54	1954-64	1964-74	1945-74	1945-54	1954-64	1964-74	1945-74
1. High Plains	20.0	5.2	2.9	8.7	39	38	58	42
Southern	25.0	3.1	-0.3	8.2	33	16	-3	19
Central	28.8	12.8	5.6	14.5	3	10	18	8
Northern	6.9	9.4	7.7	8.0	3	13	42	14
2. Eastern Oklahoma and Texas	8.0	1.9	0	3.1	12	6	0	8
3. Central Plains	7.4	6.5	6.0	6.6	7	16	51	19
4. Dakotas	6.0	3.5	2.1	3.8	1	1	1	1
5. Inter-Mountain	-0.1	1.4	-0.6	0.3	-1	22	-17	4
6. Southwest	3.1	0	0.1	1.0	6	0	0	2
7. California	4.0	0.8	0.2	1.6	28	9	4	16
8. Northwest	3.6	2.0	0.4	1.9	8	8	5	7
Western states	3.7	2.1	1.0	2.2	100	100	100	100

(Continued)

Table 2-7. (Continued)

Note:

Irrigation regions

1. High Plains

   Southern: Includes 33 Texas counties (Oldham, Potter, Carson, Gray, Wheeler, Deaf Smith, Randall, Armstrong, Donley, Parmer, Castro, Swisher, Briscoe, Bailey, Lamb, Hale, Floyd, Motley, Cochran, Hockley, Lubbock, Crosby, Yoakum, Terry, Lynn, Garza, Gaines, Dawson, Andrews, Martin, Howard, Midland, and Glasscock).

   Central: Includes 10 Texas counties (Dallam, Sherman, Hansford, Ochiltree, Lipscomb, Hartly, Moore, Hutchinson, Roberts, and Hemphill); 6 Oklahoma counties (Cimarron, Texas, Beaver, Harper, Ellis, and Woodward); 6 New Mexico counties (Lea, Roosevelt, Curry, Quay, Union, and Harding.)

   Northern: Includes 34 Kansas counties (Morton, Stevens, Seward, Meade, Clark, Stanton, Grant, Haskell, Gray, Ford, Hamilton, Kearny, Finney, Greeley, Wichita, Scott, Lane, Wallace, Logan, Gove, Trego, Sherman, Thomas, Sheridan, Graham, Cheyenne, Rawlins, Decatur, Norton, Phillips, Kiowa, Hodgeman, Ness, and Rooks); 11 Colorado counties (Baca, Prowers, Kiowa, Cheyenne, Kit Carson, Yuma, Washington, Phillips, Logan, Sedgwick, and Lincoln); 9 Nebraska counties (Dundy, Chase, Perkins, Hayes, Hitchcock, Red Willow, Furnas, Frontier, and Harlan).

2. Eastern Oklahoma and Texas: Texas and Oklahoma excluding the High Plains.

3. Central Plains: Kansas and Nebraska excluding the High Plains.

4. Dakotas: North and South Dakota.

5. Inter-Mountain: Colorado excluding the High Plains, Idaho, Montana, Nevada, Utah, and Wyoming.

6. Southwest: Arizona and New Mexico excluding the High Plains.

7. California.

8. Northwest: Oregon and Washington.

Source: U.S. Bureau of the Census, Agricultural Census, various years (Washington, D.C., GPO).

Figure 2-1.

Map of Western Irrigation Regions and Subregions.

For detailed definition of boundaries, see note to table 2-7.

describe their irrigation. As noted earlier, shortcomings of the recent census data suggest that the growth rates and percentages shown in table 2-7 should be used cautiously. Specifically, there is reason to expect that the growth rates for the 1964-74 period are understated. For examining major changes in the growth and importance of irrigation in the designated irrigation districts, the census data are instructive. Very distinctive broad trends are apparent in the data, and it is unlikely that these have been distorted significantly by the problems with the census data.

A major consideration in making the regional divisions was to isolate the High Plains, an area covering parts of six states. There is no universally accepted definition of the High Plains. For our purposes, the High Plains region is defined as those parts of Colorado, Kansas, Nebraska, New Mexico, Oklahoma, and Texas which both overlie the Ogallala groundwater formation and fall south of the Platte River.[3] This definition, which excludes parts of Nebraska and the Dakotas commonly included in definitions of the High Plains, is adopted to focus on a region where groundwater is virtually the sole water source, the aquifer is isolated from surrounding formations, and natural recharge is relatively insignificant. Thus, it spotlights an important and extensive agricultural region where irrigation is resulting in large-scale mining of its water resources. The severity of the regional groundwater depletion is noted in the Second National Water Assessment, which lists groundwater overdrafts estimated at about 14 million acre-feet per year in the High Plains among the nation's most critical water problems.[4]

Additional reasons for according the High Plains special attention are suggested by the data in table 2-7, which indicate the average annual growth rates as well as the regional contribution to the overall

---

3. Since the census data are based on political and not hydrological boundaries, the area included does not conform exactly to our criteria. The counties included in our definition of the High Plains are listed in the note to table 2-7.

4. U.S. Water Resources Council, The Nation's Water Resources 1975-2000, Second National Water Assessment, 1978, vol. 1 (Washington, D.C., GPO, December 1978) p. 78.

expansion of western irrigation of the various irrigation regions for the 1945 to 1974 period and three subperiods. The High Plains accounted for more than four of every ten new acres irrigated in the West between 1945 and 1974, and by 1974 this region had 22 percent of the total land irrigated in the West. Although the rate of growth as well as the annual change in the number of acres irrigated has declined sharply in the High Plains, this region's percentage contribution to the growth of western irrigation rose from about 38 prior to 1964 to 58 from 1964 to 1974.

Since there have been marked changes in the growth of irrigation within the High Plains, the area is further divided into three subregions. Early growth was heavily concentrated in the southern High Plains (Texas, south of the Canadian River). More recently, census data suggest irrigated acreage in this subregion has declined slightly. While the average annual rate of growth in the central High Plains (west Texas north of the Canadian River, eastern New Mexico, and the Oklahoma Panhandle) has declined roughly in half every ten years since 1945, the change in acres irrigated within this subregion as well as its percentage contribution to the total growth of irrigation in the West increased. Since 1964, the most rapid growth of irrigation has been in the northern High Plains (western Kansas, eastern Colorado, and western Nebraska south of the Platte River) which accounted for 42 percent of the total growth of western irrigation from 1964 to 1974.

Overall, there has been a dramatic change in the growth centers of western irrigation. From 1945 to 1954, 79 percent of the growth of irrigated acreage was in a southern belt including eastern Oklahoma and Texas, the southern High Plains, the Southwest, and California. In subsequent decades the contribution of this southern region to the overall growth of irrigation declined to 31 percent and then 1 percent. In contrast, the Central Plains and northern High Plains combined contribution to the expansion of western irrigation rose from 10 percent in the 1945 to 1954 period, to 29 percent in the 1954 to 1964 period, and to 93 percent in the 1964 to 1974 period, according to census data.[5]

Cropping Patterns and Trends

Acreage changes, of course, are only one aspect of understanding irrigation's contribution to the overall performance of agriculture. Considered alone the acreage estimates reveal nothing about the impacts on yields, cropping patterns, and the land required to produce a given level of output. Thus, to proceed with the analysis of the role of irrigation requires data on the crop mix and the yields of irrigated and dryland farming.

The agricultural censuses are the only sources of comprehensive acreage data for individual crops which also differentiate between irrigated and dryland. Although the total acreages of at least the most recent censuses are understated, there is no reason to expect that the census data distort the relative acreage allocated to individual crops. To the contrary, 1969 and 1974 census estimates of the percentage of total irrigated land allocated to row and close-grown crops in each of the West's farm production regions are very close to percentages projected from 1967 CNI and 1977 NRI data.[6] Consequently,

---

5. The contribution of the Central Plains and northern High Plains to overall growth in the 1964-74 period probably is overstated by these numbers. According to census data, western irrigation outside the High and Central Plains declined between 1964 and 1974 because of a 600,000 acre decline in the Inter-Mountain region and only modest increases in other regions. The combination of the CNI and NRI data contradict the conclusion that irrigation has declined outside the Central and High Plains, but these data confirm the conclusions drawn from the census data as to where most of the expansion has occurred.

6. For example, estimates for 1974 of the percentage of irrigated land in the seventeen western states allocated to various crop groups are 45.3 in row and 17.4 in close-grown crops, according to the census, and 42.5 in row and 17.5 in close-grown crops, according to a projection which starts with the 1967 CNI and 1977 NRI data and assumes the acreage of each crop group grew linearly over the decade. Row crops include all corn, all sorghum, cotton, soybeans, other field crops, vegetables, and what the census lists as "other crops." Close-grown crops include wheat, other small grains, and field seed crops.

the subsequent examination of cropping patterns and trends relies on census data to determine the percentages of irrigated land devoted to individual crops or crop groups.

In 1974 the West's irrigated lands were allocated 42 percent to grains, 22 percent to hay, 10 percent each to pasture and cotton, and 9 percent to vegetables and orchards (see table 2-8). Corn, with 18 percent of all irrigated land, was the single most important crop in terms of acreage; wheat with 9 percent and sorghum with 7 percent were also important irrigated crops.

With the exception of grains, which increased, and pasture and minor crops (listed as "all other" in the tables), which declined, there was very little change in the relative area allocated to the major crop groups from 1950 to 1974. Grains increased their share of irrigated acreage by 20 percentage points over this period, and corn, which rose from 3 to 18 percent of the total, accounted for three-fourths of the grain increase. Wheat and sorghum acreage also rose as a percentage of the total while other small grains declined. The shift to grains was particularly rapid from 1964 to 1974 when their acreage rose from 27 to 42 percent of the total.

Two underlying trends have contributed to the rise in the proportion of irrigated grains in the West--a shift in the crop mix in favor of grains and the high concentration of grain acreage in the regions with the highest irrigation growth rates. For example, the High and Central Plains, which accounted for most of the net growth of irrigated acreage in recent years, have the highest percentages of irrigated land in grains (see table 2-9). In the case of corn, which rose from 6 to 18 percent of total irrigated land in the West between 1964 and 1974, 27 percent of this percentage increase was attributable to the faster overall growth of irrigation in the traditional corn-growing areas and 73 percent was due to a change in the crop mix within the designated irrigation regions and subregions.

Impacts of Irrigation on Production and
Yields of Corn, Sorghum, Wheat, and Cotton

Irrigation, with its higher than average yields and growth, clearly has become a more important factor in the production of many

Table 2-8. Irrigated Acreage by Crop Group in the Seventeen Western
States, 1950-74

(percentages of total acres irrigated in the West)

Crop	1950	1954	1959	1964	1969	1974
Grains: total	22	24	25	27	37	42
Corn[a]	3	3	6	6	12	18
Sorghum[a]	3	6	7	8	11	7
Wheat	4	3	4	5	6	9
Other small grains	12	12	8	8	9	8
Cotton	10	11	10	9	9	10
Vegetables and orchards	n.a.	n.a.	9	8	9	9
Hay	25	25	22	23	23	22
Pasture	16	n.a.	16[b]	16	12	10
All other	n.a.	n.a.	18	17	11	8

Note: Percentages may not add due to rounding. The 1950 to 1964 percentages are based on data for all farms, whereas the 1969 and 1974 percentages are for class 1-5 farms only.

Source: Calculated from U.S. Bureau of the Census, Census of Agriculture, various years (Washington, D.C., GPO).

[a]Corn and sorghum grown for all purposes.

[b]Includes cropland irrigated but not harvested.

Table 2-9. Irrigated Acreage by Crop in Western Irrigation Regions, 1974
(percentages of total acres irrigated in each region)

Irrigation region	Total	Grains[a]				Cotton	Vegetables and orchards	Hay	Pasture	All other
		Corn	Sorghum	Wheat	Other small grains					
1. High Plains	72	29	24	18	1	16	b	3	2	6
Southern	56	12	30	12	1	34	b	1	2	7
Central	90	16	35	38	1	1	b	2	3	3
Northern	86	60	10	16	b	b	b	7	2	5
2. Eastern Oklahoma and Texas	40	b	9	4	27	27	8	11	8	6
3. Central Plains	83	77	5	1	b	b	b	8	2	7
4. Dakotas	47	34	1	8	4	b	b	39	5	10
5. Inter Mountain	23	6	1	7	9	b	1	46	19	11
6. Southwest	26	2	8	11	5	33	10	23	7	1
7. California	24	5	2	5	13	15	30	16	9	6
8. Northwest	22	3	b	15	4	b	13	33	16	17
17. Western states	42	18	7	9	8	10	9	22	10	8

Note: Percentages may not add due to rounding.

Source: Calculated from U.S. Bureau of the Census, Census of Agriculture, 1974 (Washington, D.C.,
GPO, 1978).

[a] Includes corn and sorghum grown for all purposes.

b Less than 0.5 percent.

crops. In view of the data deficiencies and the problems involved in compensating for them, analysis of the impact of irrigation on land needs and yields is limited to the production of four principal crops-- corn, sorghum, wheat, and cotton. In 1974 these crops accounted for about 44 percent of the nation's irrigated cropland and 52 percent of all harvested cropland; the West accounted for about 96 percent of the irrigated acreage of these crops. The acreage and yield estimates for 1977 along with the implied production levels are presented in table 2-10. Appendix 2-B explains how the data differentiating between irri- gated and dryland crop production and yields were derived.

Irrigation provides higher yields than the dryland alternatives for all four crops; the differences are especially large for corn and cotton and in comparison to western dryland alternatives. In the more arid areas of the West, of course, there is no viable dryland alterna- tive for these crops. Based on trend crop yields in 1977, western irrigated yields exceeded the comparable dryland West and all East yields by the following percentages:

	Corn	Sorghum	Wheat	Cotton
Dryland West	139	70	45	135
East	30	26	3	37

There were sizable increases in the production and yields of all four crops from 1950 to 1977. Indeed, although the combined acreage harvested was virtually unchanged for these four crops, average yields and production rose about 122 percent.[7] This performance was notably superior to the 68 percent increase achieved in the yield index of all

7. The average yield increase is the weighted average of the change in trend yields where the weights are the mean of the 1950 and 1977 acreage harvested. The 1950 crop acreage data for the United States, the East, and the total West are from U.S. Department of Agriculture, Agricultural Statistics 1952 (Washington, D.C., GPO, 1952). The rela- tive breakdown between western irrigated and dryland acreage is based on the data in the U.S. Bureau of the Census, Census of Agriculture, 1950 (Washington, D.C., GPO).

Table 2-10. Irrigated and Dryland Acreage, Yields, and Production of
Corn, Sorghum, Wheat, and Cotton for 1977

Crop and area	Acreage harvested (1,000 acres)	Trend yields (bushels per acre)	Production[b] (millions of bushels)
Corn[a]			
Irrigated West	8,838	115.2	1,018
Dryland West	4,572	48.3	221
East	56,596	88.6	5,014
U.S. total	70,006	89.3	6,253
Sorghum[a]			
Irrigated West	1,847	77.4	143
Dryland West	10,774	45.5	490
East	1,444	61.4	89
U.S. total	14,065	51.3	722
Wheat			
Irrigated West	3,899	39.4	154
Dryland West	49,387	27.1	1,338
East	12,930	38.4	497
U.S. total	66,216	30.0	1,989
		(bales per acre)	(1,000 bales)
Cotton			
Irrigated West	3,868	1.41	5,454
Dryland West	5,212	0.60	3,127
East	4,199	1.03	4,325
U.S. total	13,279	0.97	12,906

Sources: The total acreage estimates for the West and United States
are from U.S. Department of Agriculture, Agricultural Statistics 1978,
(Washington, D.C., GPO, 1978). Derivation of the irrigated and dryland
acreages and the trend yields are explained in appendix 2-B.

[a]For grain only.

[b]Production is calculated as the acreage harvested times the trend
yield; this is not actual production.

harvested crops.[8]   Undoubtedly the 383 percent increase in the
irrigated acreage of these four crops (compared to the approximate
doubling of total irrigated acreage) was a factor in their higher yield
increases.   The following attempt to quantify the irrigation factor
starts from table 2-11 indicating the percentage changes in acreage,
trend yields, and production of these four crops for the United States,
the irrigated West, the dryland West, and the East.

While many factors affect crop production, the focus here is
limited to the role of irrigated and dryland acreage and yields.
Western irrigation generally implies more intensive use of complementary inputs such as fertilizers and pesticides, and the higher
yields on irrigated lands are the result of the entire input package.
No attempt, however, is made to explain the impact of these other
inputs.   Indeed, the data are not available to differentiate between
the use of these inputs on irrigated and dryland farming.   At least in
the arid and semiarid West, controlled water is essential for the
introduction of high-yielding agriculture and, thus, is a controlling
element in the region's agricultural expansion.

Nationally, corn, sorghum, and wheat output at least doubled while
cotton output rose by only 18 percent.   Irrigated production generally
grew much faster than the total; for example, the percentage increases
in irrigated production were 4,748 for corn, 251 for sorghum, 470 for
wheat, and 175 for cotton.   The rapid growth of irrigated output is
partly due to relatively low base-year levels.   Thus, despite the rapid
growth, irrigation accounted for only 28 percent of the national corn
production increase, 20 percent for sorghum, and 12 percent for wheat.
Eastern cotton production declined sharply over this period, and irrigation accounted for 175 percent of the national increase in cotton.

Table 2-12 indicates the relative importance of changing acreage,
yields, and production within the irrigated West, the dryland West, and

---

8. Data on total cropland harvested and an index of crop production per
acre are in Donald D. Durost and Evelyn T. Black, Changes in Farm
Production and Efficiency, 1977, U.S. Department of Agriculture,
Economics, Statistics, and Cooperatives Service, Statistical Bulletin
no. 612 (Washington, D.C., November 1978).

Table 2-11. Changes in Irrigated and Dryland Acreage, Yields, and
Production of Corn, Sorghum, Wheat, and Cotton, 1950 to 1977

(percentages of 1950 levels)

Crop and area	Change in estimated acres harvested	Change in trend yields	Change in production
Corn			
Irrigated West	1,842	144	4,748
Dryland West	− 73	78	− 51
East	2	126	130
U.S. total	− 4	145	136
Sorghum			
Irrigated West	107	70	251
Dryland West	16	151	191
East	1,028	190	3,185
U.S. total	36	150	241
Wheat			
Irrigated West	328	31	470
Dryland West	2	96	99
East	7	77	90
U.S. total	7	92	107
Cotton			
Irrigated West	148	11	175
Dryland West	− 25	50	12
East	− 55	56	− 30
U.S. total	− 26	59	18

Note: Appendix 2-B explains the derivation of the underlying data.

Table 2-12. Sources of Corn, Sorghum, Wheat, and Cotton Production Growth, 1950 to 1977

(percentage of the change in the U.S. production of each crop)

Crop and area	Change in acres harvested	Changes in yields	Change in production
Corn for grain			
Irrigated West	19	9	28
Dryland West	-13	6	- 6
East	2	77	79
U.S. total	- 5	104	100
Sorghum for grain			
Irrigated West	12	9	20
Dryland West	9	54	63
East	11	6	17
U.S. total	26	74	100
Wheat			
Irrigated West	10	2	12
Dryland West	2	63	65
East	2	20	23
U.S. total	10	89	100
Cotton			
Irrigated West	156	19	175
Dryland West	- 44	61	17
East	-218	126	- 92
U.S. total	-182	281	100

Note: Appendix 2-B explains the derivation of the underlining data and Appendix 2-C explains the derivation of the components of the production increase.

the East on the national change in the production of these crops. Yield rather than acreage increases were the major factors underlying the national production changes. Indeed, total acreage declined for two of the four crops and, therefore, acreage changes had a negative impact on production in these cases. On the other hand, increased irrigated acreage accounted for 60 percent or more of the increases in the irrigated output of these crops.

Average yields rose for all four crops in all regions considered. Nationally, corn and sorghum yields more than doubled, wheat yields rose 92 percent, and cotton yields rose 59 percent. Both dryland and irrigated yield trends were up, and with the exception of irrigated cotton which rose 11 percent and irrigated wheat which rose 31 percent, yields rose by 50 percent or more (see table 2-11).

Four factors contribute to the change in aggregate crop yields. Three of these factors, the yield changes in the irrigated West, the dryland West, and the East, are included in table 2-12, which shows their contribution to the change in production. The fourth factor results from changes in the distribution of acreage among regions and between dryland and irrigated acreage. That is, since irrigated yields are generally higher, average crop yields rise as the percentage of the land irrigated rises. This occurs even with no change in average irrigated and dryland yields.

Table 2-13 presents the percentage changes in aggregate crop yields between 1950 and 1977 and indicates the percentage contributions of the four factors to these yield increases. It is evident from this table that the increases in yields in the East and dryland West were the dominant factors underlying the rise in national average yields. Since virtually all eastern production of these crops is dryland, we can conclude that total dryland yield increases accounted for about 80 percent or more of the total increase in corn, sorghum, and wheat yield increases and about 67 percent of the cotton yield increases. While the growth rate of yields was higher for dryland wheat, sorghum, and cotton than for irrigated production of these crops, the principal reason for the dominance of dryland yields is that nationally the great majority of the acres harvested are dryland. Thus, an increase in average dryland yields has a much greater impact on national production and yields than does a comparable increase in irrigated yields.

The importance of the ratio of irrigated to nonirrigated land is most strikingly illustrated in the case of corn. In spite of a 144 percent rise in irrigated corn yields, a 1,842 percent rise in irrigated acreage, and a 4 percent decline in total acreage, the increase in irrigated corn yields accounted for only 8 percent of the national increase in corn yields.

For corn, wheat, and cotton, the change in the acreage mix had a greater impact on aggregate yields than did the change in yields on irrigated lands (see table 2-13). The most notable case is cotton, for which the change in the acreage mix accounted for 27 percent of the national yield increase. With the exception of sorghum, the largest acreage increases were for the irrigated West; for all four crops, irrigated acreage rose as a percentage of the total. Consequently, much of the contribution to yields stemming from the changing acreage mix is attributable to the increased role of irrigation. Table 2-14 separates the contribution of the change in the acreage mix to the growth of total yields into that attributable to (1) the shift from dryland (that is, dryland West plus East) to irrigated acreage and (2) the shift from dryland West to eastern acreage.[9] Adding the impact of the increasing role of western irrigation (from table 2-14) to the impact of the change in western irrigated yields (from table 2-13), suggests the total percentage impact of irrigation on the growth

9. The impact of the increasing role of irrigation on national crop yields is determined by aggregating the dryland West and East and redoing the component analysis of yield changes described in appendix 2-C. With only two types of farming considered, irrigated West and all other, the yield impact of change in the acreage mix is equivalent to the impact of the change in the role of western irrigation. The difference between the yield changes attributable to the change in the acreage mix (from table 2-13) and that attributable to the shift from dryland to irrigated acres (from table 2-14) is due to the relative shift from dryland West to eastern production (presented in table 2-14). With the exception of cotton, all the relative shifts in acreage had positive impacts on national yields. While the changes in the role of irrigation explained 37 percent of the growth of national cotton yields, the change in relative dryland West and all East acreage reduced national yields by 10 percent over this period.

Table 2-13. Percentage Changes in Total Crop Yields and the Sources of
Changes, 1950 to 1977

| Crop | Percentage change in aggregate yield | Source of crop yield changes (percentages of total change in yields) | | | |
		Growth of yields in irrigated West	Growth of yields in dryland West	Growth of yields in East	Change in acreage mix
Corn	145	8	6	74	12
Sorghum	150	12	74	8	6
Wheat	92	3	71	23	4
Cotton	59	7	22	45	27

Note: Derivation of the underlying data is explained in appendix 2-B;
the method for differentiating between the sources of crop yield changes is
explained in appendix 2-C and in the text accompanying this table.

Table 2-14. Impact of the Change in Acreage Mix on National Crop Yields,
1950 to 1977

(percentage of the change in national yields)

Crop	Shift from dryland to western irrigation	Shift between dryland West and East
Corn	5	7
Sorghum	4	2
Wheat	4	0
Cotton	37	-10

Note: The methodology for the derivation of this table is explained
in footnote 9 of this chapter.

of national yields was 13 percent for corn, 16 percent for sorghum, 7 percent for wheat, and 44 percent for cotton.

Impacts of Irrigation on Land Use

Irrigation has two principal impacts on the supply and demand of farmland. Irrigation reduces the amount of land required to produce a given output (that is, it is a land-conserving technology) and it expands the land suitable for commercial farming (that is, it might be considered a technology for creating agricultural land.)

As noted above, yields tend to be higher on irrigated than on dryland farms, especially in the West where rainfall is low and unreliable. Improved yields stem both from the greater control irrigation provides over water and from the complementary investments in yield-increasing inputs, such as agricultural chemicals and improved seed which are profitable only where there is an assured supply of water. The capital invested in the entire package of yield-increasing inputs associated with irrigation can be viewed as a substitute for land in an agricultural production function. One way of illustrating the importance of the land-conserving impact of irrigation is to speculate on the amount of additional land that would be required to produce the 1977 level of output without irrigation. The answer, of course, depends on what happens to dryland yields both on the intensive margin (that is, the lands already in production) and extensive margin (that is, the additional lands devoted to dryland production). There is no way to know what would happen to yields under such circumstances but illustrating the implications of several assumptions provides a ballpark estimate of the land-conserving impacts of irrigation.

Assuming no change on the intensive margin and yields equivalent to the 1977 combined average of the East and dryland West, an additional 7.1 million harvested acres of dryland farming would be required to compensate for the loss of irrigated production of corn, sorghum, wheat, and cotton. This estimate contains two somewhat offsetting biases. On the one hand, the lands involved in a 25.6 million acre expansion of dryland production are likely on average to be of lower

quality than those already in production. Thus, unless farmers com-
pensated with higher levels of investment or management, average yields
on the new lands would fall below the overall dryland average. On the
other hand, this estimate makes no allowance for increasing yields on
those lands already under dryland farming. For example, if conditions
called for a major expansion of agricultural production, investment
would be directed to increasing yields on currently cropped lands as
well as to developing new farmlands. On balance, 7 million acres may
be a reasonable estimate of the land-conserving implications of the
18.5 million acres irrigated for these four crops.

The land-conserving impacts of irrigation almost certainly are
greater than 7 million acres since these four crops accounted for only
44 percent of the West's irrigated acreage in 1974. The lack of comparable data differentiating between irrigated and dryland yields of
most other crops has deterred any effort to extend this analysis to
additional crops. But even if there were no problems with the data,
comparing land requirements with dryland and irrigated production becomes more questionable when applied to some of the other crops. In
particular, the comparison ignores the difficulties of growing on dryland farms some of the high-value specialty crops which are grown
almost exclusively under irrigation.

Irrigation also expands the agricultural land base by opening up
arid and semiarid areas to high-yielding agriculture. In particular,
unirrigated arid areas have made little to no contribution to agriculture. Certainly, most of the lands in the predominantly arid states of
Arizona, Nevada, New Mexico, and Utah, much of California, and parts of
most of the other western states would not be cropped in the absence of
irrigation. A very rough estimate of the land-creating implications
suggests irrigation has expanded the acreage suitable for agriculture
by 10 to 13 million acres. The higher figure is roughly equivalent to
the 1977 irrigated cropland in Arizona, California, Nevada, New Mexico,
and Utah.

Recent interest in the commercial potential of several plants native to arid and semiarid areas raises the possibility that these lands
may contribute to the agricultural land base in the absence of irrigation. Three of the most promising such plants are jojoba, guayule, and

Euphorbia lathyris. Jojoba, a drought-resistant plant that occurs naturally in areas with 3 to 15 inches annual rainfall, produces a liquid wax which makes an excellent industrial lubricant. Guayule, a drought-tolerant plant that can be grown with 11 inches of water per year, produces a latex substance that can be partially substituted for synthetic rubber made from petroleum products. Indeed, guayule was grown in the United States as a source of rubber prior to and during World War II. Euphorbia lathyris, which also grows naturally in an arid environment, is a potential source of fuel oil. A noted University of California chemist, Melvin Calvin, is seeking to develop varieties capable of producing oil on a commercial basis.

Despite their promise, the chances that these or other crops will be grown commercially in arid areas without irrigation is highly problematical. Native arid-land plants occur naturally only in densities that are too low for commercialization. While research is likely to improve yields and other commercial properties, growing these plants profitably in arid areas may require irrigation. On the other hand, the water needs of these plants may well be much lower than the requirements of the crops commonly irrigated in arid areas, a feature which may make them increasingly attractive as water becomes scarcer.[10]

---

10. A more extensive discussion of these three as well as several other arid-land plants is available in a summary of the February 7, 1980 conference, "New Crops for California Agriculture," which has been reproduced by Continuing Education in Agricultural Sciences and Management, University Extension, University of California, Davis.

Appendix 2-A

IRRIGATION DATA PROBLEMS

Efforts to describe the past or present role of irrigation in U.S. agriculture face a fundamental problem--there is considerable uncertainty as to how many acres are currently irrigated or have been irrigated in the past. The uncertainty as to irrigated acreage is evident from the alternative estimates presented in table 2A-1. For example, the Second National Water Assessment offers alternative estimates of 45.3 and 51.9 million acres irrigated in 1975 in the United States. But even this range is not sufficiently wide to encompass alternative estimates for 1975 or neighboring years. If the 41.2 million acre estimate of the 1974 Agricultural Census were adjusted for likely expansion between 1974 and 1975, it would still fall below this range. Preliminary data of the 1978 Census of Agriculture show the United States with 50.7 million irrigated acres in 1978. This figure implies an increase of 9.5 million acres since the 1974 Agricultural Census, a very significant and unprecedented rise. The Bureau of the Census, however, suggests that a comparison of the 1978 with the 1974 and 1969 agricultural censuses overstates actual growth of irrigation.[1] The 1975 national estimates of the U.S. Geological Survey (USGS) and

---

1. In an open letter dated December 12, 1980, Arnold L. Bollenbacher, Chief, Agriculture Division, Bureau of the Census, states "Because of improvements in coverage for the 1978 census, comparisons with the previous two censuses taken by mail (1969 and 1974) must be approached with caution so that improved counts are not misinterpreted as dramatic changes occurring between censuses...."

The first draft of this study was completed before the 1978 census data were available. Indeed, the detailed state- and county-level data still are not out for most states. A major additional effort and significant delay would be required to fully analyze and incorporate the 1978 agricultural census into this study. But neither the effort nor the delay seem warranted. The preliminary data and accompanying statements from the Bureau of the Census (see, for example, Bollenbacher's statement in the preceding paragraph) support a major conclusion of this appendix--that the 1969 and 1974 agricultural censuses understate the level of irrigated acreage. While the 1978

the _Irrigation_ _Journal_ (IJ) of about 54 million irrigated acres exceed the range of the Second Assessment. Yet both of these estimates are lower than the 60.7 million acre estimate of the 1977 National Resources Inventory (NRI), even allowing for expansion from 1975 to 1977.

The seventeen western states account for 83 to 89 percent of the nation's irrigated land (depending on the data source) and for much of the uncertainty as to how many acres are irrigated. For example, the 1974 Agricultural Census shows only 36.6 million irrigated acres in the West, a figure which is more than 10 million acres below both the 1974 IJ and the 1975 USGS estimates. The preliminary 1978 agricultural census estimate shows 43.4 million acres irrigated in the West, well below the 1977 NRI figure of 50.2 million acres.

Variations in what is included as irrigated land is one possible explanation for the data differences. Indeed, the reporting of an interagency task force formed to study irrigation efficiency, concludes, "Differences occur because definitions of irrigated lands are not uniform among the different agencies."[2] Differences in definitions that might contribute to variations in irrigated acreage estimates include treatment of land which is normally irrigated but not irrigated that year, land taken out of irrigation for urban development, land which is occasionally wild flooded, and land that is double-cropped under irrigation.

The census estimates, which are generally the lowest, count as irrigated any agricultural land receiving water through artificial means in the census year. Double-cropped land is counted only once and

---

irrigation census estimates appear to be significantly improved over the previous two, underenumeration still appears likely. Although efforts were made in 1978 to include a higher percentage of actual farms in the census, the estimates still depend on responses from farmers, some of whom apparently believe it is in their interest to underreport irrigated acreage. Thus, the 1977 National Resources Inventory still is used in this study as the principal source of recent irrigation levels. Although the analysis has not been redone, references to the irrigation estimates of the 1978 census of agriculture have been added in several instances to this appendix.

2. U.S. Department of Interior, Department of Agriculture, and Environmental Protection Agency, _Irrigation_ _Water_ _Use_ _and_ _Management,_ _An_ _Interagency_ _Task_ _Force_ _Report_ (Washington, D.C., GPO, June 1979) p. 12.

Table 2A-1. Alternative Estimates of Irrigated Acreage, Various Years

(millions of acres)

Source	Year	17 Western states	U.S. total
Census of Agriculture	1964	33.2	37.1
First National Water Assessment	1965	38.8[a]	42.1
USGS	1965	39.5	44.0
Conservation Needs Inventory	1967	41.5	47.6
Census of Agriculture	1969	34.8	39.1
USGS	1970	43.7	50.0
Census of Agriculture	1974	36.6	41.2
Irrigation Journal	1974	47.0	53.3
Second National Water Assessment			
National Future[b]	1975	40.6[a]	45.3
State/Regional Future[c]	1975	46.2[a]	51.9
USGS	1975	47.3	54.0
Irrigation Journal	1975	47.6	54.0
National Resources Inventory	1977	50.2	60.7
Irrigation Journal	1977	49.9	58.5
Irrigation Journal	1978	51.3	60.7
Census of Agriculture (preliminary)	1978	43.4	50.7

Sources:

Census data: 1964 and 1969: U.S. Bureau of the Census, Census of Agriculture, 1969, vol. IV, Irrigation (Washington, D.C., GPO, 1973) table 1, p. 2. 1974: U.S. Bureau of the Census, 1974 Census of Agriculture, vol. 1, part 51, United States: Summary and State Data (Washington, D.C., GPO, December 1977), p. II-5. 1978: preliminary data released by the Bureau of the Census, U.S. Department of Commerce, undated.

National Assessment data: 1965: U.S. Water Resources Council, The Nation's Water Resources, The First National Assessment of the Water Resources Council (Washington, D.C., GPO, 1968) p. 4-4-1. 1975: U.S. Water Resources Council, The Nation's Water Resources 1975-2000: Second National Water Assessment, vol. 3: app. 1 (Washington, D.C., GPO, December 1 78) p. 59.

USGS data: 1965: C. Richard Murray, Estimated Use of Water in the United States, 1965, U.S. Geological Survey Circular 556 (Washington, D.C., 1968) table 11. 1970: C. Richard Murray and E. Bodette Reeves, Estimated Use of Water in the United States in 1970, U.S. Geological Survey Circular 676 (Washington, D.C., 1972) table 7. 1975: C. Richard Murray and E. Bodette Reeves, Estimated Use of Water in the United States in 1975, U.S. Geological Survey Circular 765 (Arlington, VA., 1977) table 7.

Conservation Needs Inventory: U.S. Department of Agriculture, Soil Conservation Service, Basic Statistics--National Inventory of Soil and Water Conservation Needs, 1967, Statistical Bulletin no. 461 (Washington, D.C., GPO, January 1971) table 3c and the a and c state tables.

Irrigation Journal data: The 1974, 1975, 1977, and 1978 IJ data from Irrigation Journal, vol. 28, no. 6, Survey/December 1978 (Elm Grove, WI.) pp. 46A to 46H.

National Resources Inventory: U.S. Department of Agriculture, Soil Conservation Service, "Basic Statistics--1977 National Resources Inventory (NRI)," Revised February 1980, in mimeograph.

[a]Regional estimates in the National Water Assessments are for water resource regions which do not correspond to state boundaries. These figures include regions 9-18.

[b] National Future--Estimates of present and future conditions as obtained primarily by participating federal agencies.

[c] State/Regional Future--Estimates of present and future conditions provided primarily by participating River Basin Commissions, state agencies, and other sponsors.

land which is normally irrigated but not irrigated in the census year is not counted.[3]

The 1967 CNI and 1977 NRI define irrigated land as "land on which irrigation water is applied by an adapted irrigation method on a recurring basis as an integral part of crop production."[4] In the 1977 survey, land was counted as irrigated if (a) the enumerator observed evidence that the land had been irrigated that year or (b) the farmer indicated the land had been irrigated at least two of the last four years.

For the First National Assessment, irrigated land was "defined as land developed for irrigation which regularly receives water for the production of agricultural products." This "includes lands which are temporarily idle for water supply or other reasons but does not include lands which do not regularly produce agricultural products."[5] In the Second Assessment, alternative estimates of 1975 irrigation are given because of the uncertainty as to the magnitude of irrigation, not because of different definitions. For both sets of estimates, irrigated farmland is defined as "pasture and cropland to which water can be expected to be applied."[6] The USGS and IJ rely on local experts for their estimates and do not define irrigated land.

---

3. Total irrigated land in the census includes harvested cropland irrigated, cropland pasture irrigated, pasture (other than cropland pasture) irrigated, and other cropland irrigated. Other cropland includes cropland in cover crops, legumes, and soil-improvement grasses, not harvested and not pastured; cropland on which all crops failed; cropland in cultivated summer fallow; and cropland idle.

4. U.S. Department of Agriculture, Basic Statistics--National Inventory of Soil and Water Conservation Needs, 1967, Statistical Bulletin no. 461 (Washington, D.C. GPO, January 1971) p. 209. Ray Dideriksen, director, Land Inventory and Monitoring, Soil Conservation Service, indicated that the 1977 NRI irrigation data are based on the same definition.

5. U.S. Water Resources Council, The Nation's Water Resources, the First National Assessment of the Water Resources Council (Washington, D.C., GPO, 1968) p. 4-4-1. This document states that the Assessment was "hampered by inconsistent data on irrigated land."

6. U.S. Water Resources Council, The Nation's Water Resources 1974-2000: Second National Water Assessment, vol. 3, Analytical Data Summary (Washington, D.C., GPO, 1978) p. 72.

The different definitions do provide reason for expecting the census estimates to be lower than the alternatives since land that is regularly irrigated but not irrigated in the census year is not listed as irrigated by the census. While the impact of the various definitions on the estimates of irrigated acreage cannot be quantified, the following analysis suggests that the major reason for the wide variations in irrigation estimates is that, with a single exception, the source of national irrigation estimates either (a) depend on the responses of farmers who may not reply or may believe it is in their interest to misstate the extent of their irrigation, or (b) rely on reports of many individuals or organizations which are asked to estimate a state's irrigation in the absence of clear guidelines or reliable primary data. In the first case, the data are systematically biased in all regions; in the second case, the magnitude and sometimes even the direction of any errors are unknown and differ among states. The only sources of irrigated acreage data which avoid both these shortcomings are the 1967 Conservation Needs Inventory (CNI) and the 1977 National Resources Inventory (NRI).

Primary Irrigation Data

The only primary sources of irrigation data which apply standardized data gathering and estimating techniques to all states are the agricultural censuses (taken about every five years), the decennial irrigation survey by the Bureau of Census (done in recent years after every other agricultural census, the 1967 CNI, and the 1977 NRI. [7]

More limited efforts to obtain primary data for estimating irrigation have been undertaken in some states. Each of the seventeen western states has an agreement with the Statistical Reporting Service of the U.S. Department of Agriculture to provide crop and livestock production estimates. Federal appropriations cover the collection and publication of these data on a state and national level only, but make no provision for distinguishing between irrigated and dryland produc-

---

7. A national soil and water inventory also was undertaken for 1958 but this did not have irrigation data.

tion. Depending on the interests of and the funds contributed by a particular state, more detailed data such as irrigated production and acreage may be collected. Most of the western State Crop and Livestock Reporting Services provide some data on the acreage and yields of principal crops under irrigation, but only a few provide data on total land irrigated in their states.[8] Variations in the detail, coverage, and reliability of the irrigation data provided by the states limit their usefulness in describing the overall role of irrigation in the West. In some cases, however, state data can provide a check on the reasonableness of alternative sources.

The most detailed and widely cited data on irrigated agriculture are those of the agricultural censuses, which include county-level irrigation figures by crop for every state. One might expect the census data to be the most accurate since they are supposed to be based on a survey of all farms. Unfortunately, this expectation is not fulfilled. There seems to be widespread agreement among those familiar with irrigation data that the 1974 agricultural census grossly understates the level of irrigated acreage in the United States. Indeed, upon releasing the preliminary 1978 census data, the Bureau of the Census itself noted that irrigated acreage was underreported in both the 1974 and 1969 agricultural censuses. This conclusion is supported by a comparison of census and other sources of irrigation data as well as by conversations with knowledgeable officials in many of the major irrigation states.[9] The failure to achieve full farm coverage is

---

8. As part of an agreement between the Statistical Reporting Service and the Federal Crop Insurance Corporation (FCIC), state statisticians do collect some irrigation data. In the West, for example, they collect data on corn in three states, wheat in fifteen states, sorghum in eight states, and cotton in four states. The state statisticians rely primarily on farmer reports for their information but the methods differ from state to state. These data are not regularly published but some states include them in their crop and livestock reports.

9. The states as well as the experts providing the USGS and IJ estimates seldom rely on census data for irrigated acreage. Based on conversations with six of the state experts providing irrigation estimates for the IJ, this situation reflects a widespread belief that agricultural census data are inaccurate. Unfortunately, as is discussed later in this appendix, rejection of the census numbers seldom means the states have better data upon which to base their estimates.

the explanation the Bureau of the Census offers for the underenumeration. But another important reason for the underenumeration may be that some farmers believe it is in their interest to understate the level of irrigation. The accuracy of a mail response system depends on individual responses which are bound to be inaccurate if farmers believe it is in their interest to distort the responses. Possible reasons why farmers might intentionally understate irrigation are that they believe their reponses will be used for tax purposes or, for farmers receiving federally subsidized water, they want to conceal how much water they actually receive. The reliance on mail responses by farmers in 1974 and 1969 as opposed to the personal interviews used in earlier censuses could account for the increase in underreporting, which appears to be greatest in 1974 and significant in 1969. The 1978 census used a direct enumeration area sample to make statistical estimates for farms missed in the initial mailing response but had no means of adjusting for underreporting among the respondents.

The 1978 agricultural census is being supplemented by the 1979 Farm and Ranch Irrigation Survey undertaken by the Bureau of the Census. This is a survey of about 10 percent of the irrigated farmers responding to the 1978 census. The survey provides more detailed farm level information on factors such as the nature of the irrigation facilities and practices, the crops grown, and their yields. This follow-up survey was undertaken in part to ease the respondent burden of the census. The data were scheduled to be available on tape about May 1981 and in published form sometime in 1982, but this schedule did not permit use of these data in this study.

The Bureau of the Census also conducts an Irrigation Census of water distributors or irrigation organizations once every ten years. The most recent were done in conjunction with the 1959, 1969, and 1978 censuses of agriculture. Historically, the irrigation censuses consistently show more acreage irrigated than do the agricultural censuses. The 1969 census indicates that the irrigation organization reports overstate irrigated area because:

"1. Some irrigation organizations report the area assessed for water, the area eligible to receive water, or the total area in farms receiving water. Usually these areas are considerably greater than the area irrigated during a year.

2. In some cases, two or more irrigation organizations provide water used to irrigate the same area. In such cases, the same area is counted by each of the organizations supplying the water."[10]

A discussion with a Census official suggests these problems persist with the more recent irrigation censuses.[11] Consequently, the acreage estimates of the irrigation censuses are not presented in this study.

The 1967 Conservation Needs Inventory (CNI) and the 1977 National Resources Inventory (NRI) also provide primary irrigation acreage estimates for all states. Although listed under different titles, these estimates represent a generally consistent effort by the Soil Conservation Service (SCS) to describe the use and conservation needs of rural land. One by-product of the 1967 and 1977 surveys is the calculation of irrigation acreages of crop groups by state and land class. Unlike the census, the CNI and NRI estimates are not dependent on farmer responses for accuracy. They are based on detailed, on-site inspection of sample points of all nonfederal rural land. The 1977 sampling rate and techniques were designed to achieve a 95 percent confidence level with a coefficient of variation of 1 to 3 percent in estimating land use such as irrigation. The sampling rate for the 1967 CNI was even higher.[12] Both surveys relied on trained personnel to gather the basic data at the randomly selected sites. The 1977 NRI data also were subjected to a quality check by a team of agronomists who resampled random sections.

The CNI and NRI irrigation data also have limitations for studying

---

10. U.S. Department of Commerce, U.S. Census of Agriculture: 1959, Final Report - Vol. III, Irrigation of Agricultural Lands, p. xxv.

11. Conversation with Fred Ruggles, U.S. Bureau of the Census, Agriculture Division, January 30, 1981.

12. For a description of the sampling techniques used for the 1967 inventory, see U.S. Department of Agriculture, Inventory of Conservation Needs, 1967, p. 203. Information on the sampling technqiues used for the 1977 inventory was provided by Ray Dideriksen of the Soil Conservation Service.

irrigation. As noted above, they include an unknown (but, at least for the West, probably small) amount of land that was not actually irrigated in the survey year. The data are not reliable at the county level, and, in states with little irrigation, the small samples result in wider percentage coefficients of variation. Furthermore, these inventories do not differentiate by crops but only by broad crop groups such as row crops and close-grown crops.

Although the 1967 CNI data were collected as described previously, other agencies, in particular the Forest Service, were allowed to adjust the data to meet their agency estimates. By allowing this adjustment process, however, the statistical properties of the survey were destroyed and its value as a primary source threatened. While the SCS staff are not sure what impact these changes had on the data, it appears that only the large groupings of land use were affected by these adjustments (that is, totals of pastureland, cropland, forestland). Apparently the irrigation acreages were unaffected by the adjustments and still can be regarded as a primary source. The 1977 data were not subject to revision by other agencies.

A comparison with other land use estimates and discussions with SCS officials suggest the CNI and NRI surveys had difficulty in distinguishing between irrigated cropland pasture and irrigated permanent pasture.[13] Although this problem does not affect the total of irrigated acres, it does indicate that the relative mix of the pasturelands should be used with discretion.

The census estimates cannot be compared directly to either the 1967 CNI or the 1977 NRI because of timing differences. However, if we assume that the change in irrigated acreage from 1967 to 1977 was linear in each state, irrigation estimates based on the CNI and NRI data can be derived for the 1969 and 1974 census years. (These projections are referred to as the CNI/NRI projections.) Table 2A-2 shows

---

13. The 1967 CNI defines rotation hay and pasture as "cropland in grasses and legumes used for hay or pasture as part of the crop rotation" and pastureland as "land producing forage plants, principally introduced species, for animal consumption." See U.S. Department of Agriculture, Inventory of Conservation Needs, 1967, p. 209.

Table 2A-2. Comparison of Estimates of Total Irrigated Acreage in the
            Seventeen Western States: 1974 and 1969 Census Estimates
            Expressed as a Percentage of the CNI/NRI Projections

State	1969	1974
Arizona	107	100
California	87	89
Colorado	77	74
Idaho	77	76
Kansas	79	73
Montana	80	69
Nebraska	71	68
Nevada	79	70
New Mexico	69	74
North Dakota	113	81
Oklahoma	92	70
Oregon	77	68
South Dakota	64	39
Texas	81	79
Utah	78	77
Washington	83	74
Wyoming	79	77
Western states	80	77
U.S. total	78	73

Sources: U.S. Bureau of the Census, Census of Agriculture, 1969,
vol. IV Irrigation (Washington, D.C., GPO, 1973); U.S. Bureau of the
Census, 1974 Census of Agriculture, vol. 1, part 51, United States:
Summary and State Data (Washington, D.C., GPO, 1977); U.S. Department
of Agriculture, Soil Conservation Service, Basic Statistics--National
Inventory of Soil and Water Conservation Needs, 1967, Statistical
Bulletin 461 (Washington, D.C., GPO, 1971); U.S. Department of Agri-
culture, Soil Conservation Service, "Basic Statistics--1977 National
Resources Inventory (NRI)," Revised February 1980, in mimeograph.

the 1969 and 1974 census data for the seventeen western states and the nation as a percentage of the CNI/NRI projections.

Nationwide the 1974 census estimate is only 73 percent of the CNI/NRI figure projected to 1974; for the West the census is 77 percent of the projection. The census figures are lower in all but one of ·the seventeen western states with the margin of difference exceeding 20 percent of the CNI/NRI figure in fourteen states. Only for Arizona is the census estimate within 10 percent of the CNI/NRI projection.

For 1969 the differences between the irrigated acreage estimates of the two sources are smaller but still substantial. The 1969 census estimate is 78 percent of the projected CNI/NRI national figures and 80 percent of the western total. In eleven of the seventeen western states the census figures are at least 20 percent below the 1969 CNI/NRI projections.[14] While there are no other primary sources of irrigation data covering all states, Nebraska, New Mexico, and Texas have estimates of total acres irrigated in either 1977 or a census year. A comparison of these state estimates (which use the census definition of irrigated land) with the census and NRI data (see table 2A-3) supports the view that the census data are grossly underestimated. This comparison also suggests that while the NRI data may provide a high estimate of irrigation in a given year, they are probably much more accurate than the census. The 1974 census estimates are 21, 33, and 23 percent below the respective state estimates for Nebraska, New Mexico, and Texas while the 1977 NRI estimates differ from the state estimates by 8 percent in Nebraska and 14 percent in New Mexico. For Texas, the state and the CNI/NRI projected estimates only

---

14. For reasons discussed in the text, we might expect that the census estimates are a lower bound on the actual amount of irrigation in a census year. Yet, in two of the seventeen states the census data actually exceed the CNI/NRI projections. Given the manner in which we have projected the CNI/NRI estimates to the census years and the statistical error that could be introduced by the CNI and NRI sampling techniques, the 5 percent difference between the CNI/NRI projections and the census figures in Arizona is not surprising. And in view of the relative insignificance of irrigation in North Dakota, the reliability of CNI and NRI irrigation estimates for that state is lower than in the other western states.

Table 2A-3. Comparison of State, Census and NRI Irrigation Estimates
for Nebraska, New Mexico, and Texas

(thousands of acres)

State	Year	NRI[a]	State sources	Census
Nebraska	1974	(5,840)	5,050	3,967
	1977	6,940	6,400 (prel.)	--
New Mexico	1974	(1,175)	1,294	867
	1977	1,167	1,358	--
Texas	1969	(8,549)	8,206	6,888
	1974	(8,334)	8,618	6,594

Sources: NRI data, U.S. Department of Agriculture, Soil Conservation
Service, "Basic Statistics--1977 National Resources Inventory (NRI),"
Revised February 1980, in mimeograph. CNI data, U.S. Department of Agriculture, Basic Statistics--National Inventory of Soil and Water Conservation Needs, 1967, Statistical Bulletin no. 461 (Washington, D.C., GPO,
1971). State data, The New Mexico and Nebraska state irrigation estimates were provided by their respective state Crop and Livestock Reporting
Services. See Nebraska Agricultural Statistics: Annual Report, 1976-1977,
p. 91 and New Mexico Agricultural Statistics: vol. VIII, p. 7. The state
irrigation estimates for Texas are from Texas Water Development Board
Report 196, Inventories of Irrigation in Texas 1958, 1964, 1969, and 1974.
October 1975, table 1, p. 60. Census data, U.S. Bureau of the Census,
1974 Census of Agriculture, vol. 1, part 51, United States: Summary and
State Data (Washington, D.C., GPO, 1977). The 1978 agricultural census
data are from U.S. Bureau of the Census, mimeograph, undated.

[a]The numbers in parentheses assume a linear trend between the 1967
CNI and the 1977 NRI estimates.

differ by 4 percent for 1969 and 3 percent in 1974. Since Texas has been noted for systematically surveying its irrigated lands, this result lends credibility to the CNI and NRI estimates.[15]

Secondary Sources of Irrigation Data

There are several secondary sources of irrigation data. Three principal ones are the Irrigation Journal (IJ) with state estimates since 1951, the U.S. Geological Survey (USGS) with state estimates every five years from 1960 to 1975, and the Water Resources Council, which published the First and Second National Water Assessments, with estimates by water resource region for 1965 and 1975. These estimates are all accorded considerable attention if not credibility--the first because the numbers are published annually in a trade journal and the other two because they are included as part of major government water studies. The derivation of these estimates and their relation to the primary data are discussed below.

Irrigation Journal

Table 2A-4 presents the Irrigation Journal's state and regional estimates of irrigated land as a percentage of the 1967 CNI and 1977 NRI estimates and the 1969 and 1974 census estimates. The census estimates are considerably lower than the IJ estimates for both census years and for virtually every state. For the seventeen western states, the IJ shows 26 percent more land irrigated in 1969 and 28 percent more in 1974 than the censuses report. In contrast, the CNI and IJ totals for the seventeen western states are virtually the same for 1967 and the NRI and IJ data differ only by 2 percent for 1977. The national

---

15. Texas conducts annual surveys of irrigation in the forty High Plains counties (which account for two-thirds of the state's irrigated land), and the Texas Department of Natural Resources in collaboration with other state agencies and the SCS has conducted state-wide irrigation surveys in 1958, 1964, 1969, and 1974. These surveys are considered to be accurate within 10 percent. Since there has been relatively little change in the state's total irrigation over the past decade, the error introduced by projections between survey years (as we have done with the CNI and NRI data) is probably small.

Table 2A-4.   Irrigation Journal Estimates as a Percentage of SCS and
Census Data

State	SCS		Census	
	1967 CNI	1977 NRI	1969	1974
Arizona	104	98	97	100
California	105	92	117	113
Colorado	83	63	114	109
Idaho	104	101	136	135
Kansas	86	98	93	117
Montana	144	117	174	193
Nebraska	119[b]	103	148	135
Nevada	104[b]	107	173	169
New Mexico	74	106	122	123
North Dakota	195	125	144	103
Oklahoma	111	114	118	147
Oregon	96	76	118	120
South Dakota	231	78	211[a]	143
Texas	93	108	126	131
Utah	89	168	133	173
Washington	103	84	119	120
Wyoming	83	88	108	123
17 western states	100	98	126	128
U.S. Total	98	95	125	129

Sources: The calculations are based on data from U.S. Department of
Agriculture, Soil Conservation Service, Basic Statistics--National In-
ventory of Soil and Water Conservation Needs, 1967, Statistical Bulletin
no. 461 (Washington, D.C., GPO, 1971); U.S. Department of Agriculture,
Soil Conservation Service, "Basic Statistics--1977 National Resources
Inventory (NRI)," Revised February 1980, in mimeograph; U.S. Bureau of
the Census, Census of Agriculture, 1969, vol. IV, Irrigation
(Washington, D.C., GPO, 1973) table 1, p. 2: U.S. Bureau of the Census,
1974 Census of Agriculture, vol. 1, part 51, United States: Summary and
State Data (Washington, D.C., GPO, 1977) p. II-5: and Irrigation Journal,
vol. 28, no. 6, Survey/December 1978, pp. 46A-46H.

[a]IJ 1969 estimate is an average of 1968 and 1970.

[b]IJ 1968 estimate is used as a proxy for 1967.

estimates of these sources differ by only 2 percent in 1967 and 5 percent in 1977. Underlying these aggregates, however, are wide variations in the estimates for individual states. The 1977 IJ acreages are within 10 percent of the NRI figures in only eight of the seventeen western states and the range is from 37 percent below the NRI level in Colorado to 68 percent above in Utah. A comparison of the 1967 IJ and CNI data shows even fewer states falling within the $\pm$ 10 percent range and the overall variations range from 26 percent below in New Mexico to 131 percent above in South Dakota.

The _Irrigation_ _Journal_'s annual irrigation surveys are based on data provided by experts in each state. Since each expert develops his own methodology for estimating state acreage, the data must be evaluated on a state-by-state basis. Since the IJ does not provide any basis for assessing the accuracy of the numbers, the individuals cited as the sources of IJ data for six states, Idaho, Kansas, Montana, Nebraska, Texas, and Utah, were contacted.[16]

Among these states, the recent IJ estimates for Texas came closest to being based on systematically acquired primary data.[17] At least in recent years the IJ Texas estimates have relied on the previously mentioned statewide and High Plains irrigation surveys; the 1974 IJ figure agrees with the 1974 Texas inventory estimate of 8.6 million acres, but the 1969 IJ estimate is 6 percent higher than the state's inventory figure.

---

16. These states were selected because they are important irrigation states with sizable discrepancies between the census and IJ estimates of irrigated acreage in 1974. For example, in the six states combined, the IJ shows 39 percent more acreage irrigated in 1974 than the census. We also attempted to include the states with the greatest percentage differences between the 1977 NRI and IJ data. Utah, for which the IJ shows 56 percent more acres irrigated than the NRI, represents one extreme. Colorado, for which the IJ shows 22 percent fewer acres irrigated, represents the other extreme. However, the 1977 _Irrigation_ _Journal_ survey lists no source for their Colorado data. Although the 1978 survey does list a source for Colorado, before this was available, we had concluded from the responses by the six state sources contacted that the IJ data did not merit further attention.

17. Wayne Keese, Extension Agricultural Engineer, Texas A&M University, is the source of IJ data for Texas.

The basis for the IJ's irrigation estimates in Kansas are highly questionable. These data are based primarily on questionnaires filled in by county agents every several years. According to Delynn Hay,[18] who is in charge of these surveys, the responses of the county agents vary from those who fill out the questionnaire quickly with little attention to accuracy to those who take the task seriously and use tax records and other available information to systematicaly develop the data. Hay concluded that about 10 percent of the 1975 county responses could not be correct since they were so far out of line with those of the previous questionnaire taken in 1972. In such cases Hay adjusted the estimates of irrigated acreage to levels considered reasonable. The 1976 IJ data are the first numbers based on the 1975 Kansas survey. Estimates for the preceding several years are projections from 1972 survey results.

In Idaho the 1966 and 1975 base figures for land use were supplied by county SCS staff. These base year figures have been updated using data furnished by power suppliers, farmer applications to bring new land into irrigated production, and records of acreage converted to irrigation by sprinkler. Dorrell Larson,[19] the source of the IJ estimates for Idaho, indicates his data are accurate within 10 percent, and a comparison with CNI and NRI estimates supports his belief. The state estimates are virtually identical to the 1977 NRI and they differ by only 4 percent from the CNI estimates. In contrast, the IJ data are 35 and 36 percent above the 1974 and 1969 census estimates for Idaho.

Until approximately 1973 Montana's irrigation estimates were obtained by updating data based on surveys taken in the 1930s. Estimated growth trends in selected counties were extrapolated to obtain state estimates for subsequent years. These estimates were known to be overstated and, indeed, the 1967 IJ estimate is 44 percent higher than the

---

18. Delynn R. Hay, extension irrigation engineer, Kansas State University, is the source of the IJ data for Kansas.

19. Larsen is an irrigation expert with the Cooperative Extension Service, University of Idaho.

CNI figure. According to J. E. Acord,[20] the source of the IJ's irrigation estimates, the state estimation techniques have improved since 1973. Montana's Water Resources Division's land classification now provides the base and this is updated by registrations of new irrigated acres. The law requiring farmers to register changes in irrigation is not strictly enforced, suggesting this method should understate the change in irrigation. Yet, the 1977 IJ estimate is still 17 percent above the NRI figure.

In Nebraska the IJ estimates of irrigated acres are compiled from the registration of water use by the state's Department of Water Resources. The data are based on farmers' registrations of the number of acres they intend to irrigate. The farmers, however, have an incentive to overstate their intentions in order to obtain larger water rights. Paul Fischbach,[21] the source of the IJ estimates, concludes that the estimates are somewhat high. And, indeed, the 1967 IJ estimate exceeds the CNI estimate by 19 percent and the 1977 IJ estimate exceeds the NRI estimate by 3 percent.

In Utah the IJ irrigation estimates rely on data from several sources including county agents and district soil conservation officials. Richard Griffin,[22] the source of the IJ estimates for Utah, explained that the IJ figure is too high because of duplication resulting from aggregating information from a variety of sources. Perhaps this explains why the 1977 IJ estimate for irrigated acreage is 68 percent higher than the NRI figure.

Inquiries into the Irrigation Journal's irrigation estimates in these six states did not instill confidence in the data. IJ data are not based on a systematic effort to survey irrigated lands. The meth-

---

20. J. E. Acord is an engineer with the Water Resources Division of the Montana Department of Natural Resources.

21. Paul Fischbach is an extension irrigation expert with the University of Nebraska at Lincoln.

22. Richard E. Griffin is an extension water resource specialist at Utah State university.

ods used to obtain the data as well as the accuracy of the data not only differ among the states but vary over time within states. The *Journal* gives no indication as to the shortcomings of its estimates. On the contrary, the publisher would have his readers believe that his data are the basic facts on irrigated acreage.[23] While some of the state estimates may be reasonably accurate, many others are not. In some cases, the sources of the estimates even felt obliged to apologize for the data. The reader of the *Irrigation Journal* had no way of discerning which state estimates to trust. While the IJ's aggregate estimates of irrigation in the United States and in the West appear to be reasonably accurate, this appears to be a fortuitous result of offsetting errors in the estimates of individual states.

The U.S. Geological Survey

The USGS has published estimates of irrigated acreage for 1960, 1965, 1970, and 1975 as part of their studies of estimated water use in the United States.[24] Table 2A-5 presents their 1970 and 1975 data as a percentage of: (1) the CNI/NRI data projected to those dates, (2) the 1969 and 1974 census data, and (3) the 1970 and 1975 *Irrigation Journal* data.

It is readily apparent from table 2A-5 that the USGS figures are not based on census data. During both periods the censuses show considerably less irrigation in virtually all states; the USGS totals for the seventeen western states and the United States range from 26 to 31 percent above the prior year census estimates. These differences are

---

23. Dick Morey, "Crystal Balling the Irrigation Industry," *Irrigation Journal* (March/April 1977).

24. These data are published in the following U.S. Geological Survey Circulars: K. A. MacKithun and J. C. Kammerer, *Estimated Use of Water in the United States in 1960*, Circular no. 456 (Washington, D.C., 1961); C. Richard Murray, *Estimated Use of Water in the United States, 1965*, Circular no. 556 (Washington, D.C., 1968) table 11; C. Richard Murray and E. Bodette Reeves, *Estimated Use of Water in the United States in 1970*, Circular no. 676 (Washington, D.C., 1972) table 7; C. Richard Murray and E. Bodette Reeves, *Estimated Use of Water in the United States in 1975*, Circular no. 765 (Arlington, VA., 1977) table 7.

Table 2A-5. A Comparison of Alternative Estimates of Irrigated Acreage

	CNI/NRI Projections[a]		USGS estimates as a percentage of Census		Irrigation Journal	
State	1970	1975	1970 USGS: 1969 census	1975 USGS: 1974 census	1970	1975
Arizona	108	121	102	121	103	122
California	104	103	120	116	101	103
Colorado	121	80	159	108	136	99
Idaho	102	98	134	133	98	94
Kansas	86	103	118	149	96	120
Montana	94	93	120	136	69	77
Nebraska	94	90	144	141	93	100
Nevada	84	75	110	111	64	65
New Mexico	93	94	134	127	110	103
North Dakota	119	138	117	183	80	141
Oklahoma	103	130	118	194	100	132
Oregon	94	89	125	135	103	108
South Dakota	57	48	101	132	71	81
Texas	98	104	120	130	100	100
Utah	99	137	127	175	95	90
Washington	91	88	114	122	96	100
Wyoming	89	90	112	116	98	93
17 western states	99	98	126	129	98	99
U.S. total	97	93	128	131	100	100

Sources: The calculations are based on data from U.S. Department of Agriculture, Soil Conservation Service, Basic Statistics—National Inventory of Soil and Water Conservation Needs, 1967, Statistical Bulletin no. 461 (Washington, D.C., GPO, 1971); U.S. Department of Agriculture, Soil Conservation Service, "Basic Statistics—1977 National Resources Inventory (NRI)," Revised February 1980, in mimeograph; U.S. Bureau of the Census, Census of Agriculture, 1969, vol. IV Irrigation (Washington, D.C. GPO, 1977) table 1, p. 2; U.S. Bureau of the Census, 1974 Census of Agriculture, vol. 1, part 51, United States—Summary and State Data (Washington, D.C., GPO, 1977) p. II-5; Irrigation Journal, vol. 28, no. 6, Survey/December 1978 (Elm Grove, WI) pp. 46A to 46H; C. Richard Murray and E. Bodette Reeves, Estimated Use of Water in the United States in 1970, U.S. Geological Survey Circular 676 (Washington, D.C., 1972) table 7; and C. Richard Murray and E. Bodette Reeves, Estimated Use of Water in the United States in 1975, U.S. Geological Survey Circular 765 (Arlington, VA., 1977) table 7.

[a] Based on a linear extrapolation of 1967 CNI and 1977 NRI data.

much too large to be explained by one year's growth of irrigated acreage.

The USGS estimates for the West are much closer to the 1970 and 1975 CNI/NRI projections based on a linear change between 1967 and 1977. For example, these estimates of total irrigated acres in the West differ by only 1 percent in 1970 and 2 percent in 1975. Again, however, the aggregates hide large variations in the estimates for individual states. The USGS estimates differ from the CNI/NRI projections by 10 percent or more in six western states in 1970 and in eleven western states in 1975.

On balance, the 1975 USGS state estimates appear more reasonable than those of the Irrigation Journal. However, these two sources have some unfortunate features in common. First, while the aggregate estimates for the nation and the West seem reasonable, this is due in large part to offsetting errors in the estimates for the individual states. Second, neither source defines irrigated land and establishes a clear methodology for estimating irrigated acreage. The USGS estimates are supplied by their district offices. The district offices in turn follow the pattern of the Irrigation Journal and rely on local experts. No primary data are collected for the USGS estimates and each district apparently develops its own methodology for making estimates.

National Water Assessments

The Water Resources Council's (WRC) 1965 and 1975 assessments of the nation's water resources include estimates of irrigated land. Comparisons with all but the USGS estimates are limited to the national totals since the WRC regions are defined along hydrological and not political boundaries.

The Second National Assessment has alternative estimates of 1975 irrigation--the National Future (NF) figure of 45.3 million acres and the State/Regional Future (SRF) figure of 51.9 million acres (see table 2A-1). An initial estimate for the assessment was made by the Department of Agriculture based on a combination of Statistical Reporting Service county data for 1971-73 and 1969 census data updated to 1972. The 1972 estimates were then projected to 1975. Representatives of the

River Basin commissions, state agencies, and others were asked to comment on the resulting 1975 estimates for their regions. This review led to the inclusion of two estimates: the National Future estimate was derived primarily by participating federal agencies and the State/Regional Future estimate incorporates the inputs of the more local groups. Despite the considerable range of these alternatives both are at least 10 percent higher than the 1974 census figure and at least 10 percent less than the CNI/NRI figure projected to 1975.

Regional comparisons of the assessment and USGS data show variations similar to those noted earlier with the comparison of alternative estimates of state irrigation, that is, similarities in aggregate figures mask wide variations in the components. For example, the high (SRF) estimate of the Second Assessment is only 3 percent less than the USGS 1975 figure. But compared to the USGS, the SRF estimates for individual water resources regions range from 50 percent less in New England to 15 percent above in the Upper Colorado.

Conclusions

The deficiencies of the census data leave us without a data base which is simultaneously detailed for crops and counties, comprehensive for the entire nation, and reliable. The 1967 CNI and 1977 NRI data appear to be the most reliable estimates available for all states. For analytical purposes, however, they have several shortcomings--they are available for only 1967 and 1977, they are not considered accurate at the county level, they do not provide data for individual crops, and they may overstate the acreage actually irrigated in the survey years since, by definition, they include lands where water is supplied as part of a cropping system. Despite these shortcomings, they appear to be the most reliable estimates of irrigated acreage, and this study relies on the CNI and NRI data whenever possible. When more detail is required, adjusted census data, state survey data, or SRS survey data are used, depending on which seems more appropriate. One method used for adjusting the census data is to assume that (1) the CNI/NRI state estimates projected to the 1969 and 1974 census years more accurately reflect the true quantity of acres irrigated and (2) the errors in the census estimates are proportional among crops.[25]

---

25. A comparison of the census crop breakdowns with the CNI and NRI percentages of row and close-grown crops suppport this second assumption at the level of the USDA's farm production regions.

Appendix 2-B

DERIVATION OF IRRIGATED AND DRYLAND PRODUCTION
AND YIELD DATA

To determine the importance of irrigation in the production of specific crops, we need production and yield data differentiating between dryland and irrigated farming. The 1969 agricultural census is the most recent source of such data which covers all states. This source, however, is neither recent nor reliable enough for analyzing the current role of irrigation on national agricultural production and land needs. Lacking any suitable single source, we combined data from the 1974 census, the 1977 NRI, and various state crop and livestock reporting boards to estimate the 1977 dryland and irrigated harvested acreage of individual crops.

The 1977 acreage estimates start with the 1974 census data on irrigated and dryland crop acreage for each of the seventeen western states. The 1974 census data are not used directly since they understate irrigated acreage. The Soil Conservation Service's 1977 NRI has irrigated and dryland acreage data for the broad categories of row and close-grown crops. For each state, the ratio of 1977 NRI irrigated (dryland) row crops to 1974 census irrigated (dryland) row crops is multiplied by the 1974 census irrigated (dryland) acreages for corn, sorghum, and cotton. The 1974 census wheat acreages of each state are adjusted by a similarly calculated ratio for close-grown crops. These adjustments are intended to compensate for three factors--the growth from 1974 to 1977, the underenumeration of the census irrigation data, and the fact that the census crop data only include farms with sales of $2,500 or more.

The above adjustment assumes that the acreage of each crop grew at the same rate as the acreage of the entire crop group. This assumption seems reasonable for wheat which comprises the great majority of the close-grown crops. A further adjustment is required, however, to allow for differences in growth from 1974 to 1977 of the individual row crops. There are only partial data available for determining these differences. For corn the ratio of irrigated (dryland) corn acreage to irrigated (dryland) row crop acreage in 1977 was divided by the comparable ratio for 1974. This ratio was then multiplied by the initial estimate of 1977 irrigated (dryland) corn acreage. Similar adjustments were made for sorghum and cotton. The state crop and livestock reporting boards are the only sources of data required to calculate these ratios but only some of the states have such data. Consequently, the available data were combined to estimate a regional adjustment factor for each of the row crops.

Since the NRI crop acreage estimates include temporarily idled land and all acreage planted, further adjustment of the 1977 crop acreages was made to convert the estimates to a harvested acreage basis. This adjustment was done by assuming that the previously calculated figures correctly reflect the ratio of irrigated to dryland acres and that the U.S. Department of Agriculture's Statistical Reporting Service data are the most accurate estimates of total harvested crop acreage.

The yield estimates are based on trends which eliminate or at least reduce the impact of short-term fluctuations resulting from the weather or other factors. Estimated yields for both irrigated and dryland production are based on fitting a linear regression to actual yields in 1950, 1954, 1959, 1969, 1974, and 1977. Census data are used for the 1950 through 1969 observations. The more recent yield data are based on crop and livestock reporting board data for all those western states providing data which differentiate between irrigated and dryland acreage and yields.

Appendix 2-C

THE COMPONENTS OF NATIONAL CROP PRODUCTION INCREASES

The changes in irrigated West, dryland West, and eastern production initially were divided into three components each: that due to
the change in acreage with yield held constant, that due to the change
in yield with acreage held constant, and that due to the impact of the
change in acreage on the change in yield, which is referred to as the
interaction effect. The sum of these three components is equivalent to
the total change in production for each category. This can be demonstrated by starting with the following definition:

$$P_t^i \equiv A_t^i Y_t^i,$$

where P_t^i is irrigated production in year t; A_t^i is irrigated acreage in
year t; and Y_t^i is the average yield on irrigated land in year t. If
indicates the change between years 0 and t, then

$$(1) \quad P^i \equiv P_t^i - P_0^i = \Delta A^i Y_0^i + \Delta Y^i A_0^i + \Delta A^i \Delta Y^i .$$

Thus, the change in irrigated production equals the sum of the three
components on the right-hand side of the equation: the change in dryland West and eastern production also can be divided into three comparable components.

Since irrigated acreage was relatively small in the initial year
(1950) and grew much faster than dryland acreage in the following decades, use of the equation in this form gives much greater weight to
nonirrigated as opposed to irrigated yield changes. Furthermore, much
of the production change is not attributed specifically to either yield
or acreage changes because of the sizable interaction term. Consequently, the interaction term has been eliminated by rewriting equation

(1) in the following but equivalent form:

$$(2) \quad \Delta P^i = \Delta A^i \, \overline{Y}^i + \Delta Y^i \overline{A}^i$$

where $\overline{Y} \equiv (Y_o + Y_t)/2$ and $\overline{A} \equiv (A_o + A_t)/2$. This equation weights the change in acreage (yield) terms by the average yields (acreages) rather than by the initial year levels. By eliminating the interaction term, the entire change in irrigated (dryland) production is divided among two terms, the change in yield and the change in acreage. The change in the total production of a given crop is equal to the sum of the changes for the irrigated West, dryland West, and East. Thus, total production change for each crop within a given region is divided into six components in table 2-11.

There are no "correct" weights for separating out the contribution of dryland and irrigated acreage and yield changes to the change in crop production. In comparison to the results presented in table 2-11, initial year weights decrease and final year weights increase the role attributed to irrigation yields.

Chapter 3

WATER AS A CONSTRAINT ON WESTERN IRRIGATION

The seventeen western states account for about five of every six gallons of the country's freshwater consumption (defined as the portion of water withdrawn for offstream use which is not returned to a surface or groundwater source). In 1975 per capita consumption in the West was 12.4 times that in the East.[1] Since the West receives only about one-fourth of the rainfall, it is not surprising that the most critical water supply problems identified by the Second National Water Assessement are located in the West.[2]

Water Development for Irrigation

With the exception of some mountainous areas and a narrow coastal strip in the Northwest, rainfall west of the 100th meridian, which roughly bisects Texas, Nebraska, and the Dakotas, is insufficient to support high productivity dryland agriculture. The combination of the sizable water requirements associated with irrigation and a deliberate government policy of encouraging western irrigation, led to the current situation where about 90 percent of western freshwater consumption is for irrigation.

The expansion of irrigation was facilitated by easy access to low cost water. Initial development was based primarily on directing surface waters to neighboring fields. Level valley lands that could be irrigated with gravity flows were the first to be developed. Subse-

---

1. C. Richard Murray and E. Bodette Reeves, Estimated Use of Water in the United States in 1975, U.S. Geological Survey Circular 765 (Arlington, Va., 1977) pp. 8-9.

2. U.S. Water Resources Council, The Nation's Water Resources 1975-2000, The Second National Water Assessment, vol. 1, Summary (Washington, D.C., GPO, December 1978) pp. 56-59.

quent expansion required canals, dams, and pumps to transport water longer distances and to increase the assured supply. Higher costs and an increasing dependence on nonrenewable groundwater supplies have resulted from this growth.

The Federal Role

The Bureau of Reclamation was established in 1902 to reclaim arid western land through irrigation. Lands receiving either full or supplementary irrigation water through federal projects rose to 400,000 acres by 1910, 3 million acres by 1930, and over 11 million acres by 1980. In recent years these projects provided at least some irrigation water to about one-fifth of the irrigated lands and full irrigation to about one-tenth of the acreage. Through time the Bureau of Reclamation's role has expanded to providing water for municipal and industrial use, hydroelectric power, water channels for navigation, flood control, and recreational facilities for the public. From 1902 through June 1975, the Bureau of Reclamation spent $6.0 billion on water related projects in the West; major accomplishments include construction of 326 storage reservoirs, 355 diversion dams, 14,320 miles of canals, and 34,290 miles of laterals.[3]

Despite the stipulation in the 1902 legislation that user charges should be sufficient to recover all the costs of constructing the projects, water from federal irrigation projects has been provided to farmers at highly subsidized rates.[4] Initial funds for construction costs were to be supplied by the sale of federal land in the West. Irrigation project costs were to be repaid by the users over a ten-year period with no interest charge; these funds then were to be used for subsequent projects. The intent of the initial legislation, however,

---

3. U.S. Department of Interior, Federal Reclamation Projects, Water and Land Resources Accomplishments, 1975, Summary Report (Washington, D.C., 1976).

4. Much of the following discussion of the evolution of federal water project policy is based on U.S. General Accounting Office, Federal Charges for Irrigation Projects Reviewed Do Not Cover Costs, PAD-81-07 (Washington, D.C., March 3, 1981) chapters 1 and 2.

bears little relation to what has transpired. The costs and problems of establishing irrigation on previously unfarmed arid lands were much greater than anticipated, and many farmers were unable to meet repayment requirements. Legislative relief came with the 1914 Reclamation Extension Act, which increased the repayment period to twenty years and provided a five-year grace period. New irrigators paid 5 percent of the costs up front and the balance in fifteen annual installments beginning in the sixth year. But even these more lenient repayment schedules were not met by many farmers, and the 1914 legislation proved to be just the first of a series of legislative and administrative adjustments to the original act that have combined to provide enormous subsidies for federal water projects. Farmers were provided with more beneficial payment terms in 1926 when about $17.3 million or 13 percent of the costs on twenty-one projects were written off and the repayment period was extended to forty years on all projects. The policy of not charging interest remained intact.

Further relief to those fortunate enough to have access to federal water came with the Reclamation Project Act of 1939. This act specified that irrigators were responsible only for that portion of the debt they were able to repay. Farm budgets are used to determine the rates farmers could afford. Implementation of the ability-to-pay criterion by the Bureau of Reclamation has been confusing but generally very beneficial to the farmers.[5] But almost regardless of the initial level of the water charge, large subsidies were ensured by extending the repayment period to as long as fifty years with a ten-year grace period and keeping the rates fixed throughout the period with no adjustment for inflation.

The objective of the earlier BR projects was almost exclusively irrigation. More recently projects have been designed to serve multiple purposes, and since the early 1950s, irrigation has been assigned

---

5. The General Accounting Office study of six federal irrigation projects found the Bureau of Reclamation's ability-to-pay "analysis to be inaccurate at times and misleading because it does not concentrate on the areas which will actually be irrigated nor on the crops which will be irrigated." Ibid., p. 2.

only part of the project costs. The amendment to the Reclamation Act allowing for separable costs intended that recreation, flood control, and fish and wildlife costs be largely nonreimbursable items; these costs were to be covered primarily by tax revenues. Irrigation costs were expected to be paid in full but without interest by the users while power, municipal, and industrial users were to repay the costs including some interest charge.

Estimates as to the level of subsidy provided irrigators on federal water projects vary depending in part on the projects considered and the interest rate used to discount future payments by irrigators. In all cases, however, dispassionate analysis indicates the subsidies have been generous.

Analysis of eighteen irrigation districts by the Office of Policy Analysis, U.S. Department of Interior shows a wide range among projects in federal subsidies. (Subsidy is defined as the difference between the full costs, which comprise all construction costs allocated to irrigation plus operation and maintenance costs with interest based on long-term government borrowing rates charged on all cost items, and the present value of past and expected future farmer payments.) The per-acre subsidies range from just $58 for Moon Lake, which receives only supplemental water, to $1,787 for the Wellton-Mohawk district; the subsidy ranges from 57 percent of the costs for Moon Lake to 97 percent for the East Columbia basin (see table 3-1).[6]

Alternative subsidy estimates by LeVeen suggest that the $3.62 billion the Bureau of Reclamation has spent for irrigation construction will be paid roughly 56.7 percent from electricity sales, 40 percent from general tax revenues, and only 3.3 percent by farmers.[7] In other words, irrigators are barely paying the operating and maintenance costs of the projects, and in some cases current charges fail to cover even these costs. For example, the cost of delivering water to the

6. U.S. Department of Interior, Acreage Limitation, Interim Report (Washington, D.C., March 1980) pp. 37-42.

7. E. Phillip LeVeen, "Reclamation Policy at a Crossroads," Public Affairs Report, vol. 19, no. 5 (October 1978) pp. 2-3.

Table 3-1. Federal Subsidies for Eighteen Irrigation Districts

Region and irrigation district	Irrigable acres in district in 1977 (1,000 acres)	Subsidy ($ per acre)	Subsidy as a percentage of full cost
Pacific Northwest Region			
1. Oroville-Tonasket	9.5	417	82
2. Black Canyon #2	53.2	762	89
3. East Columbia Basin	134.5	1,619	97
Mid-Pacific Region			
4. Cachuma Project	38.7[a]	1,378	81
5. Truckee-Carson	73.0	931	83
6. Glen	152.3[b]	101	91
7. San Luis Unit	571.9	1,422	85
8. Coachella Valley	78.5	1,000	70
9. Wellton-Mohawk	65.8	1,787	89
10. Imperial Valley	519.5	149	74
Upper Colorado Region			
11. Moon Lake	75.3[b]	58	57
12. Grand Valley	23.3	1,623	85
Southwest Region			
13. Elephant Butte	102.1	363	64
14. Lugert-Altus	47.1	675	90
Upper Missouri Region			
15. Malta	42.4	812	92
16. Lower Yellowstone #1	34.5	507	73
Lower Missouri Region			
17. Farwell	50.1	1,446	93
18. Goshen	52.5	416	74

Source: U.S. Department of Interior, Acreage Limitation, Interim Report (Washington, D.C., March 1980) pp. 38-41.

[a]A total of 38,151 acres or about 99 percent of the acreage receives only supplemental federal irrigation.

[b]This acreage receives only supplemental federal irrigation.

Westlands Water District in 1981 was projected to be $10.50 per acre-foot. Nevertheless, the present water rate of $7.50, which was determined in 1954 and implemented in 1968, will remain in effect through 2008.[8] With allowance for the effects of inflation, conservative assumptions suggest that the present value (in 1976 dollars) of the subsidy averages at least $500 per acre over all BR projects. A more definitive estimate for the Westlands Water District suggests the subsidy is three to four times that level.[9] Thus for a 160-acre farm, the total subsidy would be $80,000 at $500 per acre; in the Westlands the subsidy for such a farm might reach about $320,000. Since much of the irrigable land is owned and operated in much larger units, some landowners receive even larger subsidies. In the Westlands Water District, for example, nineteen owners have farms in excess of 1,920 acres and a subsidy of $3 million or more each. Thus, about one-half of 1 percent of the owners have 35 percent of the land in this district.[10]

A 1981 General Accounting Office (GAO) report to the Congress suggests high subsidy levels will continue with new Bureau of Reclamation projects.[11] The GAO report summarizes their assessment of six projects which were under construction but not completed at the time of the review. The total cost of these projects exceeds $2.1 billion, nearly half of which is attributed to irrigation facilities. Only a tiny fraction of these costs will be paid by irrigators. Using a 7.5 percent discount rate, the fees set by the Bureau of Reclamation imply irrigation subsidies ranging from 92.2 to 97.8 percent of the construction costs. The estimated costs of water delivered from these

---

8. U.S. Department of the Interior, Special Task Force Report on San Luis Unit, Stock no. 024-003-00123-6 (Washington, D.C., GPO, 1978).

9. LeVeen, "Reclamation Policy at a Crossroads," p. 3.

10. U.S. Department of Interior, Acreage Limitation-Draft Environmental Impact Statement (Washington, D.C., January 8, 1981) pp. 3-71 and 3-73. Distribution of federal irrigation subsidies is discussed further in chapter 4.

11. U.S. General Accounting Office, Federal Charges for Irrigation Projects.

federal projects range from $54 an acre-foot for the Fryingpan-Arkansas project, which distributes supplementary water through existing facilities, to $130 an acre-foot for the Pollock-Herreid project. Yet the charges to recover the construction costs of this water range from 27 cents (only 7 cents according to GAO calculations) to $9.82 per acre-foot.

Irrigation Water Withdrawals, 1950 to 1975

Total surface water withdrawals (defined as the water taken from surface water sources for offstream use) for western irrigation have not increased significantly from the level of 88 million acre-feet reached in 1955 (see table 3-2). Indeed, the 1955 level was not even reached again until 1975. This leveling off of stream flow diversions for irrigation reflected a number of factors including the rising costs associated with developing new supplies, the competition from nonfarm users for undeveloped supplies as well as water previously used for irrigation, and, as is demonstrated below, relatively little surface water remained to be developed within the areas with the most favorable growing conditions.[12]

Since the mid-1950s, the overall expansion of western irrigation has been based on groundwater, and the increasing importance of groundwater dates back several more decades. From negligible levels in the early 1930s, groundwater withdrawals for western irrigation rose to about 10.7 million acre-feet by 1945 and 56.0 million by 1975. Groundwater as a percentage of total irrigation withdrawals increased

---

12. Changes in surface water withdrawals may not be directly related to changes in the acreage irrigated with surface water. For example, improvements in on-farm water efficiency could increase the ratio of irrigated acreage to water withdrawn. However, since there has been little incentive for surface water users to improve irrigation efficiencies, it is not likely that there have been significant changes in this ratio. Furthermore, even if the ratio has increased, it does not necessarily follow that more land is irrigated with surface water since improvements in on-farm efficiency reduce the runoff available for use downstream.

Table 3-2. Ground and Surface Water Withdrawn for Western Irrigation, 1950-75
(per 1,000 acre-feet)

Region and source	1950	1955	1960[a]	1965	1970	1975
Northern Plains						
Groundwater	786	1,636	2,839	4,068	6,165	11,209
Surface	2,220	2,292	3,702	2,910	2,950	3,120
Total	3,006	3,929	6,540	6,978	9,115	14,329
Groundwater as						
percent of total	26	42	43	58	68	78
Southern Plains						
Groundwater	1,850	7,470	9,252	13,300	9,610	11,100
Surface	3,130	4,173	3,570	2,910	2,910	2,780
Total	4,980	11,643	12,822	16,210	12,520	13,880
Groundwater as						
percent of total	37	64	72	82	77	80
Mountain						
Groundwater	5,285	9,906	12,226	11,400	11,311	14,450
Surface	42,300	53,860	45,411	47,200	52,200	50,900
Total	47,585	63,766	57,637	58,600	63,511	65,350
Groundwater as						
percent of total	11	16	21	20	18	22
Pacific						
Groundwater	10,270	12,002	11,575	12,830	19,100	19,260
Surface	18,900	27,700	25,365	26,500	29,600	31,600
Total	29,170	39,702	36,940	39,330	48,700	50,860
Groundwater as						
percent of total	35	30	31	33	39	38
17 Western states						
Groundwater	18,191	31,014	35,892	41,598	46,186	56,019
Surface	66,550	88,025	78,047	79,520	87,660	88,400
Total	84,741	119,039	113,939	121,118	133,846	144,419
Groundwater as						
percent of total	21	26	32	34	35	39

Sources: The data are from the following U.S. Geological Survey circulars: 1950 data – Kenneth A.
MacKichan, Estimated Use of Water in the United States in 1950, circular 115 (Washington, D.C., May 1951);
1955 data – Kenneth A. MacKichan, Estimated Use of Water in the United States in 1955, Circular 398
(Washington, D.C., 1957); 1960 data – Kenneth A. MacKichan and J. C. Kammerer, Estimated Use of Water in
the United States in 1960, Circular 456 (Washington, D.C., 1961); 1965 data – C. Richard Murray, Estimated
Use of Water in the United States, 1965, Circular 556 (Washington, D.C., 1968); 1970 data – C. Richard
Murray and E. Bodette Reeves, Estimated Use of Water in the United States in 1970, Circular 676 (Washing-
ton, D.C., 1974); 1975 data – C. Richard Murray and E. Bodette Reeves, Estimated Use of Water in the
United States in 1975, Circular 765 (Arlington, VA., 1977).

[a]1960 conveyance losses are divided among ground- and surface water according to the same percentages
indicated by the 1955 data.

steadily over this period to 39 percent by 1975 (see table 3-2).[13]

Technological breakthroughs in high-speed engines and turbine centrifugal pumps helped establish deep-well pumping as a viable alternative in the mid-1930s. The combination of these technical advances and widespread drought encouraged the rapid expansion of groundwater irrigation in the late 1930s, especially in the southern High Plains. Additional technological advances as well as access to inexpensive energy for irrigation pumping further stimulated the growth of groundwater irrigation. In particular, the availability of very low cost natural gas and development of the center-pivot sprinkler system encouraged the rapid growth of irrigation in the High Plains. Although they were developed in the 1950s, the big expansion of center pivots started in the late 1960s and continued into the 1970s.

From 1945 to 1965 the largest increases in groundwater use were in the Southern Plains; more recently they have been in the Northern Plains. Annual groundwater withdrawals for irrigation in the Southern Plains rose from less than 1 million acre-feet in 1945, to nearly 2 million acre-feet in 1950, and 13 million acre-feet in 1965. This latter level resulted in substantial groundwater mining (withdrawals in excess of natural recharge), most notably within the Southern High Plains of Texas, which is examined in more detail below. Although groundwater withdrawals in the Southern Plains have declined sharply from the 1965 level, in 1975 they still accounted for 80 percent of this region's total irrigation withdrawals.

The most recent growth of western irrigation has been concentrated in the Northern Plains. While groundwater accounted for only 26 percent of 1950 Northern Plains irrigation withdrawals, over the next quarter century 92 percent of the region's increase in irrigation withdrawals were from the ground. Groundwater rose to 78 percent of their total irrigation withdrawals by 1975 (see table 3-2).

---

13. The earliest available data on groundwater withdrawals are in W. F. Guyton, "Estimated use of Ground Water in the United States--1945" (an unpublished paper prepared at the U.S. Geological Survey). Comparable surface water data are not available for 1945.

Water Supply Adequacy

There are no simple measures indicating the nature and seriousness of a region's water problems. While market price is the normal measure of scarcity, water is seldom allocated within competitive markets. But even if water were allocated competitively, the market price would not measure the social costs of water use because of the importance of third-party effects (which emerge when the buyer and seller are not the only ones affected by a water transfer) and the problems of evaluating the benefits and costs of most water uses.[14]

Further complications in assessing a region's or individual's water situation stem from the variety of factors which affect the value of a given quantity of water and the divergent impacts users can have on the supply. Quality, location, timing, and certainty of supply are all important dimensions of water value. But the importance of the various dimensions as well as the impacts of both withdrawals and re-turn flows on these factors vary widely among users. Water withdrawn for use is seldom fully consumed in that use. For example, in 1975 consumption as a percentage of withdrawals averaged 1 percent for thermoelectric power, 11 percent for other industrial uses, 23 percent for public supplies, and 56 percent for irrigation.[15] Consequently, both the portion of the water available for reuse and the characteristics of the return flows are important for determining the social costs of a particular water withdrawal.

Although there is no simple way to assess all the factors affect-ing a region's supply situation, water supply and use data from the Second National Water Assessment indicate the pressures on water re-

---

14. For a discussion of the problems encountered in managing water resources, see John V. Krutilla and Otto Eckstein, Multiple Purpose River Development (Baltimore, Johns Hopkins University Press for Resources for the Future, 1958).

15. Murray and Reeves, Estimated Use of Water in 1975, Circular 765.

sources within 20 water resource regions and 108 subregions.[16] Several
indicators of the pressures on the ten western water resources regions
are presented in the following three tables. Table 3-3 indicates the
relation between total water use, defined as the sum of instream needs
and offstream consumption, and total streamflow under average and dry
year conditions; table 3-4 indicates the relation between offstream
water consumption and total streamflow in an average year; table 3-5
indicates groundwater mining as a percentage of total annual offstream
water consumption in an average year.[17]

---

16. The regions and subregions are defined according to drainage basins
and no combination of these conforms exactly to the boundaries of the
seventeen western states. Ten of these regions, which are divided into
fifty-three subregions, include almost all of the area of the western
states. But they also include three subregions which are either
totally or largely within the eastern states and another five which
include some parts of the East. For the purposes of this section, however, there is little distortion introduced by using all ten western
water resource regions as a proxy for the seventeen western states.
The lands that are not common to both geographical groups are relatively insignificant in terms of irrigation, water use, and water supply
problems.

17. The Second National Water Assessment quantifies minimum streamflow
levels for fish and wildlife population maintenance and for navigation.
Instream need for a water resource subregion is calculated as the flow
at the discharge point of the subregion required to satisfy the higher
of the fish and wildlife or the navigational needs. In all subregions,
the fish and wildlife use is the dominant instream flow use. (U.S.
Water Resources Council, The Nation's Water Resources, vol. 1, p. 42).
    Offstream consumption is estimated as the total water that would
have been consumed or lost assuming a demand based on 1975 levels of
activity. The level of demand varies depending on the precipitation
assumptions. Average precipitation levels are those that will be
equaled or exceeded 50 percent of the time. Dry year precipitation
levels are those that will be equaled or exceeded 80 percent of the
time. The Assessment estimates only irrigation and steam electric uses
differently according to the dryness of the year.
    Groundwater mining or overdraft is the portion of groundwater
withdrawals that exceed recharge.
    Streamflow is an estimate of surface freshwater discharge rates in
the absence of offstream withdrawals at the outflow point of the
subregions.

Table 3-3. Total Water Use as a Percentage of Streamflow in Average
and Dry Years

Region number	Subregion number	Name	Average years	Dry year
09		SOURIS-RED-RAINY	62	110
	01	Souris-Red-Rainy	62	110
10		MISSOURI	87	120
	01	Missouri-Milk-Saskatchewan	82	105
	02	Missouri-Marias	82	104
	03	Missouri-Musselshell	81	102
	04	Yellowstone	96	117
	05	Western Dakotas	84	108
	06	Eastern Dakotas	82	102
	07	North and South Platte	140	160
	08	Niobrara-Platte-Loup	103	122
	09	Middle Missouri	91	107
	10	Kansas	123	191
	11	Lower Missouri	87	120
11		ARKANSAS-WHITE-RED	83	138
	01	Upper White	84	126
	02	Upper Arkansas	134	175
	03	Arkansas-Cimarron	114	243
	04	Lower Arkansas	83	152
	05	Canadian	122	261
	06	Red-Washita	129	180
	07	Red-Sulphur	83	133
12		TEXAS-GULF	101	197
	01	Sabine-Neches	85	163
	02	Trinity-Galveston Bay	89	176
	03	Brazos	142	327
	04	Colorado (Texas)	119	188
	05	Nueces-Texas Coastal	96	183
13		RIO GRANDE	136	180
	01	Rio Grande Headwaters	110	159
	02	Middle Rio Grande	140	165
	03	Rio Grande-Pecos	148	176
	04	Upper Pecos	144	177
	05	Lower Rio Grande	136	180
14		UPPER COLORADO	84	112
	01	Green-White-Yampa	87	114
	02	Colorado-Gunnison	80	106
	03	Colorado-San Juan	84	112
15		LOWER COLORADO	225	239
	01	Little Colorado	80	103
	02	Lower Colorado Main Stem	225	239
	03	Gila	304	315
16		GREAT BASIN	125	158
	01	Bear-Great Salt Lake	102	125
	02	Sevier Lake	186	204
	03	Humboldt-Tonopah Desert	177	222
	04	Central Lahontan	116	165
17		PACIFIC NORTHWEST	84	102
	01	Clark Fork-Kootenai	62	73
	02	Upper / Middle Columbia	79	94
	03	Upper / Central Snake	91	119
	04	Lower Snake	78	96
	05	Coast-Lower Columbia	85	102
	06	Puget Sound	81	96
	07	Oregon Closed Basin	101	161
18		CALIFORNIA	82	113
	01	Klamath-North Coastal	65	95
	02	Sacramento-Lahontan	76	106
	03	San Joaquin-Tulare	109	131
	04	San Francisco Bay	91	152
	05	Central California Coast	83	169
	06	Southern California	107	116
	07	Lahontan-South	243	290

Note: Total water use includes instream use and offstream consumption.

Source: U.S. Water Resources Council, The Nation's Water Resources:
The Second National Water Assessment, vol. 3, app. II (Washington, D.C.,
GPO, 1978) tables II-5 and II-6, app. IV, table IV-2.

Table 3-4. Offstream Water Consumption as a Percentage of Total Streamflow in an Average Year

Region number	Subregion number	Name	Offstream consumption as a percentage of streamflow
09		SOURIS-RED-RAINY	2
	01	Souris-Red-Rainy	2
10		MISSOURI	27
	01	Missouri-Milk-Saskatchewan	23
	02	Missouri-Marias	22
	03	Missouri-Musselshell	21
	04	Yellowstone	21
	05	Western Dakotas	24
	06	Eastern Dakotas	22
	07	North and South Platte	85
	08	Niobrara-Platte-Loup	69
	09	Middle Missouri	32
	10	Kansas	63
	11	Lower Missouri	27
11		ARKANSAS-WHITE-RED	12
	01	Upper White	1
	02	Upper Arkansas	85
	03	Arkansas-Cimarron	56
	04	Lower Arkansas	19
	05	Canadian	62
	06	Red-Washita	68
	07	Red-Sulphur	12
12		TEXAS-GULF	33
	01	Sabine-Neches	5
	02	Trinity-Galveston Bay	18
	03	Brazos	84
	04	Colorado (Texas)	82
	05	Nueces-Texas Coastal	26
13		RIO GRANDE	88
	01	Rio Grande Headwaters	69
	02	Middle Rio Grande	96
	03	Rio Grande-Pecos	102
	04	Upper Pecos	94
	05	Lower Rio Grande	88
14		UPPER COLORADO	20
	01	Green-White-Yampa	22
	02	Colorado-Gunnison	17
	03	Colorado-San Juan	20
15		LOWER COLORADO	114
	01	Little Colorado	21
	02	Lower Colorado Main Stem	114
	03	Gila	254
16		GREAT BASIN	66
	01	Bear-Great Salt Lake	44
	02	Sevier Lake	127
	03	Humboldt-Tonopah Dessert	117
	04	Central Lahontan	56
17		PACIFIC NORTHWEST	4
	01	Clark Fork-Kootenai	2
	02	Upper / Middle Columbia	8
	03	Upper / Central Snake	33
	04	Lower Snake	16
	05	Coast-Lower Columbia	5
	06	Puget Sound	<1
	07	Oregon Closed Basin	41
18		CALIFORNIA	37
	01	Klamath-North Coastal	3
	02	Sacramento-Lahontan	28
	03	San Joaquin-Tulare	89
	04	San Francisco Bay	24
	05	Central California Coast	37
	06	Southern California	101
	07	Lahontan-South	100

Source: U.S. Water Resources Council, The Nation's Water
Resources: Second National Water Assessment, vol. 3, app. II (Washington, D.C., GPO, 1978) table II-5.

Table 3-5. Groundwater Mining as a Percentage of Annual Offstream Water
Consumption in an Average Year

Region number	Subregion number	Name	Groundwater mining as a percentage of annual offstream consumption
10		MISSOURI	17
	03	Missouri-Musselshell	1
	05	Western Dakotas	2
	06	Eastern Dakotas	7
	07	North and South Platte	13
	08	Niobrara-Platte-Loup	13
	09	Middle Missouri	16
	10	Kansas	41
	11	Lower Missouri	5
11		ARKANSAS-WHITE-RED	68
	01	Upper White	2
	02	Upper Arkansas	3
	03	Arkansas-Cimarron[b]	100
	04	Lower Arkansas	2
	05	Canadian	85
	06	Red-Washita	55
	07	Red-Sulphur	1
12		TEXAS-GULF	50
	01	Sabine-Neches	8
	02	Trinity-Galveston Bay	19
	03	Brazos	78
	04	Colorado (Texas)	38
	05	Nueces-Texas Coastal	26
13		RIO GRANDE	16
	02	Middle Rio Grande	21
	03	Rio Grande-Pecos	46
	04	Upper Pecos	16
	05	Lower Rio Grande	1
15		LOWER COLORADO	53
	01	Little Colorado	7
	02	Lower Colorado Main Stem	27
	03	Gila	61
16		GREAT BASIN	16
	01	Bear-Great Salt Lake	3
	02	Sevier Lake	40
	03	Humboldt-Tonopah Desert	27
	04	Central Lahontan	3
17		PACIFIC NORTHWEST	5
	01	Clark Fork-Kootenai	2
	02	Upper / Middle Columbia	8
	03	Upper / Central Snake	4
	04	Lower Snake	7
	05	Coast-Lower Columbia	2
	07	Oregon Closed Basin	2
18		CALIFORNIA	8
	02	Sacramento-Lahontan	4
	03	San Joaquin-Tulare	10
	05	Central California Coast	10
	06	Southern California	8
	07	Lahontan-South	43

Source: U.S. Water Resources Council, The Nation's Water Resources:
The Second National Assessment, vol. 3, app. II (Washington, D.C., GPO,
1978) table II-6.

[a]Includes only subregions with percentages of 0.5 or above.

[b]The Assessment shows groundwater mining at 103 percent of offstream
consumption. Since the theoretical limit should be 100 percent, this is
the figure used here.

Surface Water

Based on the Second National Water Assessment data for average year conditions, total water use exceeds streamflow in twenty-four subregions (indicated in figure 3-1), which account for about 66 percent of the West's irrigated land. Furthermore, in most of the other twenty-nine subregions, there is little slack between streamflow and total water use. Total use is less than 75 percent of streamflow in only three subregions, and these are areas with relatively poor agricultural potential.

In a year of below average rainfall, the imbalance between supplies and estimated use is more intense and widespread. Shortfalls are more likely not only because supplies are reduced but also because demand may be higher, especially for irrigation where more water is needed to compensate for reduced precipitation. In a dry year, total water use exceeds streamflow in forty-eight of the fifty-three subregions (see table 3-3). Four of the exceptions are in the humid Pacific Northwest region and the other is the northernmost subregion of the California region. The magnitude of the supply shortfalls are particularly striking. In twenty-six of the subregions, water use exceeds streamflow by more than 50 percent, and in eight of the subregions use is more than twice dry-year streamflow.

Total water use includes an estimate of instream needs. Instream water flows can serve a number of purposes including maintaining fish and wildlife populations, outdoor recreation, navigation, hydroelectric generation, waste assimilation, and maintaining aquatic and riparian vegetation. While the second assessment estimates of instream needs reflect only the minimum flow needed to maintain fish and wildlife, a comparison of the average year percentages in tables 3-3 and 3-4 suggests the considerable importance of instream uses to the degree of water scarcity. In thirty-three of the subregions, instream flow requirements are more than half of total water use. Offstream water consumption exceeds total streamflow in an average year in only six subregions.

Figure 3-1.

Water Resource Subregions Where Total Water Use Exceeds Streamflows in an Average Year.

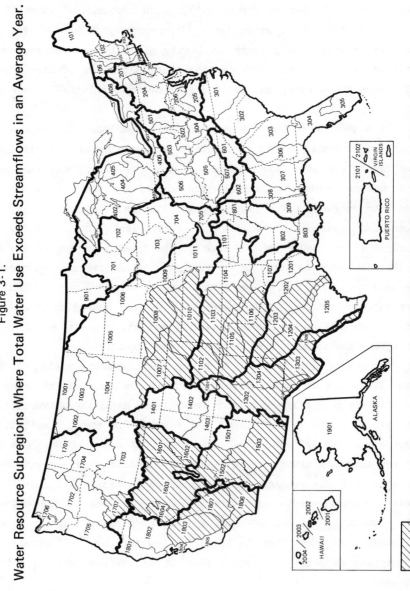

Indicates subregions where total water use exceeds total streamflow in an average year.

The absence of any consensus as to how much water should be allocated to instream uses such as fish and wildlife does not mean that including these uses in estimating total water use overstates the degree of water scarcity. There is also no general agreement as to the amount of water that should be allocated to irrigation or any other use. Society's concern as to the quantity and quality of instream flows has increased in recent years, and it may increase further in the future. Even though these uses do not compete for water in the marketplace, society must take them into account if scarce supplies are to be efficiently allocated among alternative uses.

Groundwater

Although it is customary to differentiate between ground and surface waters, the distinction between these two sources of supply is not always clear. For example, the Second National Water Assessement reports that, "about 30 percent of the Nation's streamflow, in an average year, is supplied by ground water that emerges as natural springs and other seepage. In turn, seepage from streams, rivers, canals, and reservoirs is a source of ground-water recharge. Most of the flow in many smaller streams comes from ground water during the low-flow months. In years of below normal precipitation, all the streamflow during low stage may be ground water. Ground water, therefore, is important to the continuity of steamflow."[18]

The quantity of water stored in the ground far exceeds that available in streams, lakes, and ponds.[19] Even though it will be too expensive to ever utilize most of the groundwater, the quantities economically available for use are vast. These stocks provide both a valuable source for expanding water use as well as a supplement to surface water resources during unusually dry periods. Groundwater use

---

18. U.S. Water Resources Council, The Nation's Water Resources, vol. 1: Summary, p. 18.

19. Most groundwater is a stock resource that can be depleted over time when groundwater use exceeds recharge. The fundamental differences between stock resources, which can be depleted, and flow resources, which are renewed annually, make direct comparisons of these two sources of water supplies potentially misleading.

can reduce the risk of substantial loss in a dry year, the need for costly surface storage, and the evaporation losses that result when surface storage is used. However, this is not the use to which western groundwater stocks generally have been employed. Groundwater has become the principal source of supply in many areas, not simply a dry year supplement. Consequently, enormous quantities of water are mined from western aquifers even in the wettest of years.

Mining, the net difference between extractions and recharge, exceeds 20 billion gallons per day, or 22.4 million acre-feet per year, in an average year in the seventeen western states. Just within the Texas and Oklahoma High Plains, annual groundwater mining is 14 million acre-feet, equivalent to the average annual flow of the Colorado River.[20] The annual mining from western aquifers is equivalent to 40 percent of groundwater withdrawals for irrigation in 1975 (see table 3-2) and is sufficient to irrigate 10.7 million acres based on average consumption levels.[21]

Groundwater mining is equivalent to 10 percent or more of annual off-stream consumption in twenty-one water resource subregions (see figure 3-2). Not surprisingly, there is a close parallel between these subregions and the twenty-four subregions where an average year's water use exceeds streamflow; seventeen subregions belong to both groups, and these seventeen account for about 86 percent of the total western groundwater depletions. Groundwater mining is equivalent to 30 percent or more of offstream consumption in ten subregions and 50 percent or more in five subregions. The five subregions with the highest rates of groundwater mining include most of the High Plains of Texas, Oklahoma, New Mexico, Colorado, and Kansas and Arizona's principal agricultural

---

20. U.S. Water Resources Council, The Nation's Water Resources, vol. 1, p. 18.

21. Based on the National Future estimates of the Second National Water Assessment, which indicate 86.4 billion gallons per day or 96.8 million acre-feet per year were consumed to irrigate 45.3 million acres, average consumption was 2.1 acre-feet of water per irrigated acre. Ibid., vol. 2, part III, pp. 57 and 62.

Figure 3-2.

Subregions Where Groundwater Mining is at Least 10 Percent of Offstream Water Consumption in an Average Year.

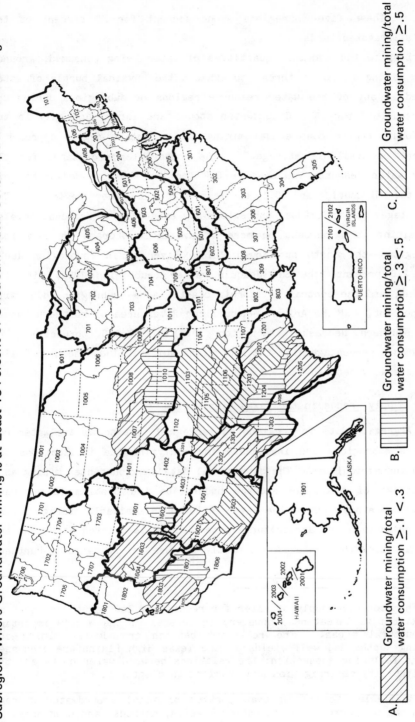

A. Groundwater mining/total water consumption ≥ .1 < .3

B. Groundwater mining/total water consumption ≥ .3 < .5

C. Groundwater mining/total water consumption ≥ .5

areas. These five subregions alone account for 20 percent of the West's irrigated lands.

Despite the enormous quantities of water being consumed, ground-water mining is not a threat to exhaust the physical supply of water stored in any of the water resource regions or subregions during the foreseeable future.[22] Groundwater stocks are large, and only in the California region does annual mining for an entire region approach 1 percent of available storage.[23] The comparable percentages for the other water resource regions are 0.4 for the Arkansas-Red-White, 0.2 for the Missouri, and 0.1 or less for all other regions. The percentages for individual subregions may exceed these regional levels, but mining is 1 percent or more of available storage in only four subregions--the North and South Platte River basin (subregion 1007) with 2.0 percent, the San Joaquin valley (subregion 1802) with 1.8 percent, and the central California coastal area (subregion 1805) with 1.0 percent, and the Arikaree-Republican River area of northern Kansas and southern Nebraska (subregion 1010) with 1.0 percent. The comparable percentages for the subregions which include the High Plains are generally between 0.6 and 1.0.

Water Supply Trends in the Texas High Plains

Aggregate data for regions as large and diverse as the water re-sources subregions are inadequate for analyzing the implications for irrigated agriculture. The subregional data on groundwater mining as a percentage of available storage understate the problem facing many irrigators since much of the water included as available storage under-lies areas with low agricultural potential or is located at depths and in quantities that make it too costly for use in irrigation. Further-

---

22. The economic supply of water for relatively low value uses such as irrigation is threatened, however, in several of the West's important agricultural areas. The relations between groundwater mining and pumping depths and well yields in the Texas High Plains are discussed in the following subsection; the relations between water costs and the profitability of irrigation are examined in chapter 5.

23. Available storage is that portion of total groundwater storage which can be tapped with conventional wells, methods, and machinery.

more, seemingly modest reductions in the groundwater stocks of a large
water resource subregion obscure the difficulties experienced by particular areas when the reductions are localized. While there are
insufficient data for a detailed analysis for the West of irrigation
water supplies and the impacts of current usage on future supplies,
studies of the Texas High Plains suggest the problems many farmers,
local communities, and regional economies may encounter.

A series of county studies by the Texas Department of Water Resources illustrates the impacts irrigation may have on future water
resources in one of the West's principal irrigated areas, the southern
High Plains. In these county studies the volume of water in storage,
the saturated thickness of the aquifer, and pumping rates and lifts are
estimated for 1974 and projected for 10-year intervals from 1980 to
2020. The projections are based on observed water use and precipitation levels between 1960 and 1972 with adjustments over time to allow
for the effects of depletion on well yields.

A twenty-four county region in the southern High Plains of Texas
is used to illustrate the impacts of groundwater mining on future water
availability.[24] Irrigation has been essential to this region's growth
and is important to its continued prosperity.

Aggregate farm income of these twenty-four counties exceeded $1.3
billion in the mid-1970s. Although irrigation's contribution to this
income is unknown, it clearly was sizable. For example, virtually all
the corn, about 80 percent of the sorghum and wheat, and 89 percent of

---

24. The twenty-four counties are Armstrong, Bailey, Carson, Castro,
Parmer, Lamb, Hale, Gaines, Gray, Randall, Swisher, Dawson, Borden,
Lynn, Garza, Terry, Yoakum, Cochran, Lubbock, Hockley, Deaf Smith,
Briscoe, Floyd, and Crosby. These counties, which comprise a
contiguous area of the southern Texas High Plains, were the only ones
for which analytical studies of the underlying Ogallala aquifer were
available. Unless otherwise stated all the information in this section
on groundwater in the Texas High Plains and the economies of these
twenty-four counties is from the series of studies published by the
Texas Department of Water Resources. These reports, which were
published between February 1976 and March 1979, are titled _Analytical
Study of the Ogallala Aquifer in --- County, Texas: Projections of
Saturated Thickness, Volume of Water in Storage, Pumpage Rates, Pumping
Lifts, and Well Yields_.

the cotton production of these counties were grown with irrigation.[25]

The water and acreage data for these twenty-four High Plains counties are aggregated and summarized in tables 3-6, 3-7, and 3-8. The Ogallala is the principal source of irrigation water for these counties. Annual pumping from the aquifer underlying these counties is projected to decline from 4.1 million acre-feet in 1974, to 3.0 million in 2000, and 2.2 million in 2020, and the water in storage is projected to fall from 145.9 million acre-feet in 1974 to 52.3 million acre-feet in 2020. Thus, even with the 46 percent decline in pumping, the projections imply that annual pumping will rise to nearly 4.2 percent of storage by 2020 compared to 2.8 percent in 1974.

Groundwater depletion is not new to this area. It is estimated that the volume of water stored in the Ogallala south of the Canadian River declined by about 100 million acre-feet or over 40 percent from 1937 to 1972.[26] While the estimates of past and projected groundwater use suggest the levels may have peaked about the mid-1970s in this region, pumping and groundwater mining as a percentage of water in storage are expected to continue to increase out to 2020.

Table 3-7 and 3-8 indicate the projected changes in the saturated thickness of the aquifer and the pumping depths for 1974, 2000, and 2020 in these twenty-four High Plains counties. These features are important determinants of water costs. Saturated thickness is directly related to well yields while pumping depth is the primary determinant of the energy required to lift water to the surface.[27] The capital

---

25. These data are based on the following publications of the Texas Crop and Livestock Reporting Service: Wheat - 1974 Texas Small Grains Statistics, p. 15; cotton - 1974 Texas Cotton Statistics, p. 16; sorghum - 1975 Texas Field Crop Statistics, pp. 67 and 71. All these publications are available from Texas Department of Agriculture, Austin, Texas.

26. U.S. Department of Interior, Bureau of Reclamation, West Texas and Eastern New Mexico Import Project. Reconnaissance Report (Washington, D.C., June 1973) pp. 18-19.

27. The pumping depth or lift is the distance from the surface to the water level in an operational well. It is equal to the depth to the static water level plus the drawdown due to pumping.

Table 3-6. Groundwater Storage and Annual Pumping in 1974, 2000, and 2020
for a Twenty-four-County Area in the Texas High Plains

(millions acre-feet)

Year	Volume of groundwater in storage[a]	Annual water pumpage
1974[b]	145.9	4.1
2000	85.2	3.0
2020	52.3	2.2

Note: Footnote 24 of this chaper lists the counties included in
these tables.

Source: Texas Department of Water Resources, Analytical Study of the
Ogallala Aquifer in --- County, Texas (Austin, Texas Department of Water
Resources, various years).

[a]These are based on estimates of the total amount of water in storage.
The quantities that can be economically recovered for use with present
technologies and costs are significantly less than the total amount in
storage.

[b]Several of the county studies from which these estimates are drawn
list 1975 rather than 1974 as the base year.

Table 3-7. Surface Area Grouped by the Saturated Thickness of the Underlying Aquifer for a Twenty-four-County Area in the Texas
High Plains

(1,000 acres)

Year	Surface area grouped the saturaged thickness of the aquifer			
	0-50 ft	50-100 ft	100-150 ft	150+ ft
1974[a]	4,636	3,471	1,883	1,787
2000	7,563	3,231	820	201
2020	9,850	1,852	121	75

Note: Footnote 24 of this chapter lists the counties included in
these tables.

Source: Texas Department of Water Resources, Analytical Study of the
Ogallala Aquifer in --- County, Texas (Austin, Texas Department of Water
Resources, various years).

[a]Several of the county studies from which these estimates are drawn
list 1975 rather 1974 as the base year.

Table 3-8. Surface Area Corresponding to Alternative Pumping Lift Intervals for a Twenty-four-County Area in the Texas High Plains
for the Years 1974, 2000, and 2020

(1,000 acres)

Pumping lift intervals (in feet)	1974[a]	2000	2020
0–25	145	143	143
25–50	374	354	354
50–75	389	383	383
75–100	548	525	525
100–125	829	780	783
125–150	1,592	1,319	1,313
150–175	1,553	1,431	1,403
175–200	1,338	1,367	1,345
200–225	1,249	1,066	1,078
225–250	1,091	552	525
250–275	839	590	571
275–300	531	776	669
300–325	360	748	644
325–350	293	488	530
350–375	204	383	445
375–400	178	240	342
400–425	110	183	181
425–450	137	138	138
≥450	82	350	473

Note: Footnote 24 of this chapter lists the counties included in
these totals.

Source: Texas Department of Water Resources, Analytical Study of the
Ogallala Aquifer in --- County, Texas (Austin, Texas Department of Water
Resources, various years).

[a]Several of the county studies from which these estimates are drawn
list 1975 rather than 1974 as the base year.

costs associated with drilling and the optimal size of the power source and well are also related to the saturated thickness and pumping depth.

In 1974 almost 3.7 million acres overlaid sections of the aquifer with a saturated thickness of 100 feet or more, the thickness generally required for well yields exceeding 1,000 gallons per minute. In comparison, the saturated thickness of the aquifer is projected to be 100 feet or more for only about 1 million acres by the turn of the century and 196,000 acres by 2020. On the other hand, the acreage overlying saturated sections of the aquifer of 50 feet or less is projected to rise from 4.6 million in 1974, to 7.6 million in 2000, and 9.9 million in 2020. These projected declines in the saturated thickness of the aquifer are particularly serious since they imply even sharper reductions in well yields. For example, a decline in the saturated thickness from 100 to 40 feet is apt to reduce the yield of a well in this region from 1,000 to 250 gallons per minute even when adjustments in the well and pump are made to reflect changes in the aquifer.[28] Since these well yield estimates are based on capability with optimal equipment, the actual reductions in well yields experienced by a typical farmer are likely to be greater. But even under the best circum-

---

28. The actual relation between well yields and saturated thickness varies depending on the physical composition of the aquifer. For example, saturated portions comprised largely of silt and clay will restrict well yields much more than will a sandy composition. For a well penetrating the total saturated section of the aquifer and sized to produce the maximum water yield, the Texas Department of Water Resources offers the following general guide relating well yield to saturated thickness in the Texas High Plains:

Saturated Thickness (feet)	Well Yield (gallons per minute)
Less than 20	Less than 100
20-40	100-250
40-60	250-500
60-80	500-800
80-100	800-1,000
More than 100	More than 1,000

Source: Texas Department of Water Resources, Analytical Study of the Ogallala Aquifer in --- County, Texas (Austin, Texas Department of Water Resources, various years) p. 9 of any of these county reports.

stances, this decline of 60 feet in saturated thickness reduces the potential irrigable acreage for this well by 75 percent. In practice the impacts of lower well yields on actual acreage irrigated have been cushioned by pumping longer hours, switching to crops with lower water requirements, or adopting other water conserving practices.

The changes in pumping lifts implied by the projected aquifer depletions are indicated in table 3-8. The most striking changes are the increases in the acreage with relatively high pumping lifts. For example, the lands with lifts of 300 feet or more are projected to rise from 1.4 million acres in 1974, to 2.5 million acres in 2000, and 2.8 million acres (23 percent of the total) in 2020.

Groundwater mining has widely differing impacts even within an area that is relatively homogeneous with respect to most factors affecting agricultural production. Despite being linked to a common aquifer, groundwater is very unevenly distributed within and among the southern High Plains counties. Also, depending on the configuration of the aquifer and its physical composition, individual lands are affected very differently by mining. For example, water table declines in the southern High Plains of Texas due to groundwater pumping from 1948 to 1967 varied from less than 20 feet to more than 120.[29] Consequently, while many farmers already have been forced to abandon irrigation, others still have relatively secure futures. (The economic implications of declining well yields and rising pumping lifts are considered in chapter 5 of this study.)

The groundwater situation in the southern High Plains is illustrative but not representative of the problems confronting many other irrigated areas. Indeed, the low rates of natural recharge, the high dependence on groundwater, and the extent and duration of the demands on groundwater all suggest that the water situation in the southern High Plains is unusually serious. On the other hand, in comparison with the arid West, irrigation requires less water and dryland farming is an alternative in the High Plains. Moreover, pumping depths in the

---

29. U.S. Department of Interior, Bureau of Reclamation, West Texas and Eastern New Mexico Import Project. p. 18.

southern Ogallala are not high compared to those of some other irrigated areas. For example, the water tables in the southern portion of
the Ogallala are often closer to the surface (although with less
saturated thickness) than those of the Ogallala north of the Canadian
River.[30] In short, there are wide differences in the impacts of
groundwater mining on individual farmers both among and between
irrigated areas.

Competition for Western Water

While irrigation continues to dominate the use of western water,
other demands for water are growing more rapidly. From 1960 to 1975,
total fresh water consumed in western irrigation grew at only one-half
the rate for all other uses combined (see table 3-9). Only in the
Northern Plains did the rate of growth of water consumption for irrigation exceed the rate for all other uses. Nevertheless, in 1975 other
water uses accounted for less than 10 percent of total fresh water consumption in all regions except the Southern Plains.

Water Consumption Projections

Future change in irrigated acreage will vary widely depending in
large part on the relation between the supply and demand for water in a
particular area. Although water is transportable, the costs of doing
so are high in relation to its value in agriculture. Consequently,
irrigators in a given area must rely largely on the water currently
available either naturally or through water importation structures
already in place. This suggests that some disaggregation of the West
according to water scarcity would be useful for forecasting likely
changes in irrigation.

---

30. In four Texas counties north of the Canadian River for which
comparable studies of the aquifer are available, 42.6 percent of the
land had pumping lifts of 300 feet or more in 1974. This compares to
only 11.5 percent of the land with such lifts in the twenty-four High
Plains counties. On the other hand, 87 percent of the land overlying
the Ogalalla in these four northern counties had a saturated thickness
of 150 feet or more compared to only 6 percent of the land in the
southern High Plains.

Table 3-9. Freshwater Consumption by Western Farm Production Region,
            1960, 1965, 1970, and 1975

(millions of gallons per day)

Region and use	1960	1965	1970	1975
Northern Plains				
Irrigation	2,866	4,730	6,060	9,930
All other	424	567	659	705
Total	3,290	5,297	6,719	10,635
"All other" as percent of total	12.9	10.7	9.8	6.6
Southern Plains				
Irrigation	6,390	11,260	8,670	11,820
All other	960	1,388	1,804	2,183
Total	7,350	12,648	10,474	14,003
"All other" as percent of total	13.1	11.0	17.2	15.6
Mountain				
Irrigation	20,960	25,500	28,200	25,000
All other	840	935	1,245	1,643
Total	21,800	26,435	29,445	26,643
"All other" as percent of total	3.9	3.5	4.2	6.2
Pacific				
Irrigation	18,100	19,400	24,500	26,200
All other	1,200	1,877	2,262	2,356
Total	19,300	21,277	26,762	28,556
"All other" as percent of total	6.2	8.8	8.5	8.3
Western states				
Irrigation	48,316	60,890	67,430	72,950
All other	3,424	4,767	5,970	6,887
Total	51,740	65,657	73,400	79,837
"All other" as percent of total	6.6	7.3	8.1	8.6

Sources: Based on data in the following U.S. Geological Survey circulars: Kenneth A. MacKichan and J. C. Kammerer, Estimated Use of Water in
the United States in 1960, Circular 456 (Washington, D.C., 1961); C. Richard
Murray, Estimated Use of Water in the United States, 1965, Circular 556
(Washington, D.C., 1968); C. Richard Murray and E. Bodette Reeves, Estimated
Use of Water in the United States in 1970, Circular 676 (Washington, D.C.,
1972); and C. Richard Murray and E. Bodette Reeves, Estimated Use of Water
in the United States in 1975, Circular 765 (Arlington, VA., 1977).

Although the Second National Water Assessment projects water use for each of the fifty-three western water resource subregions, it is nearly as instructive and conceptually much simpler to differentiate between just two areas—a water-scarce area and the rest of the West. The water-scarce area, consisting of twenty subregions, accounts for nearly 60 percent of water consumption. All twenty of these subregions (which are identified in the notes to table 3-10) have either high ratios of water requirements to streamflows or high ratios of ground-water mining to consumption, and in most both conditions prevail. Consequently, satisfying the growth of nonagricultural water demands in this region will require, with increasing frequency, diverting water out of irrigation. Furthermore, the area's heavy dependence on non-renewable water sources suggests total water use may decline by the year 2000 in some of these subregions.

The Assessment's National Future (NF) average-year projections of fresh water consumption for irrigation and other uses are presented in table 3-10.[31] Within the water-scarce area, total water consumption is projected to decline slightly (0.5 percent) over the last quarter of the century. Greater changes, however, are expected in the allocation of the water. Irrigation water consumption is projected to decline by 3 percent from 1975 to 1985 and by an additional 3 percent from 1985 to 2000. In contrast, consumption for all other purposes is projected to rise by 55 percent. But as a percentage of total consumption, the consumption of water for other purposes in the water-scarce area will rise from only 8 percent to 13 percent. These projections illustrate an important implication of the dominance of irrigation in western water use—large percentage increases in water allocations to other uses can be accommodated with relatively small percentage reductions in irrigation water consumption.

---

31. The Second National Water Assessment provides four estimates of offstream consumption for each of the years—1975, 1985, and 2000. These are the National-Future (NF) and State/Regional-Future (SRF) projections for both dry- and average-year conditions.

Table 3-10. Annual Water Consumption for Offstream Uses: National Future
Average-Year Estimates, 1975, 1985, and 2000

(millions of gallons per day)

Region and use	1975	1985	2000
20 water-scarce subregions[a]			
Irrigation	47,815	46,387	45,124
All other	4,337	5,275	6,748
Total	52,152	51,662	51,872
33 other subregions			
Irrigation	31,470	38,508	38,809
All other	4,869	6,625	9,974
Total	36,339	45,133	48,783
Total West (water resource regions 9 to 18)			
Irrigation	79,285	84,895	83,933
All other	9,205	11,900	16,722
Total	88,490	96,795	100,655

Source: U.S. Water Resources Council, The Nation's Water Resources,
The Second National Water Assessment, vol. 3, app. II (Washington, D.C.,
GPO, 1978) table II-4.

[a]This water-scarce area includes the following water resource subregions: 1007, 1010, 1102, 1103, 1105, 1106, 1203, 1204, 1302, 1303, 1304,
1305, 1502, 1503, 1602, 1603, 1604, 1803, 1806, and 1807.

In contrast to the outlook in the twenty water-scarce subregions, there are opportunities for expanding both total and irrigation water consumption in the rest of the West. Indeed, the Second National Water Assessment projects irrigation water consumption will increase a total of 22 percent between 1975 and 1985 in the other thirty-three sub-regions. However, no significant further expansion of water consumption for irrigation is projected for this region over the last fifteen years of the century. The twenty-five year projections for these thirty-three subregions suggest that water consumption will rise 34 percent and consumption for purposes other than irrigation will more than double.

Total western water consumption is projected to rise nearly 14 percent from 1975 to 2000, with irrigation accounting for 38 percent of the increase. However, the implied annual water consumption growth rates are only 0.2 percent for irrigation and 2.4 percent for all other uses.

The Assessment's National Future projections of irrigated acreage closely parallel their irrigation water consumption projections with allowance for only modest reductions in the implied consumption of water per irrigated acre. From 1975 to 2000 irrigated acreage is projected to decline about 1 percent in the twenty water-scarce subregions and to rise about 26 percent in the rest of the West for a net increase of nearly 11 percent for the West as a whole. Most of the relative regional shifts are projected to occur by 1985 as irrigation in the water-scarce region is projected to decline from 57 percent of the western total as of 1975, to 52 percent by 1985, and 51 percent by 2000.[32]

Water for Energy

Development of the West's vast energy resources, especially coal

---

32. The percentages are calculated from data in U.S. Water Resources Council, The Nation's Water Resources, vol. 3, app. 1, table 1-4.

and oil shale, are expected to place particularly heavy demands on western water. While the water consumption projections of the Second National Water Assessment include an allowance for steam electric production, petroleum refining, and fuels mining, there was concern that the Assessment had not taken adequate account of all likely energy developments and associated water requirements. This concern led to a supplementary study by the Aerospace Corporation.[33] The Aerospace Report (AR) accepts all the Assessment's water supply data and all the demand projections except those relating to energy. From four federally generated energy development scenarios, the AR determines the maximum feasible limits for energy development and the associated water requirements assuming standard size plants and no special provisions to adopt water-conserving technologies. Consequently, the AR water-for-energy estimates are higher than any likely levels. In comparison to the Assessment projections presented in table 3-10, the resulting nonirrigation water consumption levels are 7 percent higher by 1985 and 39 percent higher by 2000.

The AR estimates represent a 1 percent increase in total western water demand by 1985 and a 6 percent increase by 2000. Although these are only modest percentage changes, they would be localized and within the affected regions major new demands on water supplies are implied. Where demand already exceeds renewable supplies, any increase requires either compensating reductions among other users or additional ground-water mining.

The twenty water-scarce subregions account for about 47 percent of the consumption of water for energy projected for the turn of the century in the AR study. Within this area energy uses would rise to about 8 percent of total water consumption. If these projections are realized, water for energy would become particularly important in seven of

---

33. Aerospace Corporation, Water Related Constraints on Energy Production, Aerospace Report no. ATR-78(9409)-1 Germantown, Md., Aerospace Corporation, June 1978).

these subregions.[34] Energy uses account for 19 percent of total projected water consumption within these seven subregions, and combined
the seven subregions account for 72 percent of the projected water for
energy within the twenty water-scarce subregions.[35] However, these
seven subregions are less important in terms of their relative
contribution to irrigation. In 1975 they accounted for 28 percent of
the irrigated acreage in the water-scarce area and this percentage is
expected to decline to 20 percent by 2000. Their contribution to total
western irrigation is projected to decline from 16 percent in 1975 to
10 percent in 2000.[36]

The AR projections suggest that energy uses could become an even
more important component of water consumption in some of the subregions
where water currently does not pose such constraints to development.
In nine of these other 33 western subregions, the combined energy uses
of water account for 35 percent of total projected water use in 2000.[37]
In general, however, these nine subregions do not rank among the more
important irrigated areas; they are projected to account for only 13
percent of the water consumption and 8 percent of the irrigated land in
these 33 subregions by 2000 and 6 percent of the water and 4 percent of
the irrigated land for the West.

The water actually diverted to energy uses and away from irriga-

---

34. The seven subregions are Lahonten-South (1807) and Southern California (1806) in the California region, Humboldt-Tonopah Desert (1603)
and Central Lahonten (1604) in the Great Basin region, Middle Rio
Grande (1302) in the Rio Grande Region, and Brazos (1203) and Colorado
(1204) in the Texas Gulf region.

35. The water consumption figures in these two paragraphs are based on
data in Aerospace Corporation, Water Related Constraints on Energy
Production, table 6-2.

36. U.S. Water Resources Council, The Nation's Water Resources: The
Second National Water Assessment, vol. 3, app. 1, table 1-4.

37. The nine subregions are Western Dakotas (1005), Middle Missouri
(1009), and Lower Missouri (1001) of the Missouri region, Upper White
(1101), Yellowstone (1104), North and South Platte (1107) of the
Arkansas-White-Red region, Sabine-Neches (1201) and Nueces-Texas
Coastal (1205) of the Texas-Gulf region, and Green-White-Yampa (1401)
of the Upper Colorado region.

tion will depend in large part on the institutions, including the legal system affecting water use. These institutions vary widely among states. The earliest irrigators start from a preferred position in any struggle for water in that they commonly own the most senior water rights. Potential new irrigators have no such legal advantage, and they face a major economic disadvantage in that irrigation in general is a relatively low-value user of water. For example, water costs of $100 or more per acre-foot would be a very minor part of the total costs of mining or processing western coal while water costs of half these levels would be prohibitive for many irrigators, especially those growing relatively low-value crops. Thus, if market forces are allowed to operate, water will tend to move out of irrigation as demand starts to exceed an area's supply. Some farmers already have found it profitable to sell their water rights; many others are likely to follow suit unless they are legally constrained from doing so. (Chapter 4 examines the institutional factors affecting the use of western water.)

Indian and Federal Water Claims

Resolution of Indian and federal water claims could have significant impacts on western water use. Indian as well as federal claims on western water stem from vast landholdings and the judicially created Winters Doctrine that holds, among other things, that these lands have sufficient accompanying water rights to accomplish the purpose for which the lands were reserved.[38] A number of federal court decisions have supported the view that Indian water rights are created outside the system of state law and exist independently of it. Since virtually all western surface water has been put to use without regard for Indian rights, many existing users are threatened by resolution of Indian claims.

---

38. The 1908 Supreme Court decision in Winters v. United States held that Indian reservations had reserved water rights. Until 1955, the Winters Doctrine remained applicable only to Indian reservations. Since that time several Supreme Court decisions have extended the doctrine to any federal lands. See Heidi Topp Brooks, "Reserved Water Rights and Our National Forests," Natural Resources Journal, vol. 19 (April 1979) pp. 433-435.

Indian and federal rights remain unquantified and, in spite of President Carter's "instruction to Federal agencies to work promptly and expeditiously to inventory and quantify Federal reserved and Indian water rights,"[39] these claims are likely to remain a source of great uncertainty for western water use for years to come. (This issue is discussed further in chapter 4.)

Augmenting Water Supplies

Both the water supply and demand situations depicted above assume that there will be no major new sources of water. However, weather modifications, interbasin transfers, and icebergs are possible sources of increased supplies and water harvesting and desalinization may stretch the usable supplies in specific areas. Dams and reservoirs can increase water supplies available for specific purposes such as irrigation. Water impoundment, however, no longer is a means of significantly increasing the effective supply of western water; the limited supplies still remaining in the West's streams and rivers generally have value for fish, recreation, or preserving water quality. Thus, further construction of dams will divert water from one use to another but generally will not increase the overall supply. To the contrary, high evaporation rates from reservoirs in arid and semiarid lands reduce the effective water supply. Moreover, the best dam sites already have been exploited, and the costs of increasing irrigation water supplies through additional impoundment are high. For example, dams and reservoirs under consideration in California will cost $200 to $300 per acre-foot of water added to the effective water supply for irrigation, municipal, or industrial uses.[40] Improved farm management practices may increase the effective supply of water by enabling

---

39. A June 6, 1978 message from Jimmy Carter to the Congress of the United States accompanying the president's water policy message.

40. Personal communication with Kenneth Turner, manager, Agricultural Water Conservation Program, California Department of Water Resources, February 1980.

successful irrigation with saline or brackish water. This possibility is examined in chapter 6 on environmental impacts of irrigated agriculture.

Weather Modification

Research results have demonstrated that seeding of winter orographic clouds over mountainous areas can increase precipitation under some conditions. Generally only 20 to 50 percent of the water that is condensed in the formation of these clouds falls as precipitation; cloud seeding can increase snowfall in the mountains by as much as 20 percent.[41] More specifically, studies suggest that a coordinated program to seed the clouds of six mountain ranges in the Upper Colorado River Basin can increase snowfall sufficiently to provide an additional 1.4 to 2.3 million acre-feet of water a year to the river at a cost of about $5 to $10 per acre-foot.[42]

The promise of increasing precipitation through winter cloud seeding was noted in a 1973 National Academy of Science panel report as follows: "In the longest randomized cloud seeding research project in the United States, involving cold orographic winter clouds, it has been demonstrated that precipitation can be increased by substantial amounts and on a determinate basis."[43] This optimistic appraisal of winter cloud seeding was confirmed in a 1978 report of the Weather Modification Advisory Board. The Advisory Board's recommendations were cautious, however, and stressed the need for additional experiments to be carried out in the Colorado mountains and new studies to be initiated in other mountainous climatic regimes such as the Sierra

---

41. U.S. Department of Commerce, National Weather Modification Policies and Programs: A Report to the President and the Congress (Washington, D.C., GPO, November 1979) pp. 12-14.

42. Personal communication with Bernie Silverman, chief, Atmospheric Water Resources Management, Bureau of Reclamation, Denver, Colorado, February 1980.

43. Weather Modification Advisory Board, The Management of Weather Resources, vol. 1, Proposals for a National Policy and Program. A report to the Secretary of Commerce (Washington, D.C., GPO, June 30, 1978) p. 50.

Nevada Mountains of California.[44] Despite the apparent consensus among scientists that the technology is available for significantly increasing precipitation from winter mountainous storms at low cost, no coordinated program has been established to take advantage of this technology.

The largest potential increases in precipitation, at least in theory, lie in increasing the yield from cumulus clouds, which provide most of the precipitation in the world's principal food growing areas. An increase in our ability to control this rainfall, especially during the growing season, could be of enormous benefit to agriculture and perhaps reduce the need for irrigation. Unfortunately, increasing rainfall through summer cloud seeding has proved to be a much more difficult scientific problem than the seeding of winter orographic clouds. The complexity and variability over time and space of cumulus clouds have stymied or at least called into question the success of most efforts to increase summer rainfall. Nevertheless, there has been some encouraging evidence from seeding of summer cumulus clouds, and improved understanding of the workings of these clouds achieved in recent years should lead to better future results. In particular, scientists now have some understanding why past experiments sometimes produced negative results. Overall, however, development of a reliable technology for increasing rainfall from summer cumulus clouds is some years off and must await both better understanding of the atmospheric processes involved and further experimentation.[45]

Even if a weather modification technology is established and the economics are favorable, there will be major institutional obstacles to adoption of an extensive cloud-seeding program. Paying for the program, compensating the losers (whether real or imagined), allocating the additional water, and overcoming the fears that are sure to emerge among the people downwind from the cloud seeding are difficult problems that likely will stall efforts to increase precipitation until long

---

44. Ibid., pp. 52-53.

45. Based on the conclusions of U.S. Department of Commerce, National Weather Modification, pp. 14-17; and Weather Modification Advisory Board, Management of Weather. pp. 53-57.

after scientists and economists are comfortable with the technology. The task for winter seeding is particularly complicated since the losers (e.g., those with higher snow removal costs) are closer in both location and time to the seeding than are the beneficiaries (e.g., farmers perhaps hundreds of miles downstream who presumably receive more water many months later). Analysis of several summer cumulus seeding projects suggests that the downwind effects are uncertain. Such uncertainties are bound to inhibit adoption of any major cloud-seeding program.

In spite of these obstacles, cloud seeding is used in a few western areas today, and its use is likely to spread as the value of water increases and the technology improves. Conservative estimates suggest that winter cloud seeding might add nearly 10 percent to the flow of the upper Colorado River, which may be a reasonable target for the turn of the century. Such an increase, however, would have little impact on the overall course of western irrigation. While a 10 percent increase would be significant within that area, it would be equivalent to only 0.3 percent of total western streamflows.

Water Importation

The scarcity of indigenous water resources in relation to demand has prompted a call for water imports from more amply endowed regions. Water importation has broad support within the Lower Colorado River Basin and the High Plains areas where current activities are dependent on nonrenewable water sources. But if the net water supplies within the West's water-scarce southern belt are to be increased, the water will have to be transported long distances. The Central Arizona Project currently under construction will make it possible to transport Colorado River water into the Phoenix-Tucson area. However, this project will not increase effective water supplies within the water-scarce areas of the West. The water is already being fully utilized; the project largely will divert water to central Arizona that currently is going to southern California.

The Mississippi, Columbia, and upper Missouri rivers are the closest from which large quantities might be obtained. The availability of water for export likely would be contested vigorously in these areas. But even if there is plenty of water for export, several feasibility studies indicate that the costs of transporting it to the High Plains or Southwest would far exceed its value in agriculture. A study undertaken in the early 1970s of transporting water from the Mississippi River to the Texas and New Mexico High Plains showed only 27 cents in benefits for every $1 in costs. Even this ratio of benefits to costs probably overstates the attractiveness of the transfer since the study did not attribute any value to the water in the exporting basin and used energy costs which now appear much too low. For example, the energy costs alone at 1980 electricity prices in the area would exceed $400 per acre-foot of water delivered in the High Plains.[46] A more recent Corps of Engineers study of the feasibility of transporting water to various locations in the High Plains confirms the infeasibility of moving water long distances for agricultural uses. The Corps considered four potential import sources and routes for transferring from 1.0 to 7.2 million acre-feet per year. The estimated costs per acre-foot of water delivered to terminal storage points ranged from $352 to $880. For use in irrigation, there would be additional costs required to deliver the water to the farms.[47] In general the costs of transporting water from the Mississippi or Missouri rivers to the High Plains appear to be about an order of magnitude above the prices farmers in the High Plains currently can afford to pay for water and still irrigate profitably. Although economic feasibility has not been a necessary requirement for authorization and funding of western water projects, the economics of such a water transfer project appear poor even by the standards of other water projects.

---

46. The Bureau of Reclamation study estimated that nearly 47 billion kWh of power would be required to deliver 5,794,000 acre-feet of water to the High Plains annually. At 5 cents per kilowatt hour, approximately the average 1980 cost of electricity in Texas, the cost per acre-foot is over $400. See U.S. Department of Interior, Bureau of Reclamation, West Texas and Eastern New Mexico Import Project.

47. The data on the Corps of Engineers study, which was done as part of a larger High Plains Development study financed by the U.S. Department of Commerce and authorized by the Congress, is based on a report in The Cross Section, vol. 27, no. 3 (March 1981) published by the High Plains Underground Water Conservation District No. 1, Lubbock, Texas.

Icebergs

The availability of enormous quantities of freshwater trapped as polar ice has raised the possibility of diverting some of this water to the world's arid areas. A very optimistic assessment of the prospects for using Antarctic icebergs to supplement Southern California's water supplies came out of a 1973 study by the Rand Corporation.[48] This study concluded that delivering icebergs was both technically possible and economically attractive in comparison to some other proposals such as interbasin transfers and desalinization for supplementing water supplies. The scheme called for using nuclear tugs to tow iceberg trains attached by cables. Plastic films would supposedly reduce melting to about 10 percent per year. The operational costs of delivering a large iceberg train to California were estimated at $10 per acre-foot and the total costs of transport, conversion to water, and delivery to wholesale terminals in coastal areas were estimated at $30 per acre-foot.

More recent assessments of the technical problems and costs of delivering Antarctic icebergs to arid areas thousands of miles away have been less sanguine.[49] For example, preliminary studies of towing icebergs to Saudi Arabia were not encouraging. Geologists estimated an Artarctic iceberg would be completely melted as it passed through non-Arctic waters more than three weeks before it could reach Saudi Arabia.

The outstanding technical problems associated with the transfer and use of icebergs prevent any precise assessment as to the delivered cost of water from icebergs. But even if iceberg harvesting does show promise after allowing for technical, economic, and environmental considerations, it might be stalled by international political and legal

---

48. J. L. Hult and N. C. Ostrander, Antarctic Icebergs as a Global Fresh Water Resource. prepared for the National Science Foundation by the Rand Corporation, R-1255-NSF, October 1973.

49. Jan van Schilfgaarde and Glenn J. Hoffman, "Future Sources of Water," an unpublished paper dated October 2, 1980, provided by van Schilfgaarde.

issues concerning resource rights. Accordingly, there is little reason
to expect that icebergs will be a promising source of water for the
western United States, especially for irrigation purposes.

Water Harvesting

Harvesting rainfall by diverting the water to fields or into cist-
erns is an ancient technology which currently is used only sparingly in
the West. Its primary uses are as a water source for domestic, livestock, or wildlife purposes, seldom for irrigation. Although some
promising opportunities may have been missed by western farmers, water
harvesting for irrigation will remain very limited in terms of both the
acres having suitable topography and rainfall and the resulting increases to water supplies.

Desalinization

The enthusiasm prevalent in the 1960s for using desalted sea water
to make the deserts bloom was dampened by Clawson, Landsberg, and Alexander's conclusion that "the full and true costs of the proposed desalting projects, now and for the next twenty years, are at least one
whole order of magnitude greater than the value of the water to agriculture."[50] Although research has brought technological improvements
in desalting technology, rising energy costs have prevented significant
improvements in the economics of desalinization. Three desalting
processes are workable. A distillation process probably is best suited
to desalting sea water, while either reverse osmosis or electrodialysis
may be better suited to water with lower salt levels since the energy
requirements of these latter techniques are directly proportional to
the salinity of the water. Depending on the technology used and the
initial and final salt levels, energy costs accounted for 12 to 54
percent of total desalting costs at 1974 price levels. But even when
the process starts with brackish waters with salt levels well below
those of sea water and ends with less than pure water, the most

---

50. Marion Clawson, Hans H. Landsberg, and Lyle T. Alexander, "Desalted
Sea Water for Agriculture: Is It Economic?" Science, vol 164 (June
1969) pp. 1141-1148. Resources for the Future Reprint No. 78, July
1969.

economical methods of desalting cost from \$250 to \$300 per acre-foot in the late 1970s.[51] These are plant site costs; additional costs would be required to deliver the water to farms.

In summary, although desalting is feasible under some circumstances for some uses of water, it is not now nor is it likely to become within this century an economical means of significantly increasing irrigation water supplies. The decision of the U.S. government to construct a desalting plant in Yuma, Arizona, for the drainage waters of the Wellton-Mohawk Irrigation District was based on political rather than economic considerations. Desalinization is a very costly way of satisfying U.S. treaty obligations with Mexico regarding flows of the Colorado River. The plant, however, does enable the United States to avoid or at least postpone difficult political decisions required to implement an improved irrigation management scheme capable of accomplishing essentially the same goals at a much reduced economic cost.

Use of Low-Quality Water Supplies

The preceding discussion of water supplies implicitly has been limited to supplies of fresh water meeting current standards of most agricultural as well as domestic and industrial users. However, there are large quantities of water available in the West that do not meet these criteria, and one means of increasing effective supplies might be to make use of lower quality water. In particular, large quantities of saline water are stored in some aquifers and lakes, and all coastal areas have an essentially unlimited supply of sea water. Although (as noted above) the costs of desalinization exceed the value of water in most agricultural uses, there may be opportunities for using more saline water for irrigation.

Water qualities may be described in terms of the milligrams of

51. U.S. Bureau of Reclamation, California Department of Water Resources, and California State Water Resources Control Board, Agricultural Drainage and Salt Management in the San Joaquin Valley (San Joaquin Valley InterAgency Drainage Program, Fresno, Calif., June 1979) pp. 8-4 amd 8-5.

total dissolved solids per liter (mg per liter TDS). The higher the level of dissolved solids or salts (the term generally used to describe all these compounds) in the water, the lower the quality. All irrigation water contains some salts and concentrations of about 500 mg per liter pose no problem to most irrigators.[52] Higher concentrations start imposing costs in the form of lower crop yields, higher water requirements to prevent salt buildup in the root zone, and increased management requirements to adapt to the high salt levels. (Chapter 6 examines the problems stemming from high salt levels as well as the extent of these problems in the West.) With careful management and good drainage, up to 1,500 mg per liter TDS can be tolerated on all but the most salt sensitive crops with little loss of yield.[53] Furthermore, some crops can be irrigated successfully with water containing much higher salinity levels. Barley, a particularly salt-tolerant crop, is grown commercially in California with water containing several times these levels of salts. A field experiment has demonstrated that good cotton yields can be obtained with water containing 6,000 mg per liter TDS, and sugar beets are also tolerant of relatively high salt levels.[54] With scientists working to increase salt tolerance of a variety of crops, the options for irrigating successfully with saline waters are likely to expand in the coming decades.

A more extreme goal, but one being pursued optimistically by some researchers, is to develop a marketable crop that can be successfully grown with sea water, which has a salt level of about 35,000 mg per liter. Various types of halophytes grown experimentally with sea water have produced yields of plant matter (suitable at least as an animal

---

52. U.S. Department of Interior, Bureau of Reclamation, <u>Final Environmental Statement: Colorado River Water Quality Improvement Program</u>, vol. I (Washington, D.C., May 1977) pp. I-11 to 21.

53. Jan van Schilfgaarde and Glenn J. Hoffman, "Future Sources of Water," U.S. Salinity Laboratory, Riverside, California, unpublished paper, October 1980, pp. 10-11.

54. U.S. Bureau of Reclamation, California Department of Water Resources, and California State Water Resources Control Board, <u>Agricultural Drainage</u>, p. 3-1; and ibid., p. 11.

feed supplement) comparable to those on conventional farms.[55] Nevertheless, much research remains before sea water can be considered a suitable source of irrigation water.

In summary, the technology currently exists to make more effective use of poor quality waters widely available in the West. Furthermore, research will increase the opportunities for using these waters in irrigation. On the other hand, there are important limitations to the feasible use of highly saline water. Success requires unusually high management skills and there is a risk of severely damaging the soils with the use of such water. In addition, since the value of saline water for use in irrigation always will be less than that of better quality water, the cost that can be justified to transport low quality water to a farmer's field necessarily will be less than for fresh water.

---

55. John Neary, "Pickleweed, Palmer's Grass, and Saltwort: Can We Grow Tomorrow's Food with Today's Salt Water?" Science 81, vol. 2, no. 5 (June 1981) pp. 39-43.

Chapter 4

WATER LAWS AND INSTITUTIONS

Like labor, land, and seed, water can be viewed as another input into agricultural production. In one respect, however, it is radically different. Water is a "fugitive" resource. When it flows from one property to another, a characteristic of most surface and some ground-water supplies, it is difficult to establish a clear property right to it. Consequently, water is called a common property resource; it is accessible to many but owned by none until it is withdrawn for use. Water generally is not bought and sold in the marketplace as are other inputs. Instead, government, as guardian of public resources, allocates it by various legal and institutional means.

The federal government has not tried to establish a single legal or institutional regime to govern the country's freshwater supply. Instead, the basic task of regulating water use had been left largely to the states. The states have developed a myriad of institutions, laws, and regulations to control their waters, reflecting in part both underlying variation in the supply, demand, needs, and other circumstances surrounding water use and different views of property rights and the role of the government. Furthermore, the demands placed on water institutions have changed over time, and the history of western water law records many endeavors by states to adapt and respond to new circumstances and problems.

When water was abundant relative to demand, the states played little role in its use. As the first farmers began to settle in the valleys close to streams, they diverted the natural flow of the stream to irrigate their fields. To give greater security to irrigators and to control conflicts between rival diverters, states developed the doctrine of prior appropriative water rights, of which the basic principle is "first in time, first in right."

Once the readily accessible water was in use, expansion required dams, reservoirs, and canals to capture the heavy spring flows and carry it to undeveloped land farther away. The technical and financial demands of such projects, however, often exceeded the capabilities of private investors and even the states. These circumstances led to demands for federal assistance in constructing and financing western water projects. With these larger projects came both new opportunities for managing water resources and needs for institutions to realize their potential benefits. State laws led to the creation of irrigation districts, self-governing public corporations empowered to control water allocation within district boundaries. Likewise, advances in pump technology brought both new opportunities and institutional needs. As groundwater use increased beyond the capacity of the aquifers to recharge themselves, the states have sought ways to control withdrawals.

The rapid spread of irrigation throughout the West is at least partial evidence of the success of water laws and institutions in having met the demands placed on them. Today, however, water institutions face new challenges. Western irrigators have increasingly come into competition for water with growing urban populations and expanding industries, and unspecified Indian and federal water claims threaten established patterns of use. As the demand for water, both for irrigation and other uses, has risen, the opportunities for developing additional supplies have decreased. With most prime sites for reservoirs already developed, the costs of construction high, and little unclaimed water left, additional surface water diversion has become costly and, in many areas, of limited potential for increasing usable water supplies. An alternative response to the problem of water scarcity is to increase the physical and economic efficiency of already developed water resources. Proper incentives could encourage the adoption of conservation measures such as more efficient conveyance systems or less wasteful irrigation practices. A market-oriented allocation system would allow those with higher-valued uses to bid water away from the many lower-valued uses to which it is presently put.

Such an approach, however, often requires modifications in present water laws and institutions. So far, the legal and institutional framework governing western water has been slow to respond to this latest challenge and remains a hindrance to the task of increasing the efficiency of water use.

This chapter examines existing water laws and institutions and assesses their impacts on the allocation of western water. The first part focuses on surface water and the second on groundwater.

Surface Water

Surface Water Law

The doctrine of riparian rights provided the legal basis for the earliest western water diversions.[1] This doctrine, developed in England and employed in the relatively water-abundant eastern states, holds that an owner of land adjacent to a stream or pond has the right to make use of the water that flows by this property. The riparian water right is inseparable from the land. The holder of the right can make any "reasonable" use of this water so long as he uses it on the riparian land and does not cause a major inconvenience to other riparian users. At the same time, he is protected against the wasteful, unreasonable, or unbeneficial use of riparian waters by others. His use is correlative with other co-users, and there is no priority in right among users. Should drought cause a water shortage, all riparian users share in reducing their consumption.

Once development was required beyond the lands adjacent to the streams or modifications required in the natural streamflow to enhance supplies, the riparian doctrine proved insufficient for the needs of the West. The need to encourage and safeguard private investments and to reclaim western lands necessitated a legal system providing greater

---

1. Much of the discussion on water law is based on section 5 of George E. Radosevich, Western Water Laws and Irrigation Return Flow, a report prepared for the U.S. Environmental Protection Agency, EPA-600/2-78-180 (Ada, Oklahoma, EPA, August 1978).

flexibility in allocating water and more security in guaranteeing continued access to water sources.

The shortcomings of the riparian doctrine for western development needs led to the doctrine of prior appropriation. Under the appropriation doctrine, a party diverting water from a stream and putting it to some beneficial use can make a claim to continued appropriation of similar amounts of water from that stream. As in a mining claim, the rule of "first in time, first in right" applies. The doctrine of prior appropriation has been adopted in all seventeen western states. The Plains states of Texas, Oklahoma, Kansas, Nebraska, and North and South Dakota, along with the three Pacific Coast states, also have retained the doctrine of riparian rights in conjunction with that of prior appropriation. Only in California, however, does the riparian doctrine still have major significance. In all the other states which use a dualistic riparian-prior appropriation system of water law, new surface water claims can be made only under the prior appropriation doctrine.

In contrast to the riparian doctrine, water rights under prior appropriation are not tied to ownership of land or use of water on land bordering the stream. Instead, prior appropriation rights are acquired simply by diverting water from a stream, carrying it to the desired location and putting it to some beneficial use. At this point, the water right is created and the person can file for a permit (or license or decree depending on the state) that entitles him to continued use of the water so long as the use remains beneficial. The holder's right has priority over (or is senior to) all rights acquired after his, and is junior to all rights acquired before his. Should the streamflow fall below that needed to satisfy all appropriated rights, junior right holders would have to forego the exercise of their rights so as to allow senior holders to fully exercise theirs. The loss is not shared proportionally as it is under the riparian doctrine.

The acquired right is a real property right that can be sold, transferred, mortgaged, or bequeathed. At the same time, it is a right only to use the resource, and states place varying restrictions on the use that can be made of the water. The right arises only at the point of diversion and is contingent on the beneficial use of the water. Should the holder be unable to make good use of the water, he has no right to divert it. Also, when the diverted water leaves the property of the holder, his right to it ceases and the water returns to the status of public property. Generally, rights also exist to these return flows, that is, the return flow is often appropriated by some downstream user. Furthermore, the right pertains to a specific use and is fixed to a certain place of use. The amount of water as well as the time of year it can be diverted are generally specified.

Twelve western states also identify a ranked preference of use in their water law. Municipal and domestic uses are given top preference in all twelve states. In nine states, agricultural uses, including irrigation, get second preference. The preference rule allows preferred users to condemn the water of nonpreferred users in times of scarcity so as to satisfy the preferred need. Where preference rules exist, prior appropriation applies only within categories of users with similar preference ranking.

Besides condemnation, appropriative rights can be lost by abandonment, forfeiture, or adverse possession. If a holder fails to make use of a right for a specified period of time (usually three, five, or ten years, depending on the state), he is considered to have abandoned or forfeited his rights. Likewise, should another party make open and notorious use of someone else's water without the owner of the right taking any steps to remedy the situation within a period specified by law (usually five years), the holder may lose the right to the intruding party.

Types of Irrigation Organizations

In 1969, about 25 percent of the surface water used for irrigation was from onfarm sources.[2] By virtue of their location, these farmers independently divert water from streams and ponds for irrigation.

---

2. U.S. Bureau of the Census, Census of Agriculture, 1969, vol. IV, Irrigation (Washington, D.C., GPO, 1973) p. 70.

Generally, they were the first to arrive in a region and retained senior rights to the natural summer flow of water. There is very little land or water left in the West for expansion of this type.

The remaining 75 percent of the surface water is supplied by some type of irrigation organization. As land was irrigated farther away from the water source and reservoirs were built to increase the supply of water, irrigation organizations were developed to facilitate the delivery of water. The Census of Agriculture lists seven principal types of organizations which deliver water: unincorporated mutuals, incorporated mutuals, irrigation districts, Bureau of Reclamation (BR) constructed and operated projects, Bureau of Indian Affairs (BIA) projects, state and local government projects, and commercial enterprises. The first three types account for 95.4 percent of all water organizations and 92.2 percent of all acreage irrigated by organization (see table 4-1).[3] From 1930 to 1970, the number of irrigation organizations decreased and their average size increased as many smaller organizations consolidated to provide better, more uniform service to their members.

Unincorporated mutuals are the simplest organizations, ranging from informal verbal agreements between two farmers to build a simple diversion on a mutually held stream to several farmers who build and maintain a canal for common use. The average unincorporated mutual suppies water to seven or eight farms. While accounting for over half the number of irrigation organizations, unincorporated mutuals supply water to only 11 percent of the land irrigated by all organizations.

The incorporated mutual is simply a larger, more formal version of the unincorporated model. The users own shares in the organizations and supply water to themselves at cost. An appointed board of directors oversees the operation. This type of organization accounts for

---

3. Appendix 2-A (pp. 9-10) discusses some of the problems of the irrigation censuses as a source of irrigated acreage data. However, there is no reason to expect these data result in major distortions in the relative allocation of irrigated acreage among irrigation organizations and there are no alternative sources of such data.

Table 4-1. Types of Western Irrigation Organizations as a Percentage of
Western State Total, 1969

Organization	Percentage of all organizations	Percentage of all acreage irrigated by organization
Unincorporated mutuals	53.7	10.8
Incorporated mutuals	32.6	34.3
All districts (irrigation and other)	9.1	47.1
Bureau of Reclamation constructed and operated[a]	.7	1.8
Bureau of Indian Affairs	.7	2.9
State and local governments	.5	.2
Commercial companies	2.7	2.9
	100.0	100.0

Source: U.S. Bureau of the Census, Census of Agriculture, 1969,
vol. IV, Irrigation (Washington, D.C., GPO, 1973) p. xxv.

[a]Most Bureau of Reclamation (BR) projects are turned over to some
other type of irrigation organization once construction is completed.
Acreage serviced by BR-constructed and user-operated projects accounted
for nearly 27 percent of the acreage irrigated by other organizations.

about one-third of the organizations in number and a little more than one-third of the acreage.

Irrigation districts are organized by law as self-governing and self-financing public corporations with the powers of taxation and eminent domain. The government designates certain acreages of land which are accorded water rights. All landowners are assigned one vote regardless of acreage. While they account for only 10 percent of water organizations, they serve almost half of all land irrigated through organizations.[4]

Financial Factors Shaping the Water Industry

Over the years two factors have had a major impact on the allocation and low cost of surface water. First, most organizations are more accurately "users' cooperatives" functioning primarily to benefit farmers; commercial firms play a small part in this water industry. Second, government has played a significant role in underwriting the cost of providing water to these organizations.[5]

Typically, "users' cooperatives," provide water at cost to members. Generally, the user is charged only a nominal transaction cost for the water. The organizations compete among themselves for more dependable and cheaper water supplies instead of for new customers. This cooperative approach to providing water undercuts the opportunities for commercial firms entering the industry.

The cost structure of the industry further limits the role of commercial firms. Fixed costs, which include dams, wells, canals, ditches, and pumps, are a large portion of the total costs of delivering water. In view of the substantial economies of scale associated with constructing such facilities, the costs of delivering water tend

---

4. U.S. Bureau of the Census, Census of Agriculture 1969, vol. IV, Irrigation (Washington, D.C., GPO, 1973) p. XXVII.

5. Much of this discussion is based on the excellent study by Richard E. Caves and Julius Margolis, Northern California's Water Industry (Baltimore, Md., Johns Hopkins University Press for Resources for the Future, 1966).

to fall as the size of the water project increases. Public agencies generally are better positioned to capture these economies.

A significant portion of water industry expenses is financed not by operating revenues paid by the water user but by public taxes. This is true of both federal (BR) projects and irrigation district operations. Among the powers vested by states in irrigation districts is the power to tax nonwater users within their boundaries. For example, the Fresno Irrigation District in the Central Valley of California received assessments from landowners in the district totaling $2,162,991 in 1977. Approximately $450,000 or 22 percent was obtained from non-water users, like the city of Fresno.[6]

The evolution and magnitude of subsidies associated with federal irrigation projects was discussed in chapter 3. This discussion indicates how a series of amendments to the 1902 Reclamation Act and the administrative decisions of the Bureau of Reclamation have provided federal water to irrigators at very favorable terms. Indeed, when operating and maintenance costs are accounted for, farmers have paid only about 3 percent of the construction costs of federal irrigation projects. Inflation combined with the long-term fixed rates charged irrigators have resulted in water charges which even fall below operating and maintenance costs on some projects.

Since only some farmers benefit from these subsidies, federal policy has produced some striking contrasts among the water costs of neighboring irrigators. In Kern County, California, for example, recipients of BR water paid $3.50 per acre-foot for water in the mid-1970s while their neighbors receiving water from the California Department of Water Resources paid $22.42 per acre-foot.[7] Beneficiaries of federal water in the county receive an explicit sub-

6. Conversation between James Hanson and Howard Keck, Fresno (California) Irrigation District, July 19, 1979.

7. U.S. Department of Interior, Office of Audit and Investigation, Review of the Central Valley Project (Washington, D.C., Bureau of Reclamation, January 1978) p. 44.

sidy through interest exemption and the allocation of hydroelectric power revenues to cover part of the construction costs. Inflation and the use of forty-year repayment contracts with fixed water prices provide a sizable additional subsidy. Indeed, the differences between the prices paid by those fortunate enough to receive federal water and most all other users are likely to widen considerably over the next decade. While most of the long-term federal contracts will not expire until the 1990s, Kern County water costs on state projects are expected to rise to about $70 per acre-foot (in 1980 prices) within about five years, caused largely by higher energy costs.[8]

Government largess on such a grand scale has important implications for the wealth and competitiveness of different farmers. The 1902 Reclamation Act supposedly limited an individual to 160 acres and a farm couple to 320 acres of land receiving federal water. The intent to provide water solely for small family farms has been violated in practice through lax enforcement of the law and loose administrative practices which permit unlimited leasing and multiple ownership arrangements. While the great majority of farm operations comply with a 160- or 320-acre limitation, much of the irrigable land is operated in larger units. Of the 126,000 owners of 8.8 million irrigated acres supposedly subject to acreage limitations, nearly 91 percent own 160 acres or less and 98 percent own 320 acres or less. The remaining 2 percent, however, own 27 percent of the land. The 340 largest owners (comprising less than one-third of 1 percent of the farmers receiving water from federal projects) own 11 percent of the land receiving subsidized water.[9]

Clearly there are important equity issues involved in the distribution of federal water subsidies. But these are not of direct concern

---

8. Based on a comment by Gerald Meral, Deputy Director, Department of Water Resources, State of California, at a June 1980 water workshop held at the Ford Foundation in New York City.

9. U.S. Department of Agriculture, Farmline, vol. 1, no. 6 (September 1980) p. 4.

to this study. The distribution of the subsidies, however, is important to the extent that it affects the efficiency of water use and, thereby, total production from irrigated farms. Central to this issue is the extent to which there are economies or diseconomies of scale on irrigated farms.

Proponents of eliminating the acreage limitation emphasize that there are significant economies of size to be gained by allowing the large farmer to exist. They argue that lower food prices from these large farms benefit the consumer and discourage inflation. On the other side, limitation proponents suggest that the 160-acre limitation is necessary to distribute the subsidy among a greater number of people and to preserve the values of the small farm. Furthermore, they point to evidence suggesting that relaxation of the acreage limitation will not significantly decrease the costs of food production and aid the consumer.

Research on economies of scale of irrigated farms has been limited and inconclusive as to the implications of enforcing the 160-acre limit or some variation of it. Research published in the early 1960s indicated economies of scale existed for farms up to 600 to 1,000 acres.[10] More recently, the notion that limiting a farm to 160 or 320 acres would involve considerable economic inefficiency has been challenged by David Seckler and Robert Young, who suggest there may be no significant economies of scale on irrigated farms exceeding 180 acres.[11] A U.S. Department of Agriculture study of the effects of imposing the 160-acre limitation on farms in Nebraska, Wyoming, California, and Washington concluded that large farms in all regions did have lower production costs per unit of output than small farms. However, 98 percent

---

10. See the discussion in William E. Martin, "Economies of Size and the 160-Acre Limitation: Fact and Fancy," American Journal of Agricultural Economics, vol. 60, no. 5 (December 1978) p. 925.

11. David Seckler and Robert A. Young, "Economic and Policy Implications of the 160-Acre Limitation in Federal Reclamation Law," American Journal of Agricultural Economics, vol. 60, no. 4 (November 1978) pp. 576-588.

of the cost advantages achieved by larger operations were captured by farms which averaged between 320 and 640 acres.[12]

Although the question of economies of scale on irrigated farms remains open, it does not appear that resolution of the acreage limitation issue will have significant impacts on farm output grown with federally supplied water. Indeed, while the Congress had still not resolved the issue by the start of 1982, they seem to be moving toward increasing the acreage limitation. Illustrations of support for relaxing acreage restrictions include a bill to raise the limit to 1,280 acres, including owned and leased land, which passed the Senate in 1979, and another bill to increase the limit to 960 acres with allowance for leasing up to 2,400 additional acres which was recommended by the House Committee on Interior and Insular Affairs in June 1980.[13] In December 1981 Interior Secretary James Watt proposed eliminating restrictions on the acreage for which water from federal projects could be used but requiring irrigators to pay the full cost of any water provided for acreages exceeding 960 acres.

One result of the debate over the appropriateness of federal financing of western water projects and enforcement of the 160-acre limitation is that the BR is being forced to reexamine the policies providing such large subsidies to irrigators. As indicated in chapter 3, a major source of subsidization results from fixing the water rates for forty-year periods. The Bureau of Reclamation has responded to this problem by separating the operational and maintenance (O&M) costs from the repayment costs in its new contracts. O&M costs now are renegotiated every five years to make allowances for inflation while only the repayment costs remain fixed. These contract changes are not retroactive, however, and will only affect new contracts or old

---

12. U.S. Department of Agriculture, Economics and Statistics Service, The U.S. Department of the Interior's Proposed Rules for Enforcement of the Reclamation Act of 1902: An Economic Impact Analysis, ESCS-04 (Washington, D.C., 1980) 61 pp.

13. U.S. Department of Agriculture, Farmline. vol. 1, no. 6 (September 1980) p. 4.

contracts as they expire. In California, over 80 percent of the water delivered under current contracts will not be renegotiated until the 1992-1996 period, suggesting a considerable lag before there is much effect from this policy change.

The Federal Role

Through a series of acts in 1866, 1870, and 1877, the federal government granted each state power to distribute its water. The federal government reserved water for use on federal lands and, according to the Constitution, retained power to intervene in water use if it affected navigation.[14] While federal construction of large irrigation projects brought further federal involvement, section 8 of the 1902 Reclamation Act provided that federal projects must conform to state water laws and that nothing in the act could be interpreted as altering state water laws.[15]

Nevertheless, determining the appropriate role of the federal government in western water development and use remains controversial. The issues initially centered around the unspecified water claims for federal lands and the huge subsidies for water projects. More recently, western water has become increasingly important for achieving national objectives such as development of the West's enormous energy resources or use of some of the relatively undeveloped areas for housing new weapons systems. Critics of past policy argue for either greater federal influence over the use of distribution of the water or reduced federal support of water projects. The western states, on the other hand, are extremely sensitive to any efforts to reduce their sovereignty over water and reluctant to forego federal financing of water projects. They argue that the federal money is well spent and gener-

---

14. Radosevich, Western Water Laws, p. 38.

15. U.S. Department of Interior, U.S. Department of Agriculture, and Environmental Protection Agency, Irrigation Water Use and Management: An Interagency Task Force Report (Washington, D.C., GPO, June 1979) p. 49.

ates benefits which accrue to the nation as well as the West. They also note that the western method of water appropriation works well, having been developed over time, and any involvement by the federal government would confuse and frustrate the present system.

It was in this climate that President Carter undertook to develop a national water policy. As a presidential candidate in 1976, Carter made it clear that he regarded many water projects as environmentally destructive boondoggles, and that, if elected, he was going to bring about reform. Yet, it came as a big surprise to most people when, scarcely a month into his presidency and in the midst of a severe drought in much of the West, Carter sent Congress a revised budget for fiscal year 1978 deleting $268 million for eighteen major water projects, with a total price tag in excess of $5 billion.

Other aspects of Carter's water policy were outlined in his June 6, 1978, message to Congress and subsequent releases. Guy Martin, assistant secretary for land and water resources in the Department of the Interior, listed the primary concerns as: (1) restructuring the Water Resources Council (WRC); (2) fundamentally changing the 1902 Reclamation Act to better suit today's situation; (3) redefining the methodologies of justifying and financing water projects; (4) placing increased emphasis on water conservation; and (5) assessing new demands for water and the ability of present systems to meet these demands.[16] In January 1979, President Carter issued an executive order for the WRC to conduct an independent financial review of the water projects before Congress.

Carter's initiative proved to be both poorly timed and politically naive. The "hit list" was reported in the Denver papers the same day the western governors and recently appointed Secretary of the Interior Andrus convened a conference to discuss the problems of the drought.

---

16. Guy R. Martin, "The National Perspective" in Western Water Resources, Coming Problems and the Policy Alternatives, Federal Reserve Bank of Kansas City Symposium, September 27-28, 1979 (Boulder, Colo., Westview Press, 1980) pp. 185-198.

Although some groups in the West welcomed the President's initiative as necessary for improved management of their water, the area's political leadership was strongly opposed and saw Carter's efforts as an infringement on western water rights. This view was summarized by Utah's governor, Scott Matheson, chairman of the National Governors' Association Subcommittee on Water Management, as follows: "The options that the administration wants to pursue in the name of conservation not only could preempt the states in their traditional role in conserving water but would also emasculate the state's prerogatives in allocating water resources."[17]

Many of the Carter administration's water reform efforts were stymied by the Congress. Strong bipartisan support emerged from the long-standing congressional practice of logrolling, of putting good, bad, and mediocre projects into one big bill and resolutely fending off efforts to pare it back. Congressional response included restoring water project funds to the fiscal 1978 budget, prohibiting the Water Resources Council from spending any funds for independent project reviews, and, in legislation that passed the House of Representatives in 1980, eliminating all funding for the Council. Although the funds were authorized in 1980 to keep the Water Resources Council going, the Council has not been able to play the strong role in implementing a national water policy that the Carter administration hoped it would.

Despite these setbacks, the efforts of the Carter administration were not without impact. A number of projects were terminated, there was a definite curtailment in Congressional support for irrigation projects, and future BR projects are likely to focus much more on hydropower development and providing water for municipal and industrial use.[18] Nevertheless, federal support of new irrigation will continue. As of 1980, Congress had authorized and funded projects providing for 1.3 million additional acres of full service irrigation and 2.5 million

---

17. Scott M. Matheson, "A Western Governor Looks at Water Policy," in ibid., pp. 104-5.

18. Based on James Hanson's conversation with John Anderson, Bureau of Reclamation, Washington, D.C., March 31, 1980.

acres of supplemental irrigation which probably will be completed. The Columbia Basin Project with 500,000 acres is the primary project in this group. Congress authorized but did not fund an additional 150,000 acres of full service and 150,000 acres of supplemental service which have a good chance for being constructed. On the other hand, there are numerous projects which, though authorized by Congress, have not been funded and appear to be legislatively dead.

The Reagan administration clearly is more sympathetic to the states' views on issues involving water planning and control than was the Carter administration. But the impact of the new administration on federal support for water projects is uncertain. In a February 1981 meeting with eleven western governors, Interior Secretary James Watt reportedly asked the governors to come up with creative financing structures that would provide the states with more of a role in planning the massive water development projects they desire. He further promised to seek an end to current policy of returning unappropriated water rights to the federal government. The message received by at least one governor, John Evans of Idaho, was that the Reagan administration would be receptive to water projects.[19] Nevertheless, significant increases in federal funding for western water projects would be inconsistent with the administration's commitment to cut federal spending. Some reduction in federal funding of western water projects seems certain to result from Reagan's efforts to cut the budget. And if block grants to the states replaced federal funding that previously was tied to projects (a funding approach more consistent with the philosophy of the Reagan administration), many states may find more productive outlets for the funds than the water projects they currently support. On balance, a major expansion of federal funding for western water projects seems unlikely under the current administration.

---

19. Joanne Omang, "Western Governors Announce Accord with Secretary Watt," The Washington Post, February 26, 1981, p. A5.

Indian Water Rights

Another major issue that could affect the control and use of western water is the dispute over Indian water rights. Claims by Indians to a larger share of western water resources could change the availability and perhaps the price of irrigation water in many parts of the West. Historically, little consideration was given to the potential needs of Indians when the federal and state governments allocated western water resources. Indians are a minor consumer of water; the Bureau of Indian Affairs (BIA) projects account for only 2.9 percent of the acreage irrigated with water from irrigation organizations. However, several Indian tribes have made major claims to already appropriated surface and groundwater resources, contending that they have rights senior to those made under state law. The Navajos may lay claim to as much as a third of the flow of the Colorado River. In New Mexico, claims by several tribes to waters of the Upper Colorado Basin are many times the entitlement of the entire state to the water of the region. Even the water supply for the city of Los Angeles is endangered by Indian claims. Indeed, the problem of Indian claims has been termed ubiquitous, since almost anywhere there is an Indian reservation, there is potential for dispute. This problem has not only threatened existing reclamation and irrigation works but also casts uncertainty over the future development of water resources in the West.

The source of the conflict rests in nineteenth-century federal acts giving states jurisdiction over all nonnavigable water in the public domain. When the federal government withdrew land from the public domain for some purpose (for example, to create an Indian reservation), there existed no provision for allotting the land water rights. However, in 1908 the Supreme Court in Winters v. United States found that when the federal government withdrew lands for any purpose, it at the same time implicitly withdrew sufficient unappropriated waters from the public domain to accomplish this purpose. In the Winters case the court ruled that when the federal government created the Belknap Indian Reservation in Montana, it also appropriated sufficient water from the unappropriated flow of the Milk River to meet the needs of the reservation. The Winters doctrine allows claims to be made to any water unappropriated at the time that the land was withdrawn with priority dating back to this time. Although the priority of Indian claims has not been established clearly by either the courts or executive branch, the Winters doctrine appears to give them seniority dating from the late nineteenth and early twentieth centuries when their reservations were created.

There also has been no determination as to the quantity of water associated with Indian rights. Some claim that the quantity of water is limited to the amount needed to meet the original purpose of the land. Reservations were originally envisaged as agricultural communities and thus have rights to water commensurate with needs of irrigation, stock, and domestic use. However, Indians claim that since reservations are now regarded as the permanent homelands of their tribes, any use of water that contributes to the development of these homelands must be satisfied under the Winters doctrine. The Supreme Court ruled in one case that reservations are entitled to water sufficient to irrigate all reservation lands that can be irrigated "practically"--regardless of what the water is actually used for.[20] This decision leaves another question unanswered: if a reservation is unable to put to use its entire allotment of water, can it still lay claim to the water and lease or sell it? If so, irrigators using contested water might not actually lose their water but instead would pay royalties to the reservation for its use.

In 1979 the Carter administration stated its intention to resolve quickly all uncertainty about the quantity of water claimed for federal enclaves--including military reservations, federal lands under the Park Service, Forest Service, and Bureau of Land Management, and Indian reservations. Later, Indian claims were exempted from these discussions; federal policy on resolving Indian claims is simply to allow settlements on a case-by-case basis through negotiating among the concerned

---

20. _Arizona_ v. _California_, see Richard Sims, "Issues in Determining Indian Water Rights," in _Western_ _Water_ _Resources:_ _Coming_ _Problems_ _and_ _the_ _Policy_ _Alternatives_, p. 71.

parties or, if that fails, by litigation. As of May 1980, there were forty-seven cases in litigation dealing with Indian water rights in ten states. This process promises to be long and drawn out with, at present, little indication of how the courts will rule. In the meantime, there will be added risk to investments dependent on water resource development in areas where the rights are in dispute.

Institutional Obstacles to Water Use Efficiency

Future development in the West (for reasons examined in chapter 3) will depend increasingly on using supplies more efficiently and allocating them to higher value uses. Current and expected future conditions are very different from those that prevailed when most of the laws were written, the water rights were acquired, and the water distribution organizations were established. Consequently, it is not too surprising that there are important institutional obstacles to achieving greater efficiency in the use of western water.

Efficiency in the allocation and use of scarce water resources depends on the ease with which the resources can be transferred from one use to another in response to changing conditions and on the degree to which transfer decisions reflect social benefits and costs. Unrestricted free-market transfers are seldom permitted and, indeed, often would not result in socially efficient uses of water in view of the importance of effects on third parties. Third parties are those who are not directly a part of the transaction (that is, as buyer or seller) but are affected by the transfer. Such effects are common and often important in surface water transfers, especially since transfers tend to alter the availability of drainage waters.

Irrigation as the largest water use, holder of most of the preferred water rights, and a relatively low-value user, is central to achieving efficient water use; the incentives provided farmers to use water more efficiently and their ability to transfer water to other uses will affect both the future role of western irrigation and the overall development of the region's resources. Some features of western water law that pose obstacles to achieving a more efficient use of surface water currently used for irrigation are examined below. This discussion is followed by a brief look at an irrigation district that

has developed effective water markets and at one type of water insti-
tution that offers some promise for promoting major improvements in
water allocations but would require adjustments in the water laws of
most western states.

Irrigation water rights are "appurtenant" to only the land specified in the permit which grants the right. That is, the right attaches
to specific lands and cannot be changed without approval of the state
agency issuing the permit. In many states water rights originally were
attached to the land to help prevent fraudulent land and water sales
practices common to early settlement schemes. To the extent that these
provisions still impair transfer of water among alternative lands and
uses, they may prevent efficient water use. Generally water rights can
be transferred to other land so long as the rights of third parties are
not impaired. However, the appurtenancy rule is stricter in some
states. For example, a few states will approve transfers only for uses
other than irrigation or if continued irrigation of land to which the
right is presently appurtenant is no longer beneficially or economically practical.[21]

Some states limit the diversion of surface water out of its basin
of origin. Four states--Colorado, Nebraska, Texas, and Oklahoma--
restrict water exports to levels that will not impair present or prospective users. In the case of Texas, no water can be exported if in
the next fifty years it seems likely that it will be used within the
basin.

"Beneficial use" provisions of western water laws are intended to
prevent the wasteful use of surface water resources. These provisions
generally stipulate that both the purpose to which the water is put, as
well as the manner by which it is applied, must be beneficial. California law requires that water allocated under appropriative rights be
limited to that reasonably required for beneficial use. Likewise,
other states specify that water allocated for irrigation should not
surpass the amount required by good agricultural practices or by rea-

---

21. Radosevich, _Western Water Laws_. p. 63.

sonably intelligent and diligent use. Some states go further and impose additional criteria for establishing the amount of water to be allocated to an applicant--termed the statutory duty of water. These include quantified limits. Idaho, Wyoming, and North Dakota permit 1 cubic-foot per second (cfs) of water per 50, 70, and 80 acres, respectively. South Dakota and Nebraska allow 1 cfs per 70 acres but no more than 3 acre-feet per acre. Montana and Kansas also have quantified limits.

Beneficial use provisions are frequently vague and always difficult to enforce. Courts often have resorted to using the custom of the local community as the standard of what is beneficial and reasonable though the community's customary use may not be particularly efficient. So long as the farming methods used are deemed reasonable for that community, the farmer need not "use methods which are costly in labor and money simply because some waste can be saved thereby."[22]

Despite their intent to prevent wasteful water use, the beneficial use provisions tend to inhibit water transfers and incentives to conserve. For example, an irrigator may be unwilling to transfer his water rights temporarily to another party because he fears the transfer will be construed as evidence that he no longer can put the water to beneficial use--in which case he loses his right. The courts generally have not interpreted transfers in this manner, but this fear inhibits the exchange of water and is the basis of the "use it or lose it" philosophy influencing the use of much of the West's water.

Moreover, adopting more efficient methods does not guarantee that a user will have more water either to sell or to use himself. On the contrary, a strict interpretation of the "beneficial use" doctrine suggests that water saved from evaporation or seepage losses by some act of improvement does not automatically accrue to the person making the improvement. In the case of onfarm improvements, greater efficiency

---

22. Twin Falls Land and Water Co. v. Twin Falls Canal Co., District Court of Idaho, 1933. Cited in George Radosevich, Western Water Laws. p. 61.

in water use can mean a loss of part of one's water rights. If a farmer improves his conveyance system, distribution system, or scheduling of irrigation applications, the water saved could not be used on other lands according to the appurtenancy rule. Instead, since less water would now be needed to accomplish the intended beneficial use, the water saved could be declared in surplus of the amount needed and forfeited. Consequently, farmers may overirrigate or otherwise waste water which they are allotted rather than risk losing it through non-use.

Similarly, persons are discouraged from "salvaging" water in other ways because of the uncertainty of who will have priority for its use. Some innovative parties have tried to establish rights to water salvaged by lining canals or destroying water-absorbing plants that border canals. Courts, in some cases, have refused to grant these parties rights to the salvaged water senior to those who had prior rights to flow. In these cases, the party that had made the improvement could lose its allotment in times of shortage while the senior right holders reap the benefits of the conservation efforts. A more common judicial interpretation has been to grant the party that has made the improvement priority in right to the salvaged water. However, there is some doubt that this interpretation will hold in future contests when water is scarcer and there is greater demand for nonagricultural water uses.

Improving efficiency of water use is further complicated when the water lost by the initial appropriator makes its way back to the original stream or into a groundwater aquifer where it is appropriated by others. In some states, such as Arizona, courts have ruled that while downstream users can appropriate return flow water, they cannot prevent upstream users from adopting more efficient means that prevent this return flow. Other states have taken the opposite position, ruling that upstream irrigators cannot change their methods if the improvement will detrimentally affect downstream users who rely on runoff and seepage for their supply of water.

The rights of third parties comprise another impediment to water transfers. In general, transfers of appropriative rights are prohibited if they somehow impair third party rights. Often water transfers would affect return flows and groundwater recharge on which other farmers depend. There has been no easy method of resolving these problems and the costs of litigation often exceed benefits accrued by the transfer.

There are scattered areas in the West where at least limited water markets have developed. Most notable among these is the Northern Colorado Water Conservancy District (NCWCD). This district, which was established in 1937 to manage and distribute water from the BR's Colorado-Big Thompson project, has developed rental and water transfer markets.[23] Permanent transfers of water rights are permitted by the district as long as the new use is considered beneficial and is within the confines of the district. Temporary or seasonal transfers of water also are permitted, adding an important degree of flexibility for moving water to high-value uses in response to unforeseen events. The price of the water is arranged between the buyer and seller, and is not of concern to the district. The price of water traded within the district has risen from about $30 per acre-foot in 1962 to $1,200 in 1978.[24]

Three reasons have been cited for the success of water markets in this area of Colorado.[25] First, the irrigation company owns the water rights. Consequently, the rights are associated with shares in the company and are not attached to the land. The shares are personal

---

23. A much more detailed discussion of the Northern Colorado Water Conservancy District is available in L. M. Hartman and Don Seastone, Water Transfers: Economic Efficiency and Alternative Institutions (Baltimore, Md., Johns Hopkins University Press for Resources for the Future, 1970) chap. V, pp. 45-60.

24. Raymond L. Anderson, "Transfer Mechanisms Used to Acquire Water for Growing Municipalities in Colorado." Paper prepared for the session, Economic Issues in the Transfer of Water Rights at the Western Farm Economics Association meeting, July 24, 1978 (p. 6). Anderson suggests the effective prices may have been somewhat higher since the system does not deliver a full acre-foot per unit in most years.

25. Raymond L. Anderson, "The Irrigation Water Rental Market: A Case Study," in U.S. Department of Agriculture, Agricultural Economics Research (June 1961) pp. 54-58.

property and can be transferred freely, thus avoiding the forfeiture problem associated with the appropriation doctrine. This feature also enables the district to get around the prohibition against farmers selling water supplied from federal projects. Second, privately owned storage reservoirs provide needed flexibility in the system to accommodate seasonal and permanent transfers. And third, there are no legal problems associated with the transfer since the water comes from a transmountain transfer and, therefore, is supplemental to the natural flow of the local Big Thompson River. Although the combination of these conditions is certainly not common and may be unique within the West, the NCWCD experience demonstrates the advantages in terms of improved efficiency of water use from an institutional device facilitating water transfers.

Water banking has been proposed as a more generally applicable scheme for facilitating water transfers. A plan proposed for California would establish the local state agency in each district as the water bank.[26] Water banking would be classified as a "beneficial use" to avoid forfeiture under the appropriation doctrine. The banks would not collect the water in a physical sense but merely arrange transfers. The purchase price would rise or fall depending on the interaction of supply and demand. This particular proposal authorizes the bank to add a small charge to the price to cover any transfer costs and also to reimburse third parties for damages. Participation would be voluntary and the only required change in the water law would be to classify water banking as a beneficial use. Such a system should encourage owners of water rights to conserve water and use it on one's own land only to the point where its marginal value in use equals or exceeds the selling price. Water banking would provide a method of transferring water from lower-valued to higher-valued uses and, thereby, help re-

---

26. Sotirios Angelides and Eugene Bardach, Water Banking: How to Stop Wasting Agricultural Water? (San Francisco, Calif., Institute for Contemporary Studies, 1978).

adjust the historic misallocation created by water rights allotted on a "first come" basis at a time when water was not viewed as a scarce resource.

Groundwater Institutions

Groundwater Law

The introduction of groundwater pumping initially did not lead to situations of obvious conflict requiring legal or institutional intervention.[27] Thus, the earliest legal doctrine governing groundwater use was that of absolute ownership. Farmers' decisions based on the profitability of pumping water comprise virtually the sole determinant of use under this doctrine.

Uncontrolled groundwater use, however, has resulted in a variety of problems. Where pumping exceeds recharge, pumping lifts rise, well yields decline, seawater may intrude into and contaminate an aquifer, or land may subside, a serious problem if streets or buildings occupy the land. Furthermore, since many aquifers are interconnected to streams and rivers, groundwater pumping may jeopardize the rights of surface water users. The emergence of these problems along with improved knowledge of aquifers have brought an increased appreciation of the need for better groundwater management. Although groundwater law has developed more slowly than surface water law, a variety of legal approaches to groundwater control have emerged and further changes are being debated in the legislatures of many western states.

Texas is the sole western state to retain the doctrine of absolute ownership. Under Texas law and the judicial interpretations of the

---

27. The following discussion of groundwater law draws on several sources, especially Radosevich, Western Water Laws, pp. 42-43 and 55-58; Governor's Commission to Review California Water Rights Law, Final Report (Sacramento, Calif., December 1978) pp. 140-143; and The John Muir Institute, Inc., Institutional Constraints on Alternative Water for Energy: A Guidebook for Regional Assessments, prepared for the U.S. Department of Energy (Washington, D.C., November 1980) pp. 27-30.

state courts, essentially all groundwater is considered to be the private property of the person with title to the land above it. The water can be withdrawn for use or sale without any effective control by the state. Furthermore, the landowner is not liable for damages such as land subsidence and falling water tables that his pumping might inflict on neighbors.

Even though the state of Texas does not regulate the landowner's use of groundwater, owners overlying a defined groundwater reservoir voluntarily may adopt well regulation through mutual association in an underground water district. A number of these conservation districts have been formed, several within the High Plains.

The vast majority of western states employ the concept of prior appropriation to groundwater as well as surface water. While there is a great deal of variety as to the level of state control imposed under this system, all follow the basic principle that a person can be granted a permit or license to pump water if it does not adversely affect prior groundwater appropriations and is used in a beneficial manner in conformance with other regulations. In practice, however, this doctrine seldom has been applied to prevent depletion of an aquifer and the resulting adverse impacts mining imposes on all users of the aquifer. Laws on preference of use, priority, appurtenance, forfeiture, and abandonment apply similarly to groundwater as they do to surface water.

Nebraska employs a reasonable use doctrine for control of groundwater use. This doctrine holds that landowners overlying an aquifer have coequal rights to the water and are limited to reasonable use. Lacking any comprehensive groundwater law, application of the reasonable use doctrine recognizes the interdependence among neighboring pumpers and attempts to modify the complete disregard the absolute ownership doctrine has for the negative impacts one farmer's pumping may impose on others. This doctrine does, however, create uncertainty as to what comprises reasonable use. Limitations of the reasonable use doctrine for controlling groundwater supplies have led Nebraska to place increasing reliance on Natural Resource Districts to limit pumping. In the absence of a comprehensive groundwater law, the restrictions imposed by these districts are sure to be challenged with increasing frequency in the courts. Until passage of its Comprehensive Groundwater Act in 1980, Arizona also employed the reasonable use doctrine. However, in part as a condition for participating in the Central Arizona Project, Arizona's new groundwater act adopts the prior appropriation doctrine and pumpers will be required to have permits.

California has adopted a refined version of the reasonable use doctrine, correlative rights. This doctrine holds that every overlying landowner may make reasonable use of his groundwater as long as the water is plentiful. When supplies are threatened by overuse, each owner receives a share of the resource in proportion to his percentage of the overlying lands. All overlying uses are correlative with each other regardless of when they were initiated; there is no priority accorded early users. Transfers to another basin are permitted only where the water supply exceeds the needs of overlying properties.

Groundwater Management Organizations

Most western states have organizations with groundwater management functions ranging from administering well permits, policing water use, approving transfers, adjudicating water rights, and controlling water quality. At the state level these organizations include departments of water resources, offices of state engineers, and water commissions and boards.

In addition, many states permit the formation of special districts at the local level to regulate or manage groundwater. Locally controlled groundwater management districts are now common in areas with critical groundwater problems in California, Texas, Nebraska, Kansas, and Colorado. The example of the Texas groundwater conservation districts was mentioned above. The first and largest of these districts was established in 1951 when residents in a thirteen county area voted to form the High Plains Underground Water Conservation District No. 1. This district has the power to tax and to control well spacing and (to some extent) the use of the water. The district also helps monitor water use, pumping levels, water availability, and the long-term implications of expected water use on future water supplies and pumping levels.

The Orange County Water District in southern California illustrates the application of broad local control over groundwater resources. This district has wide ranging powers including the right to levy pump taxes and to require all pumpers to file periodic pumping statements. These powers are employed to regulate both the total quantities as well as the relative amounts of ground and surface water used within the districts.[28] This district is not typical, however, as most western groundwater is subject to little control beyond well spacing.

In some situations major improvements in water management are possible through conjunctive management of ground and surface water resources. Generally this involves utilizing surface water supplies when available either for direct delivery to users or to recharge groundwater stocks, which become the main source of supply when the less expensive but fugitive surface waters are insufficient to meet demand. Conjunctive management has been employed by some local water agencies in California for some years. As of 1970, for example, there were 261 groundwater recharge facilities within Central California. The Arvin-Edison Water Storage District, which serves 130,000 acres in Kern County has been particularly effective in conjunctively managing their water supplies. The area has very little natural surface flow but receives water from the federal Central Valley Project (CVP). However, only about 20 percent of their supply from this project is "firm" water as annual deliveries vary from about 10,000 to 350,000 acre-feet. Yet, this district has been able to increase its supply of firm water to 180,000 acre-feet by storing water in its aquifers through artificial recharge during periods of large water receipts from the CVP.[29]

---

28. Governor's Commission to Review California Water Rights Law, _Final Report_, pp. 146-147.

29. Ibid., pp. 155-156.

Efficiency of Groundwater Use

Farmers' costs have been the principal regulator of western groundwater use. Once a well is installed, farmers maximize profits by pumping until the marginal cost of pumping equals the marginal revenue that can be attributed to the use of the water. The marginal costs of pumping are essentially the costs of the energy to run the pump. These costs did not provide much of a deterrent to pumping until the early 1970s. Consequently, there has been little incentive to conserve water until recently. As is detailed in chapter 5, the rise in energy costs over the past decade has encouraged groundwater irrigators to introduce a variety of water-saving innovations.

These cost increases as well as groundwater users' ability to control the quantity and the timing of their water are important factors underlying the fact that groundwater generally is more efficiently used than surface water in western irrigation. Nevertheless, it does not follow that western groundwater resources are used efficiently. Both institutional constraints and market deficiencies may result in an inefficient use or allocation of groundwater.

Groundwater resources are likely to be used at an inefficiently rapid rate if left to market forces because of several factors. Environmental externalities, which are one possible source of market breakdown, are discussed in chapter 6. Another problem results from the cone of depression in the water table that appears in the vicinity of an operating well. Where pumps are closely spaced, this cone increases pumping depths of neighboring wells. But since a farmer does not voluntarily take into account the impacts of his pumping on others, uncontrolled pumping and well spacing can lead to a situation where the social cost of pumping exceeds the private cost. Regulations on well spacing imposed in most western states are designed in part to limit these distortions. Consequently, well spacing is not a major source of inefficiency in most of the West.

The more important source of inefficiency in groundwater use occurs when groundwater tables are falling over time. Individual farmers have no rights to water left in the ground until it is withdrawn. Consequently, the value an individual attaches to water left in

an aquifer may be less than its social value, and pumping based on private decisions may use the water at a faster rate than is socially
desirable.

At least in theory, a tax on pumping equal to the user cost, or
the value of water in storage, would equate marginal private and social
costs of pumping and result in an optimum use of the groundwater over
time. As simple as this policy seems, two problems have prevented
significant use of such a tax. First, almost any tax will be resisted
by those who will have to pay it. Second, it would be very difficult
to determine the correct tax. The optimal tax rate would decline over
the planning period if the aquifer is being depleted.[30] Well or
pumping quotas have been a more politically acceptable means of
limiting overpumping since this tends to protect the interests of the
early users. From the perspective of achieving a social optimum, there
remains the difficult problem of setting the correct quota. The
tendency is to attempt to limit pumping to the level of natural recharge so as to preserve the water in the aquifer. But such a policy
does not represent an efficient solution either. Nevertheless, a study
of Yolo County in California suggests the quota system may better
approximate the social optimum than does a policy of unrestricted
pumping.[31]

As with surface water, there are institutional constraints to
transferring water from irrigation to other uses. For example, the
Missouri Basin Power Project which involves constructing three 500-MW
generating units in Wyoming has encountered a variety of problems in
obtaining about 23,000 acre-feet of water per year for cooling purposes. Part of the water was to be supplied from groundwater rights
purchased from a neighboring rancher. The project purchased an option
permitting it to use up to 15,000 acre-feet of groundwater per year
from two different aquifers beneath the ranch. Test wells showed one

30. Jay E. Noel, B. Delworth Gardner, and Charles V. Moore, "Optimal
Regional Conjunctive Water Management," American Journal of Agricultural Economics, vol. 62, no. 3 (August 1980) p. 496.

31. Ibid., pp. 489-498.

of these aquifers contained only modest amounts of water, and while the other aquifer was potentially much more productive, it was being heavily used. To protect prior users in the area, the state engineer limited the power project's annual use to 750 acre-feet from the productive aquifer and 2,000 acre-feet from the other aquifer.[32] If market forces had been allowed to operate, the Missouri Basin Power Project would have had no difficulty in securing the needed water. The desired quantities were modest relative to agricultural uses in the area, and energy users can afford to pay much higher water prices than can farmers. The problems faced by this power project do not represent an isolated example. Indeed, institutional constraints on transferring water from irrigation to other uses are perhaps the foremost obstacle to achieving an efficient use of western groundwater resources.

The importance of the distortions resulting from uncontrolled groundwater use depend on the characteristics of the aquifer. In an aquifer with significant lateral flow, the distortions may be large since the effects of one farmer's actions are spread over a large area. In such cases, the "use it or lose it" view which distorts farmers' decisions regarding surface water use (see the discussion on p. 129) are applicable in part to groundwater. In other aquifers, such as in much of the Ogallala underlying the High Plains, there is very little lateral flow. Accordingly, the principal impacts of groundwater pumping within such an aquifer are largely contained within the area underlying the farm doing the pumping.

---

32. The John Muir Institute, Institutional Constraints on Alternative Water for Energy, p. 56. This study provides several examples of institutional constraints to obtaining sufficient water supplies for energy projects.

Chapter 5

THE CHANGING COSTS OF IRRIGATION

The preceding discussion demonstrates that the past expansion of irrigation largely relied on access to inexpensive water. Such water supplies are no longer available within the West's most favorable agricultural areas. Not only are the opportunities for expanding irrigation now limited and costly but many long-time irrigators are being confronted with sharply higher water costs. While groundwater users have been especially hard hit, nearly all farmers dependent on pumped water have been adversely affected by rising energy costs.

The overall impact of changes in water supply and energy prices on irrigation depends on the decisions of thousands of farmers responding individually to a wide variety of conditions, prices, and opportunities. Farmers are affected differently, and they can be expected to respond differently. Nevertheless, as the qualitative nature of the impacts is similar among certain classes of irrigators, insights as to the likely direction and pace of future changes in irrigation can be gained by illustrating how alternative energy prices and pumping depths affect water costs under specific assumptions.

There is no attempt in this study to provide a comprehensive analysis of the economics of irrigated farming; the focus is on only one aspect of agricultural production: water costs and the impacts of higher water costs on the relative profitability of alternative technologies. The analysis proceeds in three stages. Initially, the impacts of rising energy prices and pumping depths on the cost of getting water to the farm are examined separately for ground and surface water costs. Second, the effects of alternative energy prices on the costs of delivering water by various irrigation methods from the farmgate or wellhead to the plants are examined. Third, this cost analysis is used as the basis for assessing possible technological responses to rising water and energy costs and for drawing conclusions as to the likely changes in the relative profitability of irrigated agriculture.

Conveyance of Water to Farms

Initially, farmers irrigated their land by building crude dams and canals, allowing gravity to carry the water onto contiguous cropland. As the best lands closest to the natural water courses became fully irrigated, more sophisticated dams, reservoirs, and canals were constructed to control and transport water to fields hundreds of miles away. With the introduction of high-speed pumps in the 1930s, many farmers began pumping their water from underground aquifers or from rivers, streams, and ponds that flow on or by the farm.

The costs of gravity-carried surface water are primarily a function of the capital costs to build the necessary irrigation structures such as dams, reservoirs, and canals. Operating costs are minor. However, where water must be lifted onto a higher plain, out of a river basin, or from an aquifer, energy becomes an important cost factor and the costs increase directly with lift.

In 1977 an estimated 25.8 million acres were irrigated with onfarm-pumped groundwater (16 percent above the 1974 level) and 5.3 million acres irrigated with onfarm-pumped surface water (an increase of only 5 percent since 1974); see table 5-1. While there are no data on gravity irrigation, the combination of Sloggett's estimates of pumped irrigation and the NRI estimate of total irrigated acreage suggests that 17.3 million acres were gravity irrigated. While reliance on two different sets of data in this manner can produce some highly suspect results, it does provide a rough indication of the relationship between onfarm-pumped water and onfarm gravity irrigation. This distinction is important for examining the impacts of energy costs on profitability. However, even with onfarm gravity irrigation, pumping may be required at some point to get the water to the farmgate.

Groundwater

An important consequence of the expanded use of groundwater has been the mining of some of the region's principal aquifers. In the 1960s and early 1970s, when the rate of mining was rising rapidly, there were concerns about the effects of mining on the long-term vi-

Table 5-1. Acreage Irrigated with Onfarm-Pumped Water by Source of Water and Farm Production Region (1,000 acres)

Region	Groundwater		Surface water		Both		Total	
	1974	1977	1974	1977	1974	1977	1975	1977
Northern Plains	6,380	8,977	684	676	186	185	7,250	9,838
Southern Plains	7,770	8,320	1,491	1,569	256	256	9,517	10,145
Mountain	3,587	3,636	1,149	1,206	1,284	1,325	6,020	6,167
Pacific	4,561	4,912	1,725	1,845	0	0	6,286	6,757
17 Western states	22,298	25,845	5,049	5,296	1,726	1,766	29,073	32,907

Source: Gordon Sloggett, Energy and U.S. Agriculture: Irrigation Pumping, 1974-77, Agricultural Economic Report no. 436 (Washington, D.C., U.S. Department of Agriculture, September 1979) app. table 2.

ability of irrigation. More recently, however, the fear of depletion has been displaced by the much more immediate threat that energy prices could make irrigation uneconomical even with much of the water still in the aquifer.

Groundwater mining has two adverse effects on water costs. First, there is the increased pumping lift. On a regional or statewide basis, this may not average more than one to three feet a year, generally signifying a 1 or 2 percent per annum increase in pumping lift. On a farm-by-farm basis, however, there is a great deal of variation, and an individual irrigator may face a more rapidly declining water level. A second effect is the decrease in saturated thickness as the aquifer is mined. As saturated thickness declines, so does well yield. Eventually, additional wells and pumps are needed to maintain the flow. For example, a center pivot distribution system requires a minimum well yield of 600 gallons per minute (gpm). At lower yields, farmers must either adopt a new system requiring fewer gallons per minute, add to the number of wells, or be satisfied with less than optimum coverage. These alternatives tend to increase production costs or decrease crop yields. In Texas, where declines in saturated thickness are especially serious, some farmers have installed eight to nine smaller pumps each yielding 75 to 150 gpm to reach adequate output.[1] On farms with a center pivot or other sprinkler system, the decline in saturated thickness and its resulting problems may have a greater impact on water costs than do the increased energy costs resulting from greater pumping lifts.[2]

When water must be lifted several hundred feet, energy costs now tend to be the major component of water costs. The importance of

---

1. Personal communication with Gordon Sloggett, Oklahoma State University, February 8, 1980.

2. A Sanghi and R. Klepper, "The Economic Impact of Diminishing Groundwater Reserves on the Production of Corn Under Center Pivot Irrigation," Journal of Soil and Water Conservation, vol. 32, no. 6 (1977) pp. 282-285.

energy costs is evident in tables 5-2 and 5-3. Table 5-2 indicates the cost of the energy required to pump 1 acre-foot of water from various depths with alternative fuels and fuel prices. The alternative energy prices were selected to represent actual levels in 1970 and 1980, and projections for 2000, all in 1977 constant dollars. Alternative pumping depths of 100, 200, and 300 feet were considered; this range includes the conditions facing many but by no means all farmers. The assumptions adopted in the subsequent discussion as to fuel costs, pumping depths and other factors are most representative of the High Plains region.

The efficiency of the pumping system also affects energy costs. Pumping efficiency, which is the ratio of the theoretical to the actual energy input for a given water output, is essentially the product of the efficiencies of the pump and the power unit.[3] If properly installed, a new pump should have an efficiency of about 75 percent. The power system efficiency varies widely with the type of engine. Reasonable engine efficiencies are 90 percent for electric, 24 percent for natural gas, and 32 percent for diesel. Overall attainable efficiencies for pumping systems are about 66 percent for electric, 17 percent for natural gas, and 20 percent for diesel.[4] The estimates in table 5-2 assume a 60 percent pump efficiency and average operating conditions. The implications of different pump efficiencies on costs are examined later in this chapter.[5]

3. With internal combustion engines, the efficiency of the pumping system is likely to be reduced another 5 percent or so because of the gearhead.

4. Based on a brochure of the High Plains Underground Water Conservation District No. 1, "Overall Pump Plant Efficiency" (undated) and on High Plains Underground Water Conservation District No. 1 and the Texas Department of Water Resources, A Summary of Techniques and Management Practices for Profitable Water Conservation on the Texas High Plains, Report 79-01 (Lubbock, Texas, 1979) p. II-14.

5. Well efficiency, which is another component of overall system efficiency, also is examined later.

Table 5-2. Energy Costs to Pump 1 Acre-Foot of Groundwater with Alternative Fuels and Fuel Prices, 1970-2000

(1977 constant dollars)

Fuel	Pump lift (ft)	Energy costs under alternative fuel prices		
		1970	1980	2000
Natural gas	100	$ 1.13	$ 4.56	$ 9.12
	200	2.30	9.29	18.58
	300	3.43	13.86	27.72
Electricity	100	7.52	8.88	17.76
	200	15.03	17.76	35.52
	300	22.55	26.64	53.28
LPG	100	7.32	12.60	25.20
	200	14.65	25.20	50.40
	300	21.98	37.80	75.59
Diesel	100	5.24	14.96	29.92
	200	10.59	30.00	60.00
	300	15.74	44.96	89.92

Sources: The technical assumptions such as the amount of fuel and the pressure required to lift an acre-foot of water are based on Gordon Sloggett, Energy and U.S. Agriculture: Irrigation Pumping, 1974-77 (Washington, D.C., U.S. Department of Agriculture, September 1979). Other assumptions include a 60 percent pumping efficiency. Fuel costs in 1977 constant dollars are: natural gas ($/mcf) .39 in 1970, 1.58 in 1980, and 3.15 in 2000; electricity ($/kWh), .033 in 1970, .039 in 1980, and .078 in 2000; LPG ($/gal.) .25 in 1970, .43 in 1980, and .86 in 2000; diesel ($/gal.) .28 in 1970, .80 in 1980, and 1.60 in 2000. The 1970 prices for LPG, and diesel are a national average obtained from Agricultural Prices, Annual Summary (Washington, D.C., U.S. Department of Agriculture, June 1977). The 1970 prices for electricity are a national average obtained from Agricultural Prices, October 1977. The 1970 price for natural gas was obtained by personal communication with Delbert Schwab, OSU. The 1980 prices reflect average prices paid by farmers in Nebraska, Kansas, Oklahoma, and Texas in January 1980. The prices were obtained through phone conversations with officials in those states. Hans Landsberg, project director and co-authors (Energy: The Next Twenty Years, Cambridge, Mass., Ballinger, 1979, p. 71) conclude that, on average, real fuel prices will double by the year 2000. Although long-term contracts consummated in the last several years suggest natural gas prices may rise faster than the prices of the other three fuels, we have chosen to illustrate the implications of a doubling of all fuel prices rather than attempt to estimate differential rates of increase.

Table 5-3. Fixed and Variable Costs for Pumping 1 Acre-Foot of Groundwater
Using Different Fuels in 1980

(1977 constant dollars)

| Pumping system | Fixed cost | | Variable cost | | Total cost |
	Well	Power unit	Repair and maintenance	Energy costs for pumping	
Natural gas	3.74	3.75	.61	9.29	17.39
Electricity	3.74	2.35	.07	17.76	23.92
LPG	3.74	3.74	.61	25.20	33.29
Diesel	3.74	5.62	1.04	30.00	40.40

Note: Assumes that the cost of the well is $24,737. This includes
drilling and casing installation, 16 inch casing including perforations, an
8 inch pump assembly, and 10 inch bowls. The well was 300 feet deep with
a 900 gpm capacity, capable of irrigating 320 acres at a rate of 2 feet per
acre per year. The cost of power units includes all necessary accessories.
The motors were all capable of powering a center pivot system. Power rat-
ings for the units were: natural gas--110 h.p., V-8; electric--100 h.p.,
3 phase; LPG--100 h.p., V-8; diesel--90 to 130 h.p., V-8. Fixed costs include depreciation (no salvage value) and interest on average investment
(10.5 percent). Labor cost for operation and maintenance of materials
(oil filters, etc.) were assumed to be constant for all units except the
electrical one which required less maintenance. The Consumer Price Index
was used to render costs into 1977 constant dollars. The well, motors and
maintenance costs were taken from 1979 sources and were raised to 1980
levels using the implicit price deflator for fixed investment (7.4 percent)
for the well and motors and the CPI (11.8 percent) for the maintenance
cost. The energy costs assumed pumping from 200 feet. The technical relationship and price assumptions are shown in the footnote to table 5-2.

Sources: The cost of the well was taken from Rodney Sharp, "Economic
Adjustments to Increasing Energy Costs for Pump Irrigation in Northwestern
Colorado," M.A. dissertation, Colorado State University, 1979. Power unit
and maintenance costs were taken from Leslie Sheffield, "Energy...Is It
the Achilles Heel for Irrigated Agriculture?" Irrigation Age (September
1979).

The data indicate that the type of fuel has been as important as the pumping depth in determining a farmer's energy costs. Despite a fourfold rise in price since 1970, natural gas continues to be the least expensive means of pumping. In 1980 natural gas was only half as expensive as electricity, the next least expensive source of energy. Diesel, as a result of rapid price increases in the last two years, is now the most expensive fuel.[6] The real cost of pumping an acre-foot of water 200 feet rose an estimated $6.99 for natural gas, $2.73 for electricity, $10.55 for LPG, and $19.41 for diesel from 1970 to 1980. Cost increases are likely to be even higher over the next two decades. If real energy costs double from 1980 to 2000, as is assumed in table 5-2, the energy cost increases of pumping 1 acre-foot from a depth of 200 feet will exceed $9.00 for natural gas, $17.00 for electricity, $25.00 for LPG, and $30.00 for diesel. Under such circumstances, fuel price increases will have a greater effect on the profitability of irrigated agriculture than the additional energy costs due to declining well levels. Indeed, the impact of a doubling of fuel prices is comparable to a doubling of pumping depths.

The cost of fuel is not the only consideration in the farmer's selection of an energy source. There is considerable variation in the cost and lifetime of motors powered by different fuels. As table 5-3 demonstrates, electric motors are clearly the least expensive, followed by LPG and natural gas units. Installing, repairing, and maintaining a diesel motor is almost three times the comparable cost of an electric motor.

Besides the cost of the power unit, the fixed costs of groundwater pumping include drilling and installing the well and pump. In 1980, wells cost approximately $35 per foot to install. A properly installed

---

6. Diesel costs in Nebraska, for example, rose from 40 cents per gallon in 1978 to 85 cents per gallon in November 1979. See L. F. Sheffield, "Energy Outlook for irrigated Agriculture in 1980," Cornhusker Economics (Department of Agricultural Economics, University of Nebraska, Lincoln, Nebraska, Dec. 2, 1979).

well often extends to the bedrock at the base of an aquifer and will have a lifetime of fifty years. A vertical-drive pump is used for groundwater and is located at the bottom of the well. The type of pump and number of bowls are selected to match the conductivity of the aquifer.

When the variable and fixed costs of groundwater pumping are combined (the last column in table 5-3), the advantage of natural gas is evident. The total costs of pumping an acre-foot of water range from $17.39 in 1977 dollars for natural gas to $40.40 for diesel. If cost alone determined fuel selection, there would be an overwhelming preference for natural gas under the prices assumed in table 5-3. In fact, however, in 1977 natural gas accounted for only 35 percent of the acreage, a slight decline from 1974 (see table 5-4). Furthermore, this percentage is likely to keep declining as farmers find it increasingly difficult to arrange natural gas hookups for new irrigation. Historically, natural gas use for irrigation pumping has been limited by access to hookup rather than cost factors. Consequently, it is not surprising that 61 percent of the acreage irrigated with natural gas is found in the Southern Plains, historically the major production region for this fuel in the United States.

Electricity accounts for 50 percent of the irrigated acreage served by onfarm pumps, and within the Pacific region virtually all irrigation pumps are electric. Although table 5-3 lists electricity as only the second most economical fuel, in the pacific Northwest the availability of cheap hydropower has made it by far the cheapest fuel. Electricity also is the most important fuel in the Mountain states (74 percent) and accounts for substantial acreage in the Plains states (25 percent). Despite the 15 percent growth in electricity use between 1974 and 1977 (see table 5-4), expansion has been hindered by the fact that many electric utilities are near capacity and unwilling to add new irrigation customers because of peak-load problems. One option for such cases might be to limit new customers to pumping during non-peak hours.

Table 5-4. Acreage Irrigated with Onfarm-Pumped Water by Type of Fuel and Farm Production Region

(1,000 acres)

Region	Electricity		Diesel		Natural gas		LPG	
	1974	1977	1974	1977	1974	1977	1974	1977
Northern Plains	1,573	2,612	1,543	2,914	2,430	3,231	1,553	1,008
Southern Plains	2,007	2,347	151	166	6,742	6,949	509	568
Mountain	4,297	4,500	307	350	1,152	1,104	184	136
Pacific	6,197	6,717	4	9	84	31	0	0
17 Western states	14,074	16,176	2,005	3,439	10,409	11,315	2,246	1,712

Source: Gordon Sloggett, Energy and U.S. Agriculture: Irrigation Pumping, 1974–77, Agricultural Economics Report No. 436 (Washington, D.C., U.S. Department of Agriculture, September 1979) app. table 4.

The most rapid growth has been for diesel fuel which increased by 72 percent between 1974 and 1977. Almost all of this growth came in the Northern Plains, the only area which uses substantial amounts of this fuel. Under the 1980 fuel costs listed in table 5-2, little further growth in diesel use is expected. Diesel fuel prices have jumped dramatically since 1978 and supplies have been erratic, especially at vital periods in the growing season.

LPG use has been concentrated in the Plains states. Although its use decreased from 1974 to 1977, prospects for increased LPG use are good largely because of the supply or price problems with the alternatives. LPG prices have not risen as precipitously as either diesel or natural gas (table 5-2), and in late 1979 there was a world surplus of LPG.

Given the relative instability of the world fuel market, it is difficult to make accurate predictions about future trends. Researchers in Nebraska--the state with the most growth in pump irrigation in the last ten years and the most potential for further growth--expect that LPG and electricity will grow in importance.[7] Many farmers are switching from diesel- to LPG-powered pumps because of its ready availability and lower costs. Some have even installed LPG pumps as backups to their diesel units in case of a diesel shortage. It is projected that irrigators and electric utilities will be able to make suitable arrangements concerning peak load problems, thus allowing for some expansion of electricity use. Natural gas suppliers have relaxed restrictions on adding new customers in some areas, and recent improvements in natural gas supply conditions may result in further opportunities for irrigators to expand their use of this preferred fuel.

---

7. Personal communication with Raymond Supalla, Bruce Johnson, and others. Agricultural Economics Department, University of Nebraska, February 25, 1980.

Surface Water

There are wide differences among surface water costs. Since the original appropriators are not charged for the water itself, the cost differences depend largely on the distance and height the water must be transported to get it to a farmer's field and the extent to which these costs are paid by the farmer. Of the roughly 23 million acres irrigated with surface water, about 25 percent are supplied from onfarm sources and 75 percent from irrigation organizations.[8] The following discussion distinguishes between these types.

Onfarm Sources. The lowest water costs are enjoyed by farmers with rights to adjacent streamflows or ponds that can be exercised with inexpensive dikes and ditches. Under these conditions, water costs consist essentially of the labor required to operate and maintain the dikes and canals which probably amount to no more than a few dollars per acre-foot. Such farmers are not dependent on the cost or availability of energy or on the charges of irrigation organizations for water. Moreover, these farmers frequently possess some of the most senior rights to western waters, making their supplies secure even during a drought. While the explicit costs to such farmers are not likely to rise significantly, the implicit (or opportunity) costs for using this water will rise if there is a general increase in the scarcity of water and a right to sell the water for other uses.

Irrigation in high valleys and mountain meadows is generally of this type, involving flooding of fields by diverting streamflows through crude dikes. Since water costs are very low and independent of the quantity used, large amounts of water may be applied to relatively low-value crops in these areas. Indeed, in view of the short growing season, pasture and hay are the primary uses of water in such locations.

---

8. As noted earlier, this 23-million acre figure is a rough estimate at best. The percentage breakdown between onfarm and irrigation organization source is based on 1969 census data (see chapter 4). Since surface irrigation has not expanded much since that time, these percentages probably are still reasonably accurate.

There are about 5 million acres irrigated by pumping onfarm surface water sources.[9] The cost structure for water on such farms is
similar to that of groundwater users with two exceptions--surface water
pumping lifts are generally much less and the source is less likely to
be depleted over time. Nevertheless, although surface water pumpers do
not face the problem of drawdown as do groundwater pumpers, they may
well be confronted with low streamflows in the growing season.
Furthermore, these low flows may be associated with groundwater pumping
in the region since ground and surface waters may be interrelated such
that water pumped from an aquifer may be replaced by increased
infiltration from a river bed. While surface water pumpers are
affected by increasing energy prices, these price increases are not as
critical because of their shorter pumping lifts. In 1977, the average
pumping lift for surface water irrigators in the seventeen western
states varied from virtually nothing in Arizona to 150 feet in South
Dakota. The average for the West was 29 feet, considerably less than
the 165 feet average for groundwater pumping.

Table 5-5 illustrates the range of energy costs (with different
fuels and fuel prices) of pumping water 29 feet. At current fuel prices
the costs range from $1.34 per acre-foot to $4.35 per acre-foot, only
about one-sixth of the energy costs for pumping groundwater from 200
feet. Since the nature of the costs and the price assumptions are
similar for both ground and surface water pumping, the conclusions
regarding preferred fuels also are similar; ranging from least to most
expensive (at 1980 prices) are natural gas, electricity, LPG, and
diesel. Surface water pumpers also can be expected to shift away from
diesel to LPG or, if available, natural gas and electricity because of
cost and reliability of supply considerations.

---

9. Table 5-1 indicates 5,296,000 acres irrigated with onfarm pumping of
surface water. Personal communication with Gordon Sloggett, author of
the source of that data, indicates that very little of that acreage
involved irrigation organizations.

Table 5-5. Energy Costs to Pump 1 Acre-Foot of Surface Water a Height of
29 Feet with Alternative Fuels and Fuel Prices, 1970-2000

(1977 constant dollars)

Fuel	Energy costs under alternative fuel prices		
	1970	1980	2000
Natural gas	.33	1.34	2.69
Electricity	2.18	2.58	5.15
LPG	2.13	3.66	7.31
Diesel	1.52	4.35	8.70

Note: This assumes 29-foot lift (represents a weighted average of
lift heights for the seventeen western states, weighted by number of acres
irrigated with onfarm-pumped surface water in each state). The technical
assumptions such as the amount of fuel and the pressure required to lift
an acre-foot of water are based on Gordon Sloggett, Energy and U.S. Agriculture: Irrigation Pumping, 1974-77, Agricultural Economics Report No. 436
(Washington, D.C., U.S. Department of Agriculture, September 1979). The
fuel price assumptions are listed in the note to table 5-2.

Pumped surface water costs can be expected to rise over time,
largely in response to energy costs. Nevertheless, the cost of water
to farmers with onfarm sources will remain low relative to most groundwater users and, as is noted below, relative to many farmers receiving
water through irrigation organizations. Future water costs on farms
with onfarm sources should pose no problem to the long-term profitability of irrigation in areas with favorable climates and soils. If
given the opportunity, however, some of these farmers undoubtedly will
find it more profitable to sell their water for nonagricultural uses.

Water Supplied by Irrigation Organizations. Chapter 4 examined
the types of irrigation organizations that have emerged to deliver
surface water to farms lacking onfarm sources. As illustrated in table
5-6, water costs vary widely among irrigation organizations and, in
some cases, they vary significantly over time within an organization.

Table 5-6. Water Charges of Various Irrigation Organizations Between
1969 and 1980

(1977 dollars per acre-foot)

Location	1969	1972	1979	1980
California				
Bureau of Reclamation[a]	5.79	5.07	2.92	2.76
Department of Water[b] Resources (DWR)[b]				
Entitlement water	--	29.96	--	28.62
Surplus water	--	3.11	--	2.37
Fresno Irrigation[c] District	3.58	--	2.92	--
Lemoore Canal and[d] Irrigation Co.	7.75	--	7.51	--
Colorado[e]	--	--	1.25-6.68	--
Utah[f]	--	--	3.34	--

Note: All prices were converted to 1977 dollars using the Consumer
Price Index.

[a]The majority of Bureau of Reclamation (BR) water in California was
priced at $3.50 per acre-foot (in undeflated dollars). Eighty percent
of their water projects in California came on line between 1952-1956 and
their contracts affecting water charges will not be renegotiated until
1992-1996. In the meantime, nominal water costs for BR projects will
remain unchanged and real costs will decline. (Source: Merv Dehaas,
Bureau of Reclamation Office in California.)

[b]DWR charges all water users a base price, called the Delta price,
measured at the junction of the Sacramento and San Joaquin Rivers. In
1977 dollars this amounted to $11.65 per acre-foot in 1972 and $9.51 per
acre-foot in 1980. There is an additional conveyance cost varying by
distance from the Delta. The conveyance cost to Kern County (in 1977
dollars) was $18.31 per acre-foot in 1972 and $19.11 per acre-foot in
1980. In most years, surplus water can be purchased in an amount equal
to their entitlement at much lower rates. (Source: Lee Carter of California DWR.)

[c]Fresno Irrigation District assesses water users based on acreage.
In return irrigators receive an average of 3 acre-feet a year, the
quantity used to compute the acre-foot prices for 1969 and 1979. In the
latter year the District received 22 percent of their operating costs
from taxes collected from nonwater users with property in the District.
(Source: Howard Keck, Fresno Irrigation District.)

Table 5-6 (continued)

[d]These are the prices of water allocated to farmers on the basis of their ownership of shares in the company. Each owner receives 1 acre-foot per share. If additional water is available, it is sold at a reduced rate which varies from year to year. (<u>Source</u>: Jim Handley, Lemoore Canal and Irrigation Company, July 19, 1979.)

[e]This range of prices charged by Colorado irrigation districts is based on data in Raymond Anderson, "Transfer Mechanisms Used to Acquire Water for Growing Municipalities in Colorado." Paper presented to Western Farm Economics Association meeting, July 24, 1978.

[f]Derivation of the Utah rate is explained in the text. The data are from U.S. Department of Interior, U.S. Department of Agriculture, and U.S. Environmental Protection Agency, <u>Irrigation Water Use and Management: An InterAgency Task Force Report</u> (Washington, D.C., GPO, June 1979) p. 55.

The principal costs of these organizations are incurred in the construction and maintenance of dams, reservoirs, and conveyance canals and in the energy required to move the water. As noted earlier, however, in many cases not all of these costs are passed on to the irrigators. The Bureau of Reclamation is the extreme case where subsidies may defray 95 percent or more of actual construction costs. Water rates also may benefit from local tax subsidies and the allocation of some investment costs to other beneficiaries such as flood protection, power, and recreation.

The California Department of Water Resources (DWR) charges the highest water rates listed in table 5-6. In 1980 the state charges to Kern County users for the basic entitlement water were more than ten times the rates the Bureau of Reclamation charged California users. Although some state funds are allocated to water projects because of social benefits attributed to flood prevention, navigation, and recreation, the DWR provides irrigation water on a largely nonsubsidized basis. Users in Kern County paid $28.62 per acre-foot for their entitlement water in 1980. If available, surplus water can be purchased from DWR in an amount up to one's entitlement, at a flat rate of

$2.37 per acre-foot. Surplus water generally has been available except during the 1977 drought; since most of these farmers are conjunctive users of ground and surface water, the availability of inexpensive surface water enables them to reduce groundwater pumping. Thus, the average cost of DWR water may be considerably below the $28.62 level, and perhaps as low as $15.50 per acre-foot.

The Utah rate represents a composite of costs faced by several irrigation companies. Shareholders in a typical company pay $2.51 to $4.18 for each acre receiving water to cover operation and maintenance costs. For companies carrying on system improvements, additional costs of $6.68 to $10.02 per acre raise the average charge to $11.69 per acre. Assuming an application rate of 3.5 feet per acre, which is typical for the state, these irrigators are paying about $3.34 per acre-foot.

Conclusions on Conveyance Costs

Although surface and groundwater costs vary among farmers using different sources for their irrigation water, some useful generalizations can be made in comparing the cost of irrigation water from different sources.

Generally groundwater is much more expensive (at least to the farmer) than surface water. For example, just the energy costs of pumping an acre-foot of water from 165 feet (the average pumping depth) with electricity (the most common fuel) were about $14.65 in 1980 (in 1977 dollars). The total costs were about $20.80 per acre-foot, well above the costs to most· surface water users. Furthermore, the gap between groundwater costs and the costs charged users of existing surface water projects is likely to increase sharply as energy prices rise and groundwater tables decline. However, water supplied by new surface water projects will generally be very expensive and subsidies are apt to be less generous.

Farmers in Kern County, California, receiving DWR water also are in a relatively disadvantageous position regarding water costs. Currently, they pay much more for water than do their neighbors, especially those receiving federally subsidized water, and the differences in water rates undoubtedly will grow. Delivering state water to Kern County is energy-intensive, and one estimate suggests that DWR entitlement water may cost farmers $70 per acre-foot by the mid-1980s in current prices.[10]

The lowest water costs are enjoyed by those with onfarm surface water supplies, especially if gravity can be used to deliver it to the field, and farmers receiving federally subsidized water. Although the Bureau of Reclamation intends to adjust its rates for inflation when the forty-year contracts expire, the real costs of their water to farmers will decline for the next fifteen years.

Alternative Irrigation Systems

Once the water arrives at the farm, it then must be distributed to the fields. Sloggett's 1977 survey distinguished among four principal methods of distributing water for irrigation—surface distribution and three categories of sprinklers; center pivot, big gun, and "others."[11] About three-fourths of the West's irrigated lands use a surface irrigation system, and most of the rest use some form of sprinkler system. Virtually all the farmers receiving gravity-fed surface water supplies employ a surface irrigation system. Surface distribution also is used for 20.5 million of the 32.9 million acres irrigated with onfarm-pumped water. Center pivots and siderolls are the primary sprinkler systems used on the remaining 12.4 million acres (table 5-7). The following discussion of surface distribution methods is applicable to either onfarm-pumped water or gravity-carried surface water. The discussion of sprinkler systems, however, relates primarily to onfarm-pumped water.

---

10. Based on a statement by Gerald Meral, deputy director, California Department of Water Resources, at a workshop on western water issues in New York City, June 16, 1980.

11. Sloggett, Gordon. Irrigation Pumping, 1974-77, 1979.

Table 5-7. Acreage Irrigated with Onfarm-Pumped Water by Type of Distribution System and Farm Production Region in 1977

(1,000 acres)

Region	Surface	Center pivot	Big gun	Other sprinkler[a]	Total
Northern Plains	5,823	3,178	115	721	9,837
Southern Plains	7,426	775	108	1,837	10,146
Mountain	3,412	1,027	5	1,722	6,166
Pacific	3,821	316	39	2,581	6,757
17 Western states	20,482	5,296	267	6,861	32,906

Source: Gordon Sloggett. Energy and U.S. Agriculture: Irrigation Pumping, 1974-77, Agricultural Economic Report No. 436 (Washington, D.C., U.S. Department of Agriculture, September 1979) app. table 3.

[a]Primary component of the "other sprinkler" is the sideroll sprinkler (personal communication with G. Sloggett, April 10, 1980).

Surface Distribution

For most surface distribution systems, a farmer digs head ditches, which may or may not be lined, or lays or buries pipe along the higher edge of his farm from which water is conveyed to the field to be irrigated. The wide variations in the efficiency with which these systems deliver water to the field are examined later as part of a discussion of ways to reduce water costs. If the farmer is irrigating row crops, siphons or gated pipes, which have openings at regular intervals to match the furrows, are used to transfer water from the ditch to the furrows. For close-grown crops, such as alfalfa and small grains, the land is generally flooded and the field is bounded by levees or borders.

Low cost is a major attraction of surface distribution. If the topography of the land and soils is suitable, the initial costs to prepare the land and install the required ditches or pipe are low compared to those associated with alternative irrigation systems.

Furthermore, very little energy is required to operate a surface system once the water is delivered to the farmgate or pumped from an aquifer. Usually water is pumped only a small distance from the well or farmgate to the top of the field where gravity is used to distribute the water to the crops.

The primary factors limiting the use of surface distribution are the soil type, topography of the land, the availability of labor, and the cost of water. Since the water must flow across the field, surface distribution is inefficient on sandy soil where the water percolates too quickly. Also, to achieve uniform distribution, the field must be relatively flat. A single person is able to irrigate a maximum of 320 to 640 acres with surface distribution which is only about one-fourth of the acreage that a person could handle with center-pivot systems. Nevertheless, the costs of labor in irrigation, which tend to be a small fraction of total variable costs for all systems, are not likely to be the decisive factor in selecting among alternative irrigation systems. However, if a farmer is uncertain that labor will be available when needed, a center pivot may be favored over surface distribution.

It is commonly believed that surface systems are less efficient than sprinklers in getting water to the crops. While this view is almost certainly valid for sandy soils, on heavier soils good water management practices can increase the efficiencies of surface systems to the levels generally attained with sprinklers. The investments required to achieve major improvements in water distribution efficiency are considered below. Of course, the application efficiency--defined as the ratio of the amount of water that is retained in the root zone divided by the amount of water delivered to the soil surface--assumes greater importance as water becomes scarce or expensive. There likely will be an important difference between the efficiency of water use from the perspective of the individual farmer and the system as a whole. For example, while the application efficiency of flood irrigation may be low, the basinwide efficiency will be much higher if most of the runoff reappears and can be used downstream.

Sprinkler Irrigation

Center-Pivot Sprinklers. Center-pivot sprinklers, first patented in 1952, were irrigating 5.3 million acres in the West by 1977 (see table 5-7). With a center-pivot system, a single sprinkler-lateral powers itself in a circle around a fixed pivot. Water is supplied through the fixed pivot. The length of the lateral ranges from 200 to 2,600 feet. Most systems are designed for a quarter section of land (160 acres), but irrigate only 130 acres of that section because of the circular pattern. The system can be modified with end guns or extensions to reach the unwatered areas.

Center-pivot systems have several principal advantages over the conventional surface systems. First, center pivots can be used on hillier land (9 to 10 percent slope) and sandier soil. Second, it allows considerable savings in labor. Once a center pivot is properly adapted to its site and the automatic controls are set, one person can irrigate 10 to 15 quarter sections of land (1,300 to 2,000 acres). Finally, as noted above, center-pivot sprinklers may improve the efficiency with which water reaches the root zone. With proper calibration an application efficiency of 80 percent is possible with a center-pivot system.

The principal disadvantages of center-pivot systems involve their capital costs. A center-pivot system capable of irrigating 130 acres cost in excess of $37,000 in 1979, excluding the well and pumps. And, as is examined in some detail below, operating a center-pivot sprinkler requires considerable amounts of energy.

Big-Gun Sprinklers. Big-gun sprinklers, which are synonymous with tow and traveler systems, are used on only 267,000 acres (table 5-7). A big-gun system typically consists of one sprinkler with a large output capcity mounted on wheels. The big gun may be towed across the field with a power winch and cable or have its own motor. Although a big-gun system is by far the most energy-intensive of the various sprinkler systems, it is an attractive alternative in some situations. The big gun is readily adaptable to smaller, irregular shaped fields, its initial costs are less than those of a center pivot, and it does not have a clearance problem that makes the side-roll system unsuitable for tall crops like corn.

Other Sprinklers. The "other sprinkler" category is primarily side-roll sprinklers, consisting of a long lateral on wheels. The axle is the sprinkler line itself. These systems do not move while irrigating and must be moved from place to place between irrigations. Consequently, they are more labor-intensive but less capital-intensive than center-pivot systems.

Another system which comprises a small part of the miscellaneous sprinkler acreage is drip or trickle irrigation. In 1979, trickle systems irrigated 220,000 acres.[12] These systems use plastic tubes and drip emitters to apply small quantities of water frequently in the immediate vicinity of the plant roots. Because so much of the soil is left dry, water use is greatly reduced and application efficiency rates approach 100 percent. However, installation costs exceed $1,000 per acre, about two to three times the cost of a center-pivot system. Drip irrigation systems also are subject to rodent damage and prone to clogging.[13] Moreover, installation costs would be higher with the narrow spacing required for field crops and the pipes, which are fairly permanent, are difficult to farm around. Consequently, with present water costs, use of trickle systems is limited to high-value crops; they are particularly attractive for orchards because less tubing and fewer emitters are required (reducing investment costs).[14]

Mobile trickle systems are recent additions to the range of irrigation systems available to farmers. These involve attaching trail lines with emitters to a mobile system such as a center-pivot or side-roll sprinkler. The water is then dripped rather than sprayed onto the field. Such a system reduces evaporation losses, which average in

12. "Irrigation Survey, 1979," Irrigation Journal, vol. 29, no. 6 (December 1979).

13. High Plains Conservation District No. 1 and Texas Department of Water Resources, A Summary of Techniques and Management Practices, p. II-9.

14. Ibid.

excess of 15 percent with center pivots in the High Plains,[15] and requires less pressure and, therefore, less energy to operate than the traditional sprinkler systems. On the negative side, a mobile drip system is prone to clogging and when attached to a center-pivot system poses some threat to the plants and the soil as the trail lines move across the field. Since the system is still very much in the experimental stages, it is too early to accurately assess its potential for use in irrigating the principal row crops such as corn and cotton.

Alternative Responses to Higher Water Costs

The availability of cheap water was an important determinant not only of the rapid expansion of irrigation but of the technologies adopted on irrigated farms as well. The sharp rise in energy costs in the early 1970s increased farmer concern about the efficiency with which water is used. Even among the irrigators fortunate enough to be insulated from energy cost increases, the general scarcity of western water is increasing the opportunity cost of inefficient irrigation when the farmer has the right and means of transferring water to other uses and users.

As water costs rise, technologies and management practices that conserve both energy and water become more cost effective and often essential to the continued profitability of irrigated farming. Farmers have a wide range of opportunities for responding to high energy and water costs short of abandoning irrigation; opportunities include improving pump efficiency, installing tailwater re-use systems, reducing a sprinkler's operating pressure, irrigation scheduling, improving conveyance efficiency, alternate furrow irrigation, growing crops with lower water requirements or higher returns to water, and reducing the quantity of water delivered to a given crop.

Selection of an irrigation system is often predicated by the particular set of circumstances facing a farmer. As noted above, availability and cost of farm labor, water supply, soil type, topography,

---

15. Ibid., p. II-8.

field size, and the crops grown are important to the selection of an
irrigation system, and indeed, may limit a farmer's feasible choices.
The costs of installing and operating the system are also important
factors both for selecting the most appropriate irrigation system as
well as for determining the overall profitability of irrigation. Rapid
increases in energy prices, both past and prospective, alter the relative costs of alternative systems and increase the importance of irrigation in overall production costs. The impacts of alternative energy
prices on the costs of distributing water with different irrigation
systems are examined below.

Energy and the Costs of Alternative Irrigation Systems

Energy costs range from negligible levels for surface irrigation
to sizable sums for the more energy-intensive sprinkler systems, as
shown in table 5-8. Both the type of fuel and the costs of the fuel
have major impacts on the costs of operating center-pivot and big-gun
systems. For example, the difference between the electricity costs for
distributing 1 acre-foot with a center-pivot and a surface system increases from $11.28 at 1970 prices, to $13.33 at 1980 prices, and to
$26.67 for prices projected for the year 2000; the costs to distribute
an acre-foot with a center-pivot system at 1980 fuel costs rise from
$7.46 with natural gas, to $14.36 with electricity, to $20.38 with LPG,
and to $24.25 with diesel.

Because of differences in distribution efficiencies, comparisons
among irrigation systems should be based on the costs of delivering a
given amount of water to the root zone of the plants. For example, to
deliver 14 acre-inches of water to the root zone, a system with a 50
percent application efficiency requires an application of 28 acre-
inches while a system with an 80 percent efficiency requires only 17.5
acre-inches. For groundwater, total energy costs of pumping and distributing water through alternative systems depend on pumping depth and
relative irrigation efficiencies. The total energy requirements of a
gravity flow system may be as high as or higher than those of an
energy-intensive distribution system if water must be pumped from considerable depths and the energy-intensive distribution system has a
much higher application efficiency.

Table 5-8. Energy Costs to Distribute 1 Acre-Foot of Water with Different Distribution Systems and Alternative Fuels and Fuel
Prices, 1970-2000

(1977 current dollars per acre-foot)

Distribution system	Energy costs under alternative fuel prices		
	1970	1980	2000
Natural gas			
Big gun	4.36	17.60	35.20
Center pivot	1.85	7.46	14.92
Side roll	1.06	4.26	8.52
Trickle	.39	1.60	3.20
Surface	.13	.54	1.08
Electricity			
Big gun	28.64	33.84	67.69
Center pivot	12.15	14.36	28.72
Side roll	6.94	8.20	16.41
Trickle	2.61	3.08	6.15
Surface	.87	1.03	2.05
LPG			
Big gun	27.93	48.04	96.08
Center pivot	11.85	20.38	40.76
Side roll	6.77	11.65	23.29
Trickle	2.54	4.37	8.73
Surface	.84	1.46	2.91
Diesel			
Big gun	20.01	57.16	114.31
Center pivot	8.48	24.25	48.50
Side roll	4.85	13.86	27.71
Trickle	1.82	5.20	10.39
Surface	.61	1.73	3.46

Assumptions and Sources: Distribution PSI Assumptions: big gun
(165), center pivot (70), side roll (45), trickle (15), and surface (5).
The trickle PSI estimate is taken from Kuei-lin Chen, Robert Wensink, and
John Wolfe, "A Model to Predict Total Energy Requirements and Economic
Costs of Irrigation Systems." Paper presented to the American Society of
Agricultural Engineers, December 1976, Chicago, Illinois, mimeograph,
p. 6. The center-pivot PSI estimate is taken from Gordon Sloggett, personal communication, February 1980; and all other estimates are taken
from Sloggett, Energy and U.S. Agriculture: Irrigation Pumping, 1974-77,
Agricultural Economic Report No. 436 (Washington, D.C., U.S. Department
of Agriculture, September 1979). Other assumptions are listed in the
footnote to table 5-2.

Under the assumptions in table 5-9, total energy costs of a gravity distribution system with a 50 percent application efficiency exceed those of a center-pivot system with an 80 percent application efficiency for pumping depths of 250 feet or more. These are somewhat extreme assumptions as to comparative efficiencies of the two systems, however. Careful water management, leveling, and lining of canals can improve the application efficiencies of surface systems to 60 or perhaps 70 percent on all but sandy soils. Furthermore, as is discussed below, a tailwater recycling pit can improve the application efficiency of surface distribution to levels achieved with the best managed sprinklers. Of course, additional energy is required to pump water from the foot to the top of the field with a tailwater recycling system. On the other side, 80 percent is close to the maximum application efficiency attainable with a center pivot. In windy locations such as the High Plains, wind evaporation losses alone average more than 15 percent.[16] If the application efficiencies are 70 percent for a center-pivot and 60 percent for a gravity flow system, the pumping depths must exceed 850 feet for the energy requirements of the surface system to exceed those of the center pivot.

Improving Pumping System Efficiency

Inefficient pumping systems result in unnecessarily high pumping costs. Recent tests by the High Plains Underground Water Conservation District No. 1 in Texas showed some farmers paying twice or even three times as much for irrigation fuel as necessary. The main areas for improving pumping system efficiency involved the sizing, staging, and condition of the pump. Specifically, over-sized pumps were a major source of inefficiency. Commonly, the pumps had been designed years earlier to handle larger quantities of water than the well was now capable of yielding. Other sources of energy loss included improper staging to accommodate changes in water levels or additional lift requirements of newly installed sprinkler systems and reliance on worn-

---

16. Ibid.

Table 5-9. Total Energy Costs to Deliver 14 Acre—Inches of Groundwater to the Root Zone with Alternative Distribution Systems, Application Efficiencies, Pumping Depths, and Fuels, at 1980 Fuel Prices

Energy source	Application efficiency (percent)	Water applied (acre-inches)	Total energy costs at various pumping depths (1977 current dollars)		
			200 ft	250 ft	300 ft
Natural gas					
Center pivot	70	20.0	27.92	31.78	35.64
	80	17.5	24.43	27.81	31.18
Surface[a]	50	28.0	22.86	28.26	33.67
	60	23.3	19.04	23.54	28.05
Electricity					
Center pivot	70	20.0	53.53	60.93	68.33
	80	17.5	46.84	53.31	59.79
Surface[a]	50	28.0	43.83	54.19	64.55
	60	23.3	36.52	45.15	53.78
Diesel					
Center pivot	70	20.0	90.40	102.89	115.39
	80	17.5	79.10	90.03	100.97
Surface[a]	50	28.0	74.02	91.52	109.01
	60	23.3	61.67	76.26	90.83

Note: Total energy costs include the energy of pumping the water to the surface based on assumptions of table 5-2 and the energy of distributing the water to the root zone based on assumptions of table 5-8.

[a]Surface irrigation assumes no tailwater-recovery system. If a tailwater-recovery system is installed and the application efficiency of the surface system rises to 75 percent, then it would take a pumping depth of over 2,000 feet for the energy costs of the surface system to exceed those of the center-pivot system.

out pumps. The condition of the power unit, especially with natural gas internal combustion engines, was occasionally the source of some inefficiency, but these problems were not as severe as those involving the pumps.[17]

Table 5-10 illustrates the importance of pump efficiency on the cost of pumping 1 acre-foot of water a height of 200 feet. Energy costs rise 40 percent as the pump efficiency declines from 70 to 50 percent and costs rise another 67 percent if pump efficiency falls to 30 percent. At 1980 energy costs (deflated to 1977 constant dollars), a decline in pump efficiency to 50 percent costs a farmer an additional $3.19 per acre-foot with electricity compared to the costs with a 70 percent efficient well.

An inefficient pump commonly can be upgraded to a 70 percent efficiency level by selecting the correct number and size of bowls to fit the aquifers conductivity. In early 1980, purchasing and installing new bowls cost from $1,800 to $2,500 per well.[18] If such an investment improved pump efficiency from 50 to 70 percent, the energy savings would repay the cost in 1.9 to 2.6 years if natural gas at 1980 prices is used to pump 300 acre-feet per year. The payback period would have been shorter with any of the other fuels at 1980 price levels.

Improving Well Efficiency

The efficiency of the overall system for getting water from the ground to the surface also depends on the efficiency of the well. A properly designed well allows maximum withdrawal of water with a minimum of drawdown in the immediate well vicinity. Well efficiency is measured as a ratio of the theoretical drawdown for a given output of water (computed from the aquifer's hydraulic characteristics) and the actual drawdown. Although well efficiencies should not drop below 80

---

17. High Plains Underground Water Conservation District No. 1, Lubbock, Texas, The Cross Section, vol. 26, no. 12 (December 1980).

18. Personal communication of James Hanson with W. B. Lyle, agricultural engineer, Texas Tech University, February 15, 1980.

Table 5-10. Energy Costs to Pump 1 Acre-Foot of Groundwater 200 Feet
            with Alternative Fuels, Fuel Prices, and Pump Efficiencies

(1977 constant dollars)

Fuel	Pump efficiency	Fuel price		
		1970	1980	2000
Natural gas	70	1.97	7.96	15.93
	50	2.76	11.15	22.30
	30	4.60	18.58	37.16
Electricity	70	12.88	15.22	30.45
	50	18.04	21.31	42.62
	30	30.06	35.52	71.04
LPG	70	12.56	21.60	43.20
	50	17.58	30.24	60.48
	30	29.30	50.40	100.80
Diesel	70	9.08	25.71	51.43
	50	12.71	36.00	72.00
	30	21.18	60.00	120.00

Note: All technical and cost assumptions except for the pump
efficiences are based on the assumptions of table 5-2.

percent, apparently the majority of wells in Texas High Plains are considerably below this level.[19]   Poor well design increases the pumping
lift and may result in pumping entrained air and sand. These problems
in turn may cause rapid plugging and premature wear of the pump bowls
and the pump. Thus, over time an inefficient well hastens the decline

19. High Plains Underground Water Conservation District No. 1 and Texas
Department of Water Resources, Summary of Techniques and Management
Practices, p. II-14.

in the efficiency of the pumping system which, as noted above, leads to sizable increases in pumping costs. Lyle indicates that a well can be overhauled at approximately one-fourth to one-third the cost of a new well, or at a cost of $8-$12 per foot.[20]

The increase in energy prices over the past decade has provided a great incentive to overhaul inefficient wells and pumping plants. In many cases the savings in energy costs are sufficient to recover the investment within a year or two. And the potential savings will grow as energy costs increase, pumping depths rise, and the quantity of water pumped from the well expands. In addition to these cost savings, higher crop yields may be possible because farmers are able to apply more water in a timely fashion to their fields when pump yields are higher.

Tailwater Recovery Systems

The loss of water from runoff can be greatly reduced with a tail-water recovery system. The water is captured and stored in a pit at the end of a field from where smaller pumps can be used to pump the water back to the fields. The energy savings to the farmer can be substantial since tailwater recovery requires only about one-seventh the energy required to pump the same amount of water from a depth of 200 feet. Recovery pits are generally only practical with surface systems. Sprinklers can be adjusted so that their water output better matches the soil infiltration rate, so runoff is reduced.

Table 5-11 indicates the savings in energy costs resulting from installation of a tailwater recovery system that improves application efficiency from 50 percent to 75 percent when the alternative is pumping additional groundwater from 200 feet. Such improvements in efficiency are attainable where runoff has been a major problem. For all four fuels, energy costs are reduced by about 27 percent. The $5,000 cost of installing a tailwater recovery pit for a 160-acre field would be recovered with the energy savings in only 1.6 to 2.6 years for die-

---

20. Personal communication with W. B. Lyle, agricultural engineer, Texas Tech University, February 15, 1980.

Table 5-11. Total Energy Costs to Pump and Distribute 14 Acre-Inches of Groundwater to the Root Zone Using Surface Distribution With and Without a Tailwater Recovery System, for Alternative Fuels at 1980 Costs

Fuel and type of system	Application efficiency (percent)	Energy cost (1977 constant dollars)	Years to recover $5,000 investment costs using energy savings
Natural Gas			
Gated pipe without tailwater recovery	50	$ 22.86	--
Gated pipe with tailwater recovery	75	16.72	5.0
Electricity			
Gated pipe without tailwater recovery	50	43.83	--
Gated pipe with tailwater recovery	75	32.00	2.6
Diesel			
Gated pipe without tailwater recovery	50	74.02	--
Gated pipe with tailwater recovery	75	54.04	1.6
LPG			
Gated pipe without tailwater recovery	50	62.22	--
Gated pipe with tailwater recovery	75	44.79	1.8

Note: Gated pipe with tailwater recovery system has the following energy costs: 1) the cost of pumping 18.67 acre-inches from 200 feet at 60 percent efficiency, 2) pumping 9.33 acre-inches from a reuse pit (one-seventh cost of pumping from 200 feet), and 3) the cost of distributing 28 acre-inches through a surface system at 5 PSI. Installation cost of $5,000 to build a tailwater reuse pit. Gated pipe without tailwater recovery system has following energy costs: 1) the cost of pumping 28 acre-inches from 200 feet at 60 percent efficiency, and distributing 28 acre-inches through a surface system at 5 PSI. Other assumptions are listed in the footnote to table 5-2.

Source: Installation costs for the tailwater recovery system are from Rodney Sharp, "Economic Adjustment to Increasing Energy Costs for Pump Irrigation in Northeast Colorado," Master's thesis submitted to the Department of Economics, Colorado State University, Fort Collins, 1979.

sel, LPG, and electricity at 1980 energy prices. The cost-recovery period is five years with natural gas.

Reducing Pressure Requirements for Center Pivots

One of the disadvantages of the center-pivot system as illustrated in table 5-8 is its energy intensity. The initial systems, which required pressures of approximately 70 pounds per square inch (PSI) to operate, are particularly energy intensive. The rise in energy prices has prompted the development of systems that operated at 20 to 30 PSI. As noted in table 5-12, the energy savings per acre range from about $7 with natural gas to over $22 with diesel. Thus, the savings range from $910 to $2,860 per season for each 130 acres irrigated.

The low-pressure systems are not without problems, however. Under the lower pressure, the water comes out in larger droplets instead of the fine mist produced by the high-pressure systems. These droplets can cause difficulties under some circumstances. For instance, on soils that have slopes greater than 2 percent (and are not sandy), it is difficult to use center pivots with a PSI requirement much less than 50 to 55 because of increased runoff from the big droplets. The larger droplets increase both erosion and the variability of water application, thereby reducing yields. Systems which require 50 to 55 PSI provide much lower energy savings, and may not justify the high cost of conversion. The costs of converting engines, pumps, and a center pivot can range between $4,000 to $5,000.[21] Also, if the center-pivot system is water driven, then high pressure (65 to 75 PSI) is required to move the system and conversion is not even possible.

Irrigation Scheduling

Formerly it was fairly common for farmers to apply more water than could be effectively used. The costs of such profligacy are not limited to the irrigation costs. Excessive irrigation increases ero-

---

21. Personal communication with Paul E. Fischbach, University of Nebraska, Lincoln, August 21, 1980.

Table 5-12. Energy Costs for Pumping and Distributing 14 Acre-Inches of
Groundwater to the Root Zone Using Center-Pivot Systems with
Different PSI and Alternative Fuels in 1980

(1977 dollars)

System	Natural gas	Electricity	Diesel	LPG
Center pivot (70 PSI)	24.43	46.84	79.10	66.47
Center pivot (25 PSI)	17.45	33.38	56.38	47.36
Savings in energy costs	6.98	13.46	22.72	19.11

Note: Technical relationships and price assumptions are listed in
the footnotes for tables 5-2 and 5-8. The pumping lift is 200 feet.

sion and the loss of nutrients in the root zone and, in some instances,
may have reduced crop yields. These costs were either unknown or ignored by farmers as long as water was inexpensive.

High energy and water costs have led to more careful scheduling of
water applications. Some improvements were readily attained as cost
considerations led farmers to eliminate obvious waste such as shutting
off their pumps before the roads surrounding their fields were flooded.
But the potential for improved scheduling extends well beyond what is
likely to be gained through reliance solely on common sense and intu-
ition. By limiting water applications to the times and quantities that
can be used most effectively by the plants, often water use can be reduced while yields are increased.

Irrigation scheduling services have emerged in many areas of the West to assist farmers with irrigation decisions. Typically, these services utilize computers to analyze data affecting water needs. A farmer provides the service with information on the crop grown and the soil type. With daily weather records and technical information on soil moisture capacity and levels, infiltration and evaporation rates, and the water needs and responsiveness of particular crops, a computer calculates evapotranspiration and crop water requirements and recommends the timing and rate of water applications. Currently, most scheduling services charge $4 to $5 an acre which includes a field inspection by trained personnel. If the service results in reduced pumping, much of this charge could be recovered by savings in fuel costs. For example, under the assumptions of table 5-11, a 25 percent reduction in fuel use for a system combining gated-pipe distribution with tailwater recovery would justify a $4 an acre cost regardless of the fuel used. In most instances, irrigation scheduling offers greater cost savings where sprinklers are used. And if improved timing of the water applications also increases yields, scheduling becomes even more attractive to farmers. Unfortunately, scheduling services are not available to many farmers, and they only help when a farmer can control the timing and quantity of water use.

Onfarm Conveyance Systems

Surface irrigation commonly involves delivering water from the well or farmgate to the fields through unlined ditches and siphon tubes. This method results in very low application efficiencies which can be improved by about 16 percent by installing underground pipe to convey water to the field's edge and using gated pipes to deliver it to the furrows. The cost of such an arrangement depends largely on the distance which the water must be conveyed and the configuration and number of lateral pipes. A configuration designed to irrigate field crops in the Texas High Plains uses 20 feet of pipe per acre at a cost of $62.74 per acre.[22] A gated pipe system proposed for field crops in northeast Colorado uses over 48 feet of pipe per acre and costs $120 per acre.[23] Assuming the irrigator is pumping groundwater from 200 feet and applying 28 inches per acre, a 16 percent increase in efficiency from adopting an underground and gated pipe system would save annually $3.67 per acre with natural gas, $7.01 with electricity, $9.95 with LPG, and $11.85 with diesel. The cost (excluding interest) of the less expensive system would be recovered in 5.3 years by the irrigator using diesel fuel; 6.3 years with LPG; 9.0 years with electricity, and 17.2 years with natural gas. Recovering the cost of the more expensive system would take nearly twice as long. At times the federal government has provided cost-sharing funds for onfarm water conservation constuction. The availability of such funding, of course, would make investments in improved conveyance systems more attractive to farmers.

Alternate Furrow Irrigation

Experiments suggest water use can be decreased by almost 33 percent by irrigating alternate furrows instead of every furrow. Most of the water savings, however, occur on the lower part of the field. The resulting unequal water distribution can adversely affect yields, perhaps outweighing the savings in water costs. As energy prices increase and research improves the technology, alternate furrow irrigation may become increasingly widespread.

---

22. This system is described in James E. Osborne, Alan M. Young, Otto C. Wilke, and Charles Wendt, Economic Analysis of Trickle Distribution Systems-Texas High Plains (Lubbock, Texas Agricultural Experiment Station, Texas A&M University, October 1977). The system covers 96 acres, using 1,637 feet of underground pipe and 12 twenty-foot spans of gated aluminum pipe. Total cost is $6,023.

23. This system is described in Rodney Sharp, "Economic Adjustment to Increasing Energy Costs for Pump Irrigation in Northeast Colorado." Master's thesis submitted to the Department of Economics, Colorado State University, Fort Collins, 1979. This system covers 300 acres using 3,960 feet of connecting pipe and 10,560 feet of gated pipe. The total cost is $36,000.

Switching Crops

Crops vary in their requirements for and sensitivity to water. Thus, as water becomes more expensive, farmers can be expected to switch to crops requiring less water or providing higher returns per unit of irrigation water.

Corn requires a "full" irrigation to obtain high yields and does not yield well under reduced levels of irrigation. In the High Plains region 20 to 28 acre-inches are typically applied. Sorghum, wheat, and soybeans, on the other hand, do not require as much water as corn and retain most of their yielding ability when irrigation is reduced. Farmers typically apply 12 to 16 acre-inches of water to sorghum. While relative prices and yields continue to make corn the predominant irrigated grain crop, high water costs in the southern High Plains have prompted some switching out of corn in recent years and these substitutions could become much more common.[24]

Irrigated soybeans are still relatively insignificant in the West. However, soybeans use 2 to 4 acre-inches less water than corn and, in recent years, prices for soybeans have averaged three times the levels of corn prices. Until now, soybean yields have not been very responsive to irrigation; however, experiments with a dwarf variety in Nebraska show irrigated yields in the range of 65 bushels per acre compared to dryland yields of about 30 bushels per acre.[25] These yield increases together with high energy prices could make soybeans an attractive alternative to corn on irrigated lands in eastern Nebraska.

In the High Plains irrigation increases wheat yields by about 50 percent compared to the 300 and 150 percent increases common with irrigated corn and sorghum respectively. Irrigated wheat, however, does

24. Ronald G. Cummings, "Scenarios for 1985 Grains/Soybeans Production in the High Plains Area." Report prepared for Resources for the Future, 1978, p. 43.

25. Personal communication with Ray Supalla, Bruce Johnson, and others, University of Nebraska, Agricultural Economics Department, February 25, 1980.

have some advantages which could lead to its future expansion. As noted, wheat does not require as much water as corn. Since winter wheat is grown largely in the off-season, in locations where the growing season is long enough, irrigated wheat may be expanded without installing a new pump or abandoning another crop. Furthermore, irrigated wheat can be grazed by livestock and still grown out for its grain without much loss of yield.[26]

Local researchers suggest the following trends in cropping patterns are likely. In the north Texas High Plains, where irrigated corn is now grown, irrigated sorghum and wheat will displace corn as energy prices and pumping lifts continue to increase.[27] In Nebraska, high water costs or limits on water withdrawals would prompt a substitution of irrigated sorghum for irrigated corn in the western part of the state and irrigated soybeans for corn in the east. Currently, about 92 percent of Nebraska's irrigated acreage is in corn. While changes in crop mix may reduce water withdrawal and pumping costs, crop prices are a key variable for any permanent change in cropping patterns.

Reducing Water Applications Below Yield-Maximizing Levels

In addition to the opportunities discussed above for improving irrigation efficiency or switching to less water-intensive crops, a farmer may reduce water costs simply by applying less water. Indeed, for any given crop and irrigation system, the quantity of water that maximizes farm profits declines as the cost of the water rises.

Agricultural scientists have tended to focus their efforts on obtaining maximum yields. A principal concern of irrigation research has been to determine the quantity and timing of water flows that maximize the yield of a given crop. The emphasis on physical yield has been reinforced by irrigation management services, both public and

---

26. Personal communication with Herbert Grubb, Texas Water Development Board, February 28, 1980.

27. Ibid.

private, which almost invariably base their water use recommendations on yield-maximizing criteria. Yet the quantity of water that maximizes physical yields is the same as the quantity that maximizes farm profits only if the cost of water is zero. Where water is inexpensive, the differences between these two water quantities are slight. For example, one study suggests that the difference between the profit- and yield-maximizing water applications is two acre-inches or less for cotton and wheat with water costing $6 per acre-foot. But when water costs increase 5 to 10 fold, profit maximization calls for applying 4 to 14 acre-inches less water per acre than the yield-maximizing levels.[28]

Of course, neither the farmer nor the researcher knows with precision how crop yields in a given year will respond to varying water levels. The response undoubtedly varies among farms. Nevertheless, higher water prices are likely to prompt lower water applications which, other things being equal, generally reduce yields and thus irrigated production.

Future Technological Change

The above discussion focused on adjustments with existing management skills and technology. Future technological innovation also will help farmers offset the impacts of higher water and energy prices. One area with great potential involves developing crop varieties requiring less water. When water was inexpensive, research emphasized increasing yields regardless of the water applied. Only within the last decade or so have researchers paid much attention to developing varieties for irrigation that can use less water without reducing yields. The change in research emphasis that has come with rising water costs undoubtedly

---

28. The study cited is reported in Harry W. Ayer, Paul G. Hoyt, and Melvin Cotner, "Crop-Water Production Functions in Economic Analysis," in American Society of Civil Engineers, Irrigation and Drainage: Today's Challenges, Proceedings of Specialty Conference (Boise, Idaho, 1980) pp. 336-345.

will bring at least marginal improvements in the ability of plants to produce with less irrigation water. However, scientists still have only a very incomplete knowledge of the factors affecting the efficiency of plant transpiration and resistence to drought. Sizable gains in yields to water may have to await further development of this basic knowledge which may require several decades. While some knowledge will provide farmers the means of increasing the returns to irrigated water, it also should improve the productivity of dryland farming in the semi-arid West. The net result might well be an increase in the relative productivity of dryland compared to irrigated agriculture in this area.

Technological advances likely will improve the effectiveness and profitability of many of the cost-sharing and yield-increasing techniques discussed above. Further advances in computerized irrigation scheduling, new or better designed irrigation methods (such as perfecting a mobile trickle system for use on the principal irrigated crops or improving water flow through row damming), and development of evaporation suppression methods and chemicals will enable farmers to make more effective use of scarce and expensive water supplies. A water-efficient irrigation system of the not too distant future may automatically schedule the quantity and timing of irrigations based on a computerized system which assimilates detailed information on soil moisture derived from a neutron probe and the crop's responsiveness to water at each point in its productive cycle. A neutron probe measures the hydrogen ions in the soil which are directly related to the quantity of water in the soil.[29]

Research to develop salt-tolerant varieties and farm management techniques appropriate for irrigating with low quality water supplies will limit yield losses in areas where salinity levels are rising and may expand the water supplies suitable for irrigation to include brackish and highly saline waters (see chapter 6). Hail suppression

---

29. David Sheridan, Desertification of the United States (Washington, D.C., GPO, 1981) p. 113.

techniques and improved windbreaks may reduce crop losses and, thereby, increase returns to water. And advances in weather modification may increase the useful water supplies for both irrigated and dryland farming in the West. This listing is not intended to be exhaustive but merely suggestive of the range of relevant research that undoubtedly will expand the capability of western farmers to respond effectively to rising water and energy costs.

Profitability of Irrigated Agriculture

While the focus of this analysis is on water costs, these costs are just one element of farm profitability. Factors such as farm management, weather, soil, crop prices, and the prices of other inputs are all important determinants of the return to irrigated agriculture. Nevertheless, it is the control over water that distinguishes irrigated from dryland farming and the cost of the water is a crucial determinant of the relative profitability of irrigated and dryland agriculture.

The impact of higher water and energy costs on the profitability of growing alternative crops in various regions of the West are illustrated with the aid of the 1977 crop budgets developed as part of the U.S. Department of Agriculture's Enterprise Data System (FEDS). These budgets, which are developed from surveys, represent averages for the farms surveyed in each region. Thus, the data reflect local production costs, crop prices, yields, and water sources and costs. There are, of course, other factors affecting farmers' cropping plans that are not reflected in these budgets. Crops may be grown as part of a rotation designed to preserve productivity, reduce erosion or control pests, or they may be complementary to other aspects of the overall farm enterprise. For our purposes, however, the profitability measures in the FEDS do illustrate important factors influencing the impact of water and energy prices on the course of irrigated agriculture in the coming decades.

Table 5-13 shows net returns and irrigation costs for several crops in several western regions. With a single exception, the illus-

Table 5-13. Water Costs, Yields, Crop Prices and Returns for Several Crops and Locations, 1977

Crop	Location [a]	Source	Water [b] Cost ($/ac. ft.)	Water [b] Ac.-Ft. applied	Yield [c] (bu/acre)	Price [c] ($/bushel)	Net returns ($/acre) to Land, management, overhead, risk [d]	Risk [e]
Corn	Central California (400)	S	12.00	3.75	119.1	3.36	187.76	55.80
	Eastern Nebraska (500)	G	27.72	1.00	107.4	2.62	143.17	55.72
	South Western Nebraska (200)	G	26.40	1.67	108.3	2.62	125.66	32.17
	Texas Pan-handle (100 & 200)	G	45.60	2.17	109.8	3.04	115.14	73.58
	Eastern Kansas (200 & 300)	G	31.44	1.75	105.3	2.69	107.00	62.35
	Western Kansas (100)	G	36.12	2.00	106.8	2.69	91.75	44.40
Sorghum	Central California (400)	S	15.84	2.08	70.4	3.13	51.92	-40.39
	Texas Rio Grande (600)	S	12.84	1.50	59.3	2.67	42.33	- 3.72
	Eastern Nebraska (500)	G	26.04	1.00	75.5	2.38	82.30	18.45
	Eastern Kansas (200 & 300)	G	31.44	1.33	80.2	2.38	64.54	27.44
	Texas Panhandle (100)	G	43.20	1.83	84.3	2.67	63.38	23.01
	Western Kansas (100)	G	36.12	1.50	76.0	2.38	46.02	15.35
	Arizona (200)	G	26.52	3.17	66.1	3.07	14.56	-82.27
Winter wheat	Central California (400)	S	17.16	1.17	72.9	3.63	146.22	57.66
	Snake Basin (Id.) (400)	S	9.12	2.50	62.9	3.50	128.52	44.31
	Arizona (200)	S	20.88	3.33	70.2	3.39	53.31	- 3.56
	Columbia Basin (Wash.) (401)	G	47.76	1.50	77.0	3.83	132.82	23.92
	Eastern Oklahoma (300)	G	49.32	1.00	32.5	3.60	23.68	-20.18
	Western Kansas (100)	G	35.16	1.17	36.8	3.41	24.34	-13.86
	Texas Panhandle (100)	G	42.84	1.33	28.8	3.55	-16.91	-71.74
Cotton	S. Central California (500)	S	36.24	3.33	1014/lb lint 1635.5 lb seed	.621/lb lint .063/lb seed	294.56	154.28
	Texas Rio Grande (600)	S	12.84	1.50	472.3/lb lint 748.8/lb seed	.472/lb lint .052/lb seed	- 9.84	-94.53
	Arizona (200)	G	40.20	4.92	1127.8/lb lint 1887.2/lb seed	.597/lb lint .061/lb seed	268.55	149.61
	Central Texas (300)	G	34.92	2.00	416.0/lb lint 648.0/lb seed	.480/lb lint .052/lb seed	40.59	-30.94
	Texas Panhandle (200)	G	58.80	1.17	351.7/lb lint 568.7/lb seed	.472/lb lint .052/lb seed	26.71	-32.40
	Eastern Oklahoma (300)	G	48.36	2.00	509.0/lb lint 810.0/lb seed	.437/lb lint .056/lb seed	13.02	-66.16

Source: U.S. Department of Agriculture, Economic Research Service. "Farm Enterprise Data System (FEDS)," computer printouts prepared in cooperation with and available from the Department of Agricultural Economics, Oklahoma State University, Stillwater, Oklahoma.

[a] The numbers in parentheses are the FEDS area identification numbers for the respective states.

[b] Water costs include fixed and variable costs. The sources are S for surface water and G for groundwater.

[c] Crop yields and prices are region-specific averages for 1974-77 and are calculated from FEDS data. Crop prices are adjusted to 1977 dollars.

[d] Returns to land, management, overhead and risk are calculated as the difference between total receipts and the sum of total variable costs and the depreciation, taxes, interest, and insurance on machinery and equipment. Costs are based on 1977 FEDS budgets adjusted to the 1974-77 average yields.

[e] Returns to risk also deduct land charges, management, and overhead from total receipts. Land charges are calculated as either cash rents, share rents, or are based on land prices. Management charge is calculated as 10 percent of all costs except land. Overhead reflects costs for building and fence repairs, accounting, telephone, farm organization dues, and other such costs.

trated surface water costs are much less than the groundwater costs. The exception is cotton grown in south central California where the surface water costs include the cost of pumping a considerable height and distance from the Sacramento Delta. The average (with equal weights for each region) surface cost across crops and regions is $17.16 per acre-foot, less than half the average groundwater cost of $38.28 per acre-foot. Consequently, water costs tend to be a significantly higher percentage of total production costs for groundwater users. For the four crops and twelve locations, water costs as a proportion of total production costs averaged 22 percent for surface water and 38 percent for groundwater.

Under the assumptions of table 5-13, cotton and corn tended to be the most profitable crops. Profitability, however, varies widely depending on location, and relative profitability depends only in part on differences in water costs. The profitability rankings are consistent with a priori expectations based on the acreage planted to the various crops. Corn is both the dominant crop in terms of acreage and relative profitability in the Plains States; cotton, which is important in western Texas, Arizona, and California, is profitable in these areas; and irrigated wheat, which is the primary irrigated grain grown in the Northwest is profitable in that region. In contrast, irrigated wheat is generally unprofitable and not very important in the Plains. Differences in regional net returns to wheat are due largely to yields which averaged 32.7 bushels per acre in the three High Plains locations compared to 70.9 bushels per acre in California, Idaho, and Washington.

The impacts of rising energy costs and pumping lifts on relative profitability are illustrated in table 5-14, which compares the returns of the major irrigated and dryland crops in a region under alternative cost assumptions. The cost alternatives are selected to depict possible changes in pumping depths and energy prices between 1977, 1980, and 2000. Four comparisons are provided: irrigated corn compared to dryland corn in eastern Nebraska, irrigated corn compared to dryland wheat in both western Kansas and the north Texas High Plains, and irrigated cotton compared to dryland cotton in the south Texas High

Table 5-14 Returns to Irrigated and Dryland Farming in Selected Locations with Alternative Energy Costs and Pumping Lifts

(1977 dollars)

Location	1977			1980			2000		
	Irrigated	Dryland	Difference (irrigated-dryland)	Irrigated	Dryland	Difference (irrigated-dryland)	Irrigated	Dryland	Difference (irrigated-dryland)
Eastern Nebraska [a]	(corn)	(corn)	(corn)	(corn)	(corn)	(corn)	(corn)	(corn)	(corn)
Return to L,M,O,R ($ per acre)[e]	143.17	35.89	107.28	138.45	32.44	106.01	121.88	23.70	98.18
Return to risk ($ per acre)	55.72	-22.55	78.27	51.00	-26.00	77.00	34.43	-34.74	69.17
Water costs ($ per acre-ft)	27.72			32.40			48.96		
Western Kansas [b]	(corn)	(wheat)	(corn)	(corn)	(wheat)	(corn)	(corn)	(wheat)	(corn)
Return to L,M,O,R ($ per acre)[e]	91.75	45.41	46.34	78.60	42.35	36.25	30.66	35.21	- 4.55
Return to risk ($ per acre)	44.40	16.29	28.11	31.25	13.23	18.02	-16.69	6.09	-22.78
Water costs ($ per acre-ft)	36.12			42.72			66.72		
North Texas High Plains [c]	(corn)	(wheat)	(corn)	(corn)	(wheat)	(corn)	(corn)	(wheat)	(corn)
Return to L,M,O,R ($ per acre)[e]	115.14	17.33	97.81	108.52	14.75	93.77	77.80	8.71	69.09
Return to risk ($ per acre)	73.58	- 4.47	78.05	66.96	- 7.05	74.01	36.24	-13.09	49.33
Water costs ($ per acre-ft)	45.60			48.72			62.88		
South Texas High Plains [d]	(cotton)	(cotton)	(cotton)	(cotton)	(cotton)	(cotton)	(cotton)	(cotton)	(cotton)
Return to L,M,O,R ($ per acre)[e]	26.71	20.19	6.52	20.04	14.28	5.76	- 3.42	2.26	- 5.68
Return to risk ($ per acre)	-32.40	-35.14	2.74	-39.07	-41.05	1.98	-62.53	-53.07	- 9.46
Water costs ($ per acre-ft)	58.80			64.56			84.60		

Source: USDA, Firm Enterprise Data System, 1977.

[1] Between 1977 and 2000, energy prices increased according to assumptions made in table 5-2, pumping depths increased according to the cropping situation description, and all other factors affecting profitability are left unchanged. Water costs are based on fixed and variable costs. Fixed and variable costs (excluding energy prices and pumping depth) remained unchanged between 1977 and 2000. Yields and prices are averages of 1974-1977 FEDS data.

[2] Eastern Nebraska: Irrigated corn (107.4 bu/A) vs. dryland corn (45.7 bu/A). Irrigation water (12 ac.-in.) was pumped from 100 ft. and distributed through gated pipe using electricity. Pumping depth increased .5 ft./year. Corn prices: $2.62 bushel.

[3] Western Kansas: Irrigated corn (106.8 bu/A) vs. dryland wheat (25.7 bu/A). Irrigation water (24 ac.-in.) was pumped from 215 ft. and distributed through gated pipe using natural gas. Pumping depth increased 2 ft./year. Corn prices: $2.69 bushel; wheat prices: $3.41/bushel.

[4] North Texas High Plains: Irrigated corn (109.8 bu/A) vs. dryland wheat (13.6 bu/A). Irrigation water (26 ac.-in.) was pumped from 200 ft. and distributed through gravity flow system using natural gas. Pumping depth increased 3 ft./year. Corn prices: $3.04 bu. Wheat prices: $3.55/bushel.

[5] South Texas High Plains: Irrigated cotton (351.7 lbs. lint/A and 568.7 lbs. seed/A) vs. dryland cotton (230.3 lbs. lint/A and 366.2 lbs. seed/A). Irrigation water (14 ac.-in.) was pumped from 150 ft. and distributed thorough gravity flow system using natural gas. Pumping depth increased 3 ft./year. Cotton prices: $.472/lbs. lint and $.052 lbs. seed.

[6] Returns to land, management, overhead, and risk.

Plains. The irrigated alternative was more profitable than the dryland at all four locations with the 1977 pumping and cost assumptions (table 5-14). However, if pumping depths and energy prices increase over time according to the assumptions and all other factors affecting profitability are unchanged, then the dryland alternative becomes increasingly attractive relative to the irrigated alternative. In two of the locations with significant groundwater mining, western Kansas and the south Texas High Plains, the dryland alternatives are more profitable in the year 2000.

Crop prices are assumed to remain unchanged throughout the time period covered in table 5-14. Altering this assumption shows that relatively modest increases in crop prices can compensate for expected increases in pumping costs. Changes in crop prices necessary to cover the increase in water costs due to greater pumping depths and higher energy prices from 1977 through 2000 are 20 cents per bushel for corn in eastern Nebraska, 46 cents per bushel for corn in western Kansas, 35 cents per bushel for corn in the north Texas High Plains, and 7.8 cents per pound for cotton lint in the south Texas High Plains.

The preceding discussion of profitability overstates the likely impacts on irrigated agriculture by not allowing for adjustments to cost changes. Many farmers already have made major adjustments to higher energy and water costs by adopting some of the water-saving techniques discussed above. And over the next several decades, new technologies will provide farmers with an even wider range of options for adjusting to higher water costs.

Crop price levels are also an important determinant of the relative profitability of irrigated and dryland farming. Higher crop prices, of course, increase the profitability of all farming. But since irrigated yields tend to be higher than dryland yields, the impacts of a given change in crop prices are greater with irrigated farming. For example, the assumptions of table 5-14 suggest irrigated corn yields in eastern Nebraska are more than double the yields from the region's dryland corn alternative. If water costs double from the 1977 base year level in that region, a 45 cents per bushel or 17 percent increase in corn prices would be sufficient to restore the base level profit differential between irrigated and dryland corn production

in the region. Higher corn price increases would increase the relative
returns to irrigated production despite the doubling of water costs.

The example of cotton in the south Texas High Plains suggests that
in some cases rising water costs may require much larger compensating
crop price increases to restore the relative profitability of irrigated
farming. Water costs are higher in the Texas High Plains than in eastern Nebraska and the assumed differential between irrigated and dryland
cotton yields is not as high as the corn differential (see table 5-14).
Consequently, a doubling of water costs on the irrigated cotton alternative would require a doubling of cotton lint and cottonseed prices to
restore the base year differential between the profits of irrigated and
dryland cotton.

Consequently, the impacts of rising energy and water costs on the
relative profitability of irrigated and dryland farming will depend
largely on the adjustments farmers can make to changes in relative
factor prices and the level of crop prices. In the absence of higher
crop prices, the available technological adjustments to higher energy
and water costs are unlikely to be sufficient to prevent some decline
in the profitability of irrigated relative to dryland farming. On the
other hand, if the sharp increases in agricultural prices predicted by
some analysts are realized,[30] the returns to western irrigation may
increase faster than those to western dryland farming. Nevertheless,
limited water supplies would prevent these higher returns from being
translated into a rapid expansion of irrigated acreage in the West.

---

30. For example, the Global 2000 Report concludes that real food prices
will double by the year 2000. Council on Environmental Quality and the
Department of State, The Global 2000 Report to the President: Entering
the Twenty-First Century, vol. 1 (Washington, D.C., GPO, 1980) p. 2.

Chapter 6

ENVIRONMENTAL IMPACTS OF IRRIGATED AGRICULTURE

Nature of the Problems

Erosion and the unintended impacts of fertilizer and pesticide use are the principal environmental problems associated with dryland farming, and uncontrolled water movements are their primary cause. Even though irrigation implies some control over water, similar environmental problems stemming from excessive water applications are not uncommon on western irrigated lands. When large quantities of water are applied, either naturally or artificially, then soil, fertilizers, and pesticides may be transported into streams and rivers or nitrates may leach out into the groundwater. Both the farmlands, where soil and nutrients are lost, and the recipient water bodies, where the quality of the water deteriorates, are damaged in the process.[1]

In addition to the unintended transport of soil, fertilizers, and pesticides, there are several environmental issues peculiarly associated with irrigation. These are salinity and the problems related to streamflow reduction, groundwater mining, and water development projects.

All water used for irrigation carries salts, and the salt content of the water increases as water evaporates, is consumed by the plants, or passes over saline soils. Salts both in the water and the soil create problems for agriculture; they inhibit plant growth and in extreme cases render the land useless for agriculture. Where drainage is adequate, salts can be flushed from the root zones if there is sufficient rainfall or additional irrigation water is applied for this

---

1. Pierre R. Crosson and Kenneth D. Frederick, The World Food Situation: Resource and Environmental Issues in the Developing Countries and the United States (Baltimore, Md., Johns Hopkins University Press for Resources for the Future, 1977) chap. 5.

purpose. But this seldom eliminates the salinity problem. If the salts are washed off the land with additional water applications, the return flows have higher salt concentrations. This may adversely affect the plant and wildlife dependent on the river as well as downstream users. In areas lacking good drainage, repeated irrigation may raise the water table. If the water table reaches the root zone of the plants, capillary action carries water close to the soil surface, where it evaporates and leaves a salt residue. In time this process, if uncorrected, greatly reduces or even destroys the productivity of the land. In addition, salinity increases management and operating costs and accelerates corrosion of equipment.

As the area's major water consumer, irrigation is the primary contributor to the depletion of western river and streamflows. About 90 percent of the nearly 90 billion gallons of water consumed per day for offstream uses is for irrigation. As a result many former perennial streams are now dry or reduced to a trickle for much of the year. As streamflow declines, pollutant concentrations and temperatures rise. Both can have devastating effects on riverine flora and fauna. Moreover, the flow of fresh water into estuaries and tidal marshes is diminished, reducing the productivity of these ecologically vital and commercially valuable resources. Lagoons on the Texas and California coasts have been particularly vulnerable to such damage.[2]

In addition to its impact on pumping costs and future water supplies, groundwater mining may result in subsidence or saltwater intrusion. The costs stemming from subsidence become particularly important when settled areas are affected. For example, subsidence due to groundwater withdrawals in the Houston-Pasadena-La Porte areas of Texas and in Las Vegas has reached the point where city streets and buildings are threatened. Saltwater intrusion occurs when the fresh water of coastal aquifers is mined and replaced by seawater. As a wedge of

---

2. U.S. Water Resources Council, The Nation's Water Resources, 1975-2000; Second National Water Assessment (Washington, D.C., GPO, 1978) p. 73.

saltwater intrudes into the aquifer, the value of the remaining fresh-water, as well as the storage value of the aquifer, may be destroyed. Saltwater intrusion is a problem along parts of both the California and Texas coasts.

There are also important environmental impacts associated with water projects. The dams, reservoirs, and canals required for large-scale surface irrigation projects have major impacts on ecological systems. Such projects commonly flood valuable lands, reduce down-stream sediment loads, and alter the timing and quantity of river flows to the possible detriment of the riverine ecology. Unintended conse-quences may include loss of animal habitats and potentially damaging effects on coastal fisheries. In developing countries large water projects often have led to spread of waterborne diseases, especially schistosomiasis. All such impacts should be taken into account in evaluating the environmental implications of irrigation projects.

The environmental impacts of irrigation are not all negative. In arid and semiarid areas irrigation may produce a better vegetative cover which in turn reduces erosion and runoff. Irrigation may either reduce or increase the amount of sediment in the water. In the High Plains, for example, irrigation has helped reduce wind erosion which has been a serious problem during periods of extended drought. These beneficial effects, however, often have been countered by the removal of windbreaks to make room for large sprinkler systems. From a na-tional perspective, irrigation has greatly expanded the land base suitable for high-productivity agriculture; the high yields generally attained on irrigated lands enable some highly erodable lands to remain under permanent vegetative cover. Changes in the overall level of irrigation affect the total number and the location of the cropped and pastured acres required to produce a given output. Since the marginal lands that would be brought into production with any general expansion of dryland farming may be environmentally fragile, the level of irrigation has important implications for the nature, location, and magnitude of the environmental impacts associated with national agri-cultural production.

The direct environmental impacts of irrigated agriculture can be divided into (1) those such as salinity, erosion, and water quality degradation from fertilizers and pesticides associated with onfarm water management, and (2) those such as low flows, subsidence, salt-water intrusion, and the need for water development projects associated with the overall demands irrigation places on limited water supplies. Our focus in this chapter is on the first group--the impacts that stem from and might be controlled by the water management practices of farmers. Of course, improved onfarm water management may reduce the water withdrawn and consumed for irrigating a given acreage and, thus, might increase streamflows, and reduce subsidence and saltwater intrusion. On the other hand, any such water savings might be diverted to other offstream uses as expanding the irrigated acreage or other water-consuming activities rather than increasing instream flows. The environmental issues associated with the overall level of irrigation and water use are considered in the concluding chapter in the context of examining the implications of alternative irrigation trends on the overall environmental impacts of U.S. agriculture. Analysis of the environmental impacts of low flows, subsidence, saltwater intrusion, and water projects is beyond the scope of this study.

Extent of the Environmental Problems

Salinity

Salinity is the most pervasive environmental problem stemming from irrigation in the United States. All western river basins except the Columbia are confronted with high and generally rising salt levels. In much of the Lower Colorado, parts of the Rio Grande, and the western portion of San Joaquin river basins, the salt concentrations in either the water or the soils are approaching levels that threaten the viability of their traditional forms of irrigated agriculture. Groundwater salinity, which may result from the infiltration of irrigation waters or from the intrusion of seawater as the fresh water is pumped out of coastal aquifers, is not a widespread problem in the West. However, the problem is growing and already is serious in parts of California, New Mexico, Montana, and Texas.[3] Although groundwater tables are less susceptible than surface waters to pollution, the problems are much more difficult to correct underground.

An informed guess suggests that 25 to 35 percent of the irrigated lands in the West have some type of salinity problem, and the problems are getting worse.[4] Two large irrigated areas where salinity already is a serious problem are the Lower Colorado River Basin and the west side of the San Joaquin Valley in California. The underlying cause of the problem differs in these cases. The salt content of the Colorado increases progressively downstream because of the salt-concentrating effects of irrigation and the addition of salts picked up as the water passes over saline formations. About two-thirds of the salts delivered to the Colorado are from natural sources, and these deliveries only can be eliminated through expensive investments to divert the river and its tributaries around some of the areas contributing the salts of desalinization plants. Irrigation accounts for most of the remaining salts which could be curtailed greatly by reducing irrigation return flows. Annual damages from salinity in the Colorado River have been estimated between $75 and $104 million in 1980 and $122 and $165 million in 2000 if no control measures are taken. While most of the damages would be incurred by municipal and industrial users, farmers would face decreased crop yields, increased leaching requirements, and higher management costs. Four initial control projects costing a total

---

3. See U.S. Department of Interior, *Westwide Study Report on Critical Water Problems Facing the Eleven Western States* (Washington, D.C., Bureau of Reclamation, April 1975) pp. 116-118; and Ibid., vol. 1, summary, p. 65.

4. Personal conversation with Jan van Schilfgaarde, director, U.S. Salinity Laboratory, Riverside, Calif., February 1980.

of $125 million have been proposed to reduce but not eliminate the salt problems.[5]

In the San Joaquin Valley the principal salinity problem results from poor drainage preventing salt-laden waters from being carried away from the fields. High water tables already threaten the productivity of about 400,000 acres and ultimately more than 1 million acres in the valley may be similarly affected. A $1.26 billion drainage system to carry irrigation runoff from the western side of the valley to the Delta has been proposed as a solution to the problem. Since farmers would have to install their own underground drainage to get the waters to the central drain, the total costs of an effective system would be considerably higher than this figure.[6]

Erosion and Sedimentation

Erosion and sedimentation are viewed as problems in many areas of the West. With a few exceptions, however, it is not clear that irrigation is an important contributor to these problems. Even though human activities altering the natural ground cover may greatly accelerate erosion and sedimentation, in the eleven most western states "most of the rapidly eroding range, grassland and forest-covered soils occur where natural geologic erosion is dominant."[7] The human contribution to erosion probably has been more important in the Plains States, but as noted earlier the impacts of irrigation are mixed.

---

5. U.S. Department of Interior and U.S. Department of Agriculture, Final Environmental Statement: Colorado River Water Quality Improvement Program, vol. I (Washington, D.C., Bureau of Reclamation, May 1977) section 1.

6. U.S. Department of Interior, California Department of Water Resources, and California State Water Resources Control Board, Agricultural Drainage and Salt Management in the San Joaquin Valley, Final Report (Fresno, Calif., San Joaquin Valley InterAgency Drainage Program, June 1979).

7. U.S. Department of Interior, Westwide Study Report, p. 127.

On the positive side, in dry areas irrigation may provide a better vegetative cover to protect the soil from the wind. Also, land leveling, which may be done with the installation of an irrigation system, reduces erosion, and irrigation may reduce sediment in streams where the natural loads are heavy.

On the negative side, center-pivot irrigation has led to cropping hilly, sandy soils that are highly erodable and the wheel tracks of the large mobile sprinkler systems may lead to the start of large gullies. Some of the soils that were placed under irrigated crops become extremely vulnerable to wind erosion if irrigation is terminated. Since the high cost of water in the southern High Plains has forced some farmers to eliminate winter irrigation for a cover crop, wind erosion has been increasing.[8] But the most extensive erosion from irrigation arises when flood and furrow systems are used on lands which have not been adequately leveled.

While there are no data on leveling, the 1977 National Resources Inventory differentiates between crop and pasture lands which are and are not susceptible to erosion and indicates how much of the acreage in each subclass was planted to various crop groups and how much was irrigated by gravity and pressure systems. Tables 6-1 to 6-3 summarize some of these data for farm production regions.

In 1977, 35 percent of the West's irrigated cropland and 34 percent of the irrigated pasture was in subclass e, that is, susceptible to erosion; 21 percent of the cropland and 28 percent of the pasture was highly erodable (see table 6-1). The percentages of irrigation on erodable lands varied widely among states with Oklahoma (69 percent) and Washington (57 percent) at the high end and Arizona (1 percent), Nevada (2 percent), and California (8 percent) at the low end. While the NRI data suggest that erosion may be a problem on many of the lands irrigated in the West, the potential problems are much more extensive on dryland cropland, 64 percent of which was in subclass e.

---

8. Personal communication with Herbert Grubb, Texas Department of Water Resources, February 28, 1980.

Table 6-1. 1977 Irrigated Cropland and Pasture on Erodable Soils, by Farm Production Region

Region	Cropland		Pasture	
	Erodable acres irrigated (1,000)	Percent of all irrigated cropland	Erodable acres irrigated (1,000)	Percent of all irrigated pasture
Northern Plains				
Erodable[a]	4,405	41	41	33
Highly erodable[b]	2,599	24	23	19
Southern Plains				
Erodable[a]	4,076	47	183	46
Highly erodable[b]	2,055	24	140	35
Mountain				
Erodable[a]	5,713	38	750	38
Highly erodable[b]	3,772	25	625	32
Pacific				
Erodable[a]	2,160	18	320	23
Highly erodable[b]	1,391	12	274	20
17 Western states				
Erodable[a]	16,354	35	1,294	34
Highly erodable[b]	9,817	21	1,062	28

Source: U.S. Department of Agriculture, Soil Conservation Service, "Basic Statistics: 1977 National Resources Inventory (NRI)," Revised February 1980, tables 3a and 4a.

[a]"Erodable" includes all subclass e lands. These are defined as those soils where susceptibility to erosion or past erosion damage is the dominant problem or hazard in their use.

[b]"Highly erodable" includes class III-e soils or worse. Class III-e soils have moderately steep slopes and are highly susceptible to water or wind erosion or have suffered severe erosion in the past.

Table 6-2. 1977 Irrigated Row Crops on Erodable Soils, by Farm Production
Region

Region	1,000 acres	Percent of irrigated row crops	Percent of total irrigated-erodable or highly erodable cropland
Northern Plains			
Erodable	3,510	41	80
Highly erodable	2,002	23	77
Southern Plains			
Erodable	3,143	53	77
Highly erodable	1,423	24	69
Mountain			
Erodable	1,690	41	30
Highly erodable	924	22	24
Pacific			
Erodable	305	7	14
Highly erodable	52	1	4
17 Western states			
Erodable	8,648	37	53
Highly erodable	4,401	19	45

Note: definitions of "erodable" and "highly erodable" are provided
in table 6-1.

Source: U.S. Department of Agriculture, Soil Conservation Service,
"Basic Statistics: 1977 National Resources Inventory (NRI)," Revised
February 1980, tables 3a and 4a.

Table 6-3. 1977 Use of Gravity (Flood or Furrow) Irrigation on Erodable
Soils, by Farm Production Region

Region	1,000 acres	As percentage of that category
Northern Plains		
Erodable	1,375	30
Highly erodable	498	19
Southern Plains		
Erodable	2,315	53
Highly erodable	787	35
Mountain		
Erodable	4,380	64
Highly erodable	2,828	60
Pacific		
Erodable	835	33
Highly erodable	590	35
17 Western states		
Erodable	8,905	49
Highly erodable	4,703	41

Note: definitions of "erodable" and "highly erodable" are provided in table 6-1.

Source: U.S. Department of Agriculture, Soil Conservation Service, "Basic Statistics: 1977 National Resources Inventory (NRI)," Revised February 1980, table 9a.

A comparison of the Soil Conservation Service's 1967 CNI and 1977 NRI data suggest the potential erosion problem on irrigated lands increased substantially over the decade. While total irrigated acreage rose by nearly 9.7 million acres or 23 percent, erodable irrigated cropland rose by 5.8 million acres or 50 percent. Irrigated cropland in subclass e rose from 29 to 35 percent of the total. The Northern Plains region, which accounted for nearly 60 percent of the total increase in irrigated acreage, accounted for half of the increase in erodable irrigated acreage. The Southern Plains accounted for 24 percent, the Mountain region 23 percent, and the Pacific region only 2 percent of the total increase in erodable irrigated acreage over the decade. The most dramatic change was in the Southern Plains where subclass e soils rose by 1.4 million acres even though total irrigation in the region grew by only 0.2 million acres.

The threat of erosion depends on the use of the land as well as on its susceptibility to erosion. Since row crops represent the agricultural use most likely to lead to erosion, it is significant that more than one-half of the irrigated-erodable cropland was in row crops (see table 6-2). In 1977, 8.6 million irrigated-erodable acres were planted to row crops, and more than half of this land was highly erodable. These data suggest that 37 percent of all irrigated row crops in the West were on erodable lands, and 19 percent were on highly erodable lands. The combination of planting row crops on erodable soils is particularly common in the Plains states which accounted for more than three-fourths of the total for the seventeen western states. In contrast, the Pacific region accounted for only 4 percent of the West's total row crops planted on erodable soils.

The type of irrigation system also influences the likelihood of erosion. As noted above, the combination of gravity irrigation on erodable soils is particularly vulnerable to serious erosion. Gravity is the sole means of irrigating 66 percent of the West's irrigated acreage, and on another 4 percent gravity is combined with a pressure irrigation system. Table 6-3 indicates that 49 percent of the erodable irrigated soils (17 percent of all western lands) and 41 percent of the highly erodable irrigated soils (9 percent of the total) are irrigated with gravity. Nearly half of this acreage is in the Mountain region where 64 percent of the erodable and 60 percent of the highly erodable irrigated acreage uses gravity distribution.

In summary, although the data are not available to link irrigation crop and water management practices directly to the West's overall erosion problems, the data do indicate potential for major problems of erosion on irrigated lands, especially within the Plains and Mountain states. On the other hand, there is twice as much highly erodable land in dryland row crops in the West as there is in irrigated row crops. Moreover, this comparison does not just reflect the larger acreage in dryland crops; 27 percent of the dryland row crops were on highly erodable soils compared to 19 percent of the irrigated row crops.

Agricultural Chemicals

The Second National Water Assessment identified the principal pollutants of the nation's surface and groundwater supplies. Agricultural chemicals are identified as a "significant" source of surface water pollution in three areas in the West but the Assessment does not indicate whether dryland or irrigated farming is the principal culprit and there are no data to make this distinction. In comparison to the rest of the country, which has twenty-four locations where agricultural chemicals are identified as a significant surface water pollutant, this problem is not very extensive in the West. The only water quality problems directly linked to irrigation return flows by the Assessment are groundwater pollution and surface water salinity, and groundwater pollution is only deemed "significant" in Southern California.[9] Percolating irrigation water has been blamed for leaching large quantities of nitrates into underlying aquifers in Southern California.

---

9. U.S. Water Resources Council, The Nation's Water Resources, 1975-2000: Second National Water Assessment, vol. I: summary, pp. 62-65.

In the Santa Maria Valley it was estimated that 39 percent of the nitrates applied to irrigated fields were leached below the root zone.[10] Likewise in the Upper Santa Ana Valley, nitrate pollution of groundwater was prevalent, especially under sandy, coarse irrigated soils. While nitrate contamination spreads very slowly, decontamination is equally slow to occur.[11]

The projected expansion of irrigation in the Sandhills of Nebraska poses a potentially serious groundwater pollution problem in that region. Since the soil is quite sandy, agricultural chemicals are easily leached through the soil into the groundwater. The water table averages 100 feet beneath the surface, and where there is irrigation (primarily center pivots), nitrate-N levels have risen to 20 ppm, twice the public health standard for drinking water. With good irrigation management the concentration of nitrate-N is expected to level out around 20 to 25 ppm. But given the sandy nature of the soil, it is unlikely that any lower levels can be maintained with an expansion of irrigation and much higher concentrations are clearly possible.[12]

The emerging pollution problem in the Sandhills is in contrast to many parts of the High Plains where the agriculture chemicals move very slowly through the soil. In the Texas High Plains, for example, there are still no recordable pollution problems in the groundwater after almost forty years of irrigation.[13]

---

10. L. J. Lund, J. C. Ryden, R. J. Miller, A. E. Laag, and W. E. Bendixen, "Nitrogen Balances for the Santa Maria Valley," in P. F. Pratt, editor, National Conference on Management of Nitrogen in Irrigated Agriculture (Riverside, University of California, 1978) p. 411.

11. R. S. Ayers, "A Case Study--Nitrates in the Upper Santa Ana River Basin in Relation to Groundwater Pollution," in Ibid., pp. 355-367.

12. Personal communication with Darryl Watts, University of Nebraska, July 15, 1980.

13. Personal communication with Herbert Grubb, Texas Department of Water Resources, March 3, 1980.

Managing Environmental Problems

Conceptually, the way to eliminate erosion, sedimentation, and water quality degradation stemming from irrigation is simple--limit the rate and quantity of water applied to a field to levels that can be fully absorbed within the root zone. Without runoff, chemicals and sediments are not washed or leached into neighboring streams, lakes, or aquifers. There is a catch, however, in that reduced runoff may lead to salt accumulations in the soil.

Moreover, there is no mystery as to the technical means for at least reducing and perhaps eliminating runoff. The most serious problems of erosion and sedimentation are associated with flood and furrow irrigation. Land leveling, and the adoption and proper operations of sprinkler, drip, or subsurface irrigation systems reduce or eliminate runoff. While these technologies are expensive and not always cost effective to farmers, there are a wide variety of other measures that can reduce runoff and help control the resulting environmental damages. These include reduced tillage, altering the length and size of the furrow stream, changing the frequency and duration of irrigations, managment of crop residues to reduce erosion and evaporation, controlling the tail waters and sediments at the end of the field, and lining of canals.

The nature of the return flow problems as well as the best methods for handling them vary widely depending on factors such as soil type, land gradient, irrigation technique, water quantity and quality, and drainage conditions. A National Conference on Irrigation Return Flow Quality Management reported on the effectiveness of alternative farming practices for controlling return flow quality under a wide range of conditions.[14] For example, a study of the cost effectiveness of

---

14. The proceedings of this conference held at Colorado State University in May 1977 have been published in James P. Law and Gaylord V. Skogerboe, editors, Proceedings: National Conference on Irrigation Return Flow Quality Management (Fort Collins, Colorado State University, 1977).

reducing onfarm sediment losses in southern Idaho concluded that, on a cost per ton of sediment saved basis, sediment ponds, vegetative strips, and then mini-basins were the most cost effective. Side-roll sprinklers and flow cutbacks were the most expensive.[15] A more general conclusion from another study of farms in southern Idaho is that any practice which increases irrigation efficiency generally decreases sediment loss. In this particular study a 20 percent decrease in water applied to a gravity irrigated field resulted in an 85 percent decrease in sediment loss.[16] An evaluation of surface irrigation return flows in California's Central Valley concludes that return flows are nearly nonexistent where water is scarce or expensive.[17] Indeed, a general conclusion that might be drawn from these site-specific studies is that the return flow problems are significantly reduced when the cost of the water provides an incentive for efficient use. What comprises efficient use, however, varies widely depending on the specific conditions of the region and even the individual farmer.

Unfortunately, eliminating runoff will not solve all the environmental problems associated with irrigation. The high rates of water consumption required for plant growth necessarily leave higher salt concentrations. The salts must be deposited somewhere. If water applications are limited to the absorptive capacity of the soil, the salts accumulate in the soil; if additional water is applied to leach the salts out of the root zone, the salts may show up in either the underlying aquifer or the neighboring streams.

---

15. Karl H. Lindeborg, Larry Conklin, Roger Long, and Edgar Michalson, "Economic Analysis of On-Farm Methods for Controlling Sediment and Nutrient Losses," in ibid., pp. 193-201.

16. D. W. Fitzsimmons, C. E. Brockway, J. R. Busch, G. C. Lewis, G. M. McMaster, and C. W. Berg, "On-Farm Methods for Controlling Sediment and Nutrient Losses," in ibid., pp. 183-191.

17. Kenneth K. Tanji, James W. Biggar, Robert J. Miller, William D. Pruitt, and Gerald C. Horner, "Evaluation of Surface Irrigation Return Flows in the Central Valley of California," in ibid., pp. 167-173.

Nevertheless, improved farm management techniques can go a long way toward reducing some salinity problems and obviating the need for some of the costly structural solutions under consideration. Efficient water and agronomic management can reduce (but not eliminate) the salt concentrations by limiting evaporation and evapotranspiration. A closer than normal spacing of cotton rows, for example, hastens the maturity of the plant and reduces the time required to develop a full canopy. Consequently, early evaporation losses are reduced and the season for evapotranspiration is shortened; the resulting water savings reduce the salt concentrating effects of the irrigation.[18]

Curtailing the water applied for leaching reduces the dissolution of salts from the soil. Downstream users benefit from a reduction in the mass of salt appearing in the drainage water but the farmer is left with higher salt precipitation in his soils. However, research results reported by van Schilfgaarde suggest that the adverse impacts of these salts may be kept within acceptable levels through careful water management. Under some circumstances salinity in the lower portion of the root zone can be permitted to build up considerably more than suspected without adversely affecting yields as long as good quality water is applied in the upper zone.[19]

Since water and agronomic management practices alone will not eliminate the presence of and problems resulting from salts, additional steps may be required to preserve the long-term productivity of irrigated agriculture under many circumstances. Engineering solutions such as basinwide drainage systems or desalting plants exist but, as noted above, the costs are high. A promising alternative for many situations is growing plants adapted to high levels of water and soil salinity. Barley has long been grown successfully with salt levels that would kill most plants. And in recent years scientists have developed varieties of wheat and tomatoes with high tolerance to salt. Genetic re-

---

18. A letter to the author from Jan van Schilfgaarde, director, U.S. Salinity Laboratory, Riverside, California, October 31, 1980.

19. Jan van Schilfgaarde, "Minimizing Salt in Return Flow by Improving Irrigation Efficiency," in Law and Skogerboe, Proceedings, pp. 81-98.

search to combine salt tolerance, high yield, and desirable market characteristics in a single variety is likely to further expand the opportunities for successful irrigation with saline water and soil and to become increasingly important to the future of irrigated agriculture.[20]

Improved basinwide water management also has great potential for mitigating salinity problems. Where poor drainage prevents salt-laden waters from being carried away from the field, artificial drainage is required to prevent eventual loss of productivity. But the extent of the drainage needs can be greatly reduced through good management. Van Schilfgaarde suggests that the San Joaquin Valley drainage problem could be reduced to one-third or less of current levels and a long-term equilibrium reached through an integrated irrigation system whereby the best water is used first on salt-sensitive crops with the increasingly salt-laden runoff applied to increasingly salt-tolerant crops. The remaining highly saline waters would be reduced to quantities that could be disposed of through a greatly scaled down drainage system or perhaps in evaporation ponds.[21] A major, if not insurmountable, difficulty in implementing such a scheme would be to get some farmers to accept lower quality water.

Federal Efforts to Control Irrigation
Runoff and Some Policy Lessons

Although there had been a long history of water quality legislation, it was not until passage of the Federal Water Pollution Control Act Amendments of 1972 (FWPCA) that the federal government was granted

---

20. Emanuel Epstein, Jack C. Norlyn, Dale W. Rush, Ralph W. Kingsley, David B. Kelley, Glen A. Cunningham, Anne F. Wrona, "Saline Culture of Crops: A Genetic Approach," Science vol. 210 (24 October 1980) pp. 399-404.

21. Personal communication with Jan van Schilfgaarde in February 1980 and October 1980.

the power and mandate to pursue specific water quality goals. Under the FWPCA, water quality control was based primarily on setting effluent standards for point source discharges. Polluters were required to have permits for the discharge of pollutants, and target dates were established for the adoption of improved treatment technologies. The federal legislation required each state to develop a water quality control program; once a state's program is approved by the Environmental Protection Agency (EPA) as being consistent with federal provisions, administration of the permit system is turned over to that state.[22]

Congress recognized that control of point sources of pollution would not be sufficient to meet the established goals. Thus, section 208 of the Act charged the states with developing and implementing "areawide waste treatment management plans" which also were to include "a process to (i) identify, if appropriate, agriculturally and silviculturally related nonpoint sources of pollution...and (ii) set forth procedures and methods (including land use requirements) to control to the extent possible such sources."[23]

The first federal initiative to control the quality of irrigation return flows stems from the 1972 Act. The legislation was not clear as to whether agricultural pollutants were to be classified as point or nonpoint sources. This was left up to EPA. In July 1972 EPA ruled that irrigation return flows from sources of less than 3,000 acres were exempted from the permit requirement unless the EPA Regional Administrator or the head of a state water pollution control agency identified a particular source as a significant polluter. The EPA ruling, which was prompted in part by the administrative difficulties of attempting to issue permits to all point sources, was challenged in court by the

---

22. This discussion of federal water quality control is based largely on George E. Radosevich and Gaylord V. Skogerboe, _Achieving Irrigation Return Flow Quality Control Through Improved Legal Systems_, EPA-600/2-78-184 (Ada, Ok., Environmental Protection Agency, December 1978) section 7.

23. _Federal Water Pollution Control Act Amendments of 1972_, Report No. 92-1465, House of Representatives, 92 Congress, 2 sess. (1972).

Natural Resources Defense Council. In July 1975 the court upheld the challenge and ordered EPA to extend the permit system to include all agricultural point sources.

Partly in response to this court decision, a series of EPA actions between February 1976 and February 1977 classified most agricultural water pollution as nonpoint sources. Irrigation return flows through ditches and drains to navigable waters were an exception; these were to be subjected to general rather than individual water pollution control permits. Subsequent legislation changed this and placed all agricultural return flows under the 208 planning process, which has yet to make significant progress in curbing the water quality damages from irrigated farming.

During the period of the 1970s when it appeared irrigation discharges might be classified as point sources and be subject to the permit system, six states issued permits for irrigation return flows. These permits, however, were used only for monitoring (not for controlling) discharges.[24] Nevertheless, just the hint of federal regulation was sufficient to prompt challenges to their legality. The permits generally were for irrigation districts. But in most cases the only effective way to control the discharges is at the farm level, and the authority of irrigation districts to control onfarm water management through discharge permits is uncertain at best. Legal issues almost surely will stymie attempts to control irrigation discharges in this manner.

A step toward establishing a firmer legal basis for farm-level water quality control has been made in California and Oregon where water quality provisions have been attached to new, extended, or transferred water rights.[25] While it is desirable to attach quality

---

24. Radosevich and Skogerboe, <u>Achieving Irrigation Return Flow Quality Control</u>, p. 119.

25. Ibid., p. 117.

considerations to new and altered water rights, this represents a slow and piecemeal approach to controlling return flows and will be inadequate for meeting most water quality objectives.

Even if there were no legal issues associated with a permit system, there are questions as to the practicality of designing and enforcing onfarm water management regulations. Conditions vary so much among farms and regions that blanket standards will be extremely inefficient and costly. Yet, government agencies lack the specific knowledge of the relationships between farming practices, soils, weather conditions, and water quality to design an efficient and effective system for achieving predetermined water-quality objectives. Furthermore, the number of actors is so large and the distances among them so great that it would be extremely difficult and costly to enforce effectively any permit system without the cooperation of the farmers.

The voluntary approach to controlling the quality of irrigation return flows generally starts with a recognition that success depends on gaining farmer cooperation. Amidst the confusion that followed the Federal Water Pollution Control Act Amendments of 1972 regarding responsibility for controlling agricultural irrigation discharges, several states did initiate projects designed to encourage farmers to adopt better water and farm management practices. Two states, Idaho and Montana, developed demonstration projects to show how improved conservation and management practices can reduce erosion and sedimentation. The most comprehensive effort to develop and implement a voluntary approach has been in the Sulphur Creek area of the State of Washington. This project relies primarily on education and technical assistance to encourage farmers to adopt best management practices; regulations on farmers may be used at a later date only if and where a voluntary approach does not work. The program is structured to provide local control to meet the program's objectives of conserving soil and water and improving water quality, fertilizer and pesticide application, and crop production. Initial results suggest that attitude changes stemming from improved education and information and reliance on local inputs and control are key elements in reducing pollution discharges. It is too soon, however, to assess the effectiveness of the program in controlling environmental damages.[26]

As long as the desired changes are in the farmer's interests, education, technical assistance, and demonstration projects are likely to be extremely effective means of inducing innovation. But since the environmental benefits of innovation are external to the farm, the educational approach alone may not be sufficient to induce farmers to adopt the most socially desirable practices. On irrigated farms, the gap between the farmers' and society's benefits and costs are likely to be great if water is inexpensive. In such cases additional inducements are required to encourage adoption of water management practices that will reduce discharges and their associated environmental problems. A variety of financial incentives and disincentives might be used to promote improved water management, but the most direct and effective is likely to be through the cost of water. Where water is expensive, runoff and the associated environmental problems tend to be very small. There is a strong correlation between the irrigation practices that are profitable when water is expensive and those that are advisable for reducing the environmental damages. As the economic analysis of chapter 4 illustrates, expensive water makes it economically advantageous for farmers to adopt practices such as tailwater recovery systems, sprinkler irrigation, and irrigation scheduling. With these practices farmers can reduce the intake of water to levels more in line with the water needs of the crops. This in turn reduces discharges which are the major source of the environmental problems of irrigated farming.

As was noted in chapter 4, many surface water irrigators are insulated from the forces pushing up the social cost of water in the West. Consequently, such farmers have little incentive to adopt im-

---

26. John Spencer, Marc Horton, and Jim Gleaton, "The Sulphur Creek Pilot Project: A Practical Approach to Control of Pollutants Leaving Irrigated Farmlands," in Law and Skogerboe, Proceedings, pp. 307-319. A more recent assessment of the Sulphur Creek project was provided by Marc Horton in a July 1980 conversation with the author.

proved water management practices. Any effort to raise the cost of water to these farmers would meet with strong resistance as well as legal obstacles. However, improved water use on such farms might be encouraged and farmer opposition muted by measures to improve the marketability of water and allow the sale of unused water. While such changes would not increase the price these favored farmers paid for water, they would increase the opportunity costs of using water and, thereby, provide incentive to use it efficiently.

Even when farmers pay market water prices, environmental problems associated with runoff may occur which keep the social costs above the private costs. In most areas, however, the remaining environmental problems are likely to be greatly reduced if not inconsequential. When significant problems persist, they could be addressed by programs designed to meet the problems and conditions of a specific area. With the overall problem reduced in scope, a program focused on the remaining priority problem areas would be much more manageable than any comprehensive effort to control irrigation return flows.

Federal policies have failed to provide any effective control to the quality of irrigation return flows. Radosevich and Skogerboe offer several explanations for this failure. Officials in charge of implementing water quality and water rights laws in the seventeen western states were almost unanimous in the view that "relative to other water pollution problems, degradation from irrigation return flow as a statewide problem is not significant or has not been adequately identified.[27] Many states felt the EPA approach was not workable and others became turned off by the gyrations and uncertainties in the legal treatment of irrigation return flows. And finally, even when there has been agreement that a problem does exist, adoption of a suitable remedy has been deterred by both the physical difficulties of dealing with it and the philosophical resistance to federal controls.[28]

---

27. Radosevich and Skogerboe, _Achieving Irrigation Return Flow Quality Control_, p. 114.

28. Ibid., p. 124.

Despite the general lack of success of past efforts to control the quality of irrigation return flows, these efforts do provide some important lessons that could be useful for designing future policies. Considerations that should be taken into account in formulating such policies include: (1) the elusive nature of irrigation return flows makes them very difficult to control with an effluent approach such as permits; (2) there is considerable potential for mitigating environmental damages of erosion and water runoff through improved onfarm management of irrigation water; (3) farmers (along with almost everyone else) act in ways they perceive to be in their own best interests, and environmental costs are ignored in farmer's plans as long as the damages are borne by others; (4) farmers' aversion to controls combined with their large numbers and spatial dispersion make it difficult and expensive to direct farmer behavior through controls; (5) the nature of the problems, their importance, and the appropriate corrective measures vary widely among and within regions, making most national standards and control measures inefficient and costly.

Analysis of past efforts and the problems confronted led Radosevich and Skogerboe to develop and advocate an "influent control approach" to irrigation return flow quality control which relies primarily but not exclusively on incentives to encourage voluntary compliance.[29]   Their approach calls upon the states to undertake the following eight steps.   (1) Designate problem areas for focusing the state's efforts and an area entity (such as an existing irrigation organization) that would be responsible for monitoring, discussing ways to alleviate unreasonable water quality degradation, and encouraging voluntary changes in agricultural practices by those farmers identified as significant sources of pollutants within the designated problem

---

29. Their approach, which is briefly summarized here, is presented in Radosevich and Skogerboe, "An Influent Control Approach to Irrigation Return Flow Quality Management" in Law and Skogerboe, Proceedings, pp. 423-434, as well as in Radosevich and Skogerboe, Achieving Irrigation Return Flow Quality Control, section 8.

area. (2) Develop standards and criteria for beneficial use of water
that are consistent with the state's concept of a water right. (3)
Introduce incentives to use water more efficiently. Incentives might
be in the form of cost-sharing funds and technical assistance for
improvements in onfarm water management or permitting and encouraging
the trading, leasing, or selling of water saved through the adoption of
more efficient irrigation practices. (4) Include water quality provisions in new, transferred, or changed water rights. (5) Adopt and
enforce a reporting and recording system for water rights in order to
improve a state's ability to manage water quality. (6) Recognize that
some reasonable degradation of water quality will result from agricultural water use and that it would be excessively expensive and detri-
mental to irrigation to completely eliminate all pollutants. (7) Adopt
an agricultural practices act which includes sediment and erosion control, licensing and control over application of agricultural chemicals
to include pesticides and artificial fertilizers, and creation of an
agricultural practices control board. (8) Promote the cooperation or
integration of the various state agencies involved in water quantity
and quality issues.

While all eight of these suggestions merit careful consideration,
the highest returns may lie with step (3), introducing incentives to
use water more efficiently. As noted in chapter 5, where water is expensive, it is profitable for farmers to adopt a wide variety of water
conservation practices. And, as noted in this chapter, these water-
conserving irrigation practices generally are the most effective means
for reducing runoff, the source of most of the erosion and water quality contamination associated with irrigated farming. In most cases the
necessary incentives can be provided by eliminating the institutional
obstacles preventing water from being valued in accordance with its
scarcity value (see chapter 4). In a few cases the social costs of a
farmer's water use might remain well above the private costs even after
introduction of water markets. In such cases it might be desirable to
supplement the market mechanism with taxes designed to equate private
and social costs of water use. Or, if taxes are politically unaccept-

able, more direct measures could be used to guide farmer behavior towards socially more desirable farming practices. Although water markets would not eliminate the environmental problems associated with irrigation, those remaining after the obstacles to water transfers are eliminated would be less extensive than at present and, thus, more amenable to correction through specifically targeted state programs. And in addition to going a long way towards curbing the negative environmental impacts of irrigation, more active water markets would encourage a more efficient allocation of the West's increasingly valuable water resources.

Chapter 7

SUMMARY AND CONCLUSIONS

Previous chapters have examined the factors most likely to influence the future of irrigated agriculture in the West. Among the
factors examined are past trends in irrigated acreage, availability of
and emerging demands for water, water institutions, impacts of rising
energy costs and pumping depths on water costs and profitability,
emerging technologies, and environmental problems associated with irrigation. The principal objectives of this chapter are to consider the
implications of these various factors on the future of western irrigation and the overall policy implications of the analysis. First, the
factors affecting the future role of irrigation are briefly reviewed
and the irrigated acreage projections of several major government
studies are presented and discussed. Then projections as to both the
quantitative and qualitative changes likely to occur in western irrigation over the next several decades are made, based on the analysis of
this study. Some concluding comments on the broad environmental implications of these trends and the policy implications of the changing
water situation are presented.

Review of the Factors Affecting
the Future of Irrigation

Past Trends

Irrigation of about 25 million additional acres in the West was an
important factor in raising U.S. crop production by 70 percent from
1950 to 1977 without any net increase in total harvested acreage in the
United States. A very rough estimate of the impact of irrigation of
four principal crops on agricultural land use suggests that the higher
average yields on these irrigated lands reduced the harvested land
required to produce the 1977 national output of corn, sorghum, wheat,

and cotton by 7 million acres. Furthermore, by making high productivity farming possible in arid areas, irrigation has expanded the
acreage suitable for agriculture by about 10 to 13 million acres.

While western irrigation had a significant impact on the yields of
corn, sorghum, wheat, and cotton, it was not the principal factor
underlying the impressive increases in national average yields of the
four principal crops from 1950 to 1977. The combination of the improved yields on irrigated farms and the increase in the relative
acreage devoted to irrigation accounted for 13 percent of the national
rise in corn yields, 16 percent for sorghum, 7 percent for wheat, and
44 percent for cotton. Irrigation's contribution to production increases was even greater; 28 percent of the national increase in corn
production over this period was on irrigated lands, 20 percent for
sorghum, 12 percent for wheat, and 175 percent for cotton.

Two broad trends have dominated the rate and location of the
growth of western irrigated acreage for the past twenty-five years and
both are likely to continue in the future. First, the rate of growth
of irrigated acreage, which has declined steadily over the last three
decades, will continue to decline and second the locus of the growth,
which has moved from south to north, will remain in the north. From
1945 to 1954, 79 percent of the growth of irrigated acreage was in a
southern belt extending from Texas and Oklahoma to California. In
subsequent decades, this region contributed 31 percent and then only 1
percent of the overall growth of western irrigation. Analysis of the
water supply and demand conditions and the adverse impacts of rising
energy prices suggest that irrigated acreage has probably started or
will soon start to decline in this southern belt. In contrast, the
central and northern High Plains contribution to the expansion of
western irrigation rose from about 10 percent from 1945 to 1954 to over
90 percent from 1964 to 1974. Since Nebraska is one of the few western
states for which significant further expansion of irrigated acreage
appears likely, this percentage is likely to rise even further.

Water Supplies

Total surface water withdrawals for irrigation have fluctuated around a level trend since the mid-1950s, and the combined impact of several factors suggests this situation may continue for several more decades. First of all, total water requirements exceed average year streamflows within the West's principal irrigated areas, and there is little water available for expansion in most of the other areas. Where there is water for expansion, the increases will go primarily to non-agricultural users who can afford to pay higher water costs.

The comparative stability of surface water use for irrigation in the face of increasing water scarcity reflects in part the insulation of most surface water costs from both market considerations and rising energy costs. Undoubtedly, there will be transfers of water from agricultural to other uses, particularly within the water-scarce areas, as farmers are presented with increasing opportunities to sell their water rights. However, since large percentage increases in other water uses can be accommodated with small changes in irrigation water use, at least over the next several decades, the impacts of such transfers on irrigation will be gradual and relatively minor from the perspective of the entire West. Moreover, transfers of water rights from irrigation to other uses in the water-scarce areas are likely to be offset in part by modest increases in irrigation within the regions where surface water is still available for appropriation. Federal irrigation projects, which are encountering increasing resistance to their high investment costs and the high opportunity costs of diverting more scarce water to irrigation, will not make any further significant contribution to the expansion of western irrigation.

For several decades the growth of western irrigation has been based on groundwater withdrawals which rose threefold between 1950 and 1975. Currently groundwater withdrawals, which account for about 39 percent of all western irrigation water, result in the mining of more than 22 million acre-feet per year from western aquifers. Even though groundwater stocks are still large in relation to current use, and mining is not a threat to exhaust physically the water stored in any of the water resource regions or subregions in the foreseeable future, the combination of the overdrafts and rising energy costs threaten the economic supply of water for many irrigators. In some regions, especially the High Plains, the combination of increased pumping depths, lower well yields, and higher energy costs already has started to curtail pumping and irrigated acreage. In the absence of sharp increases in real crop prices, future expansion likely will be limited to areas with relatively low pumping depths or access to energy supplies under relatively favorable terms. But combining one or both of these conditions with favorable growing conditions will become increasingly rare.

The water available for irrigation is not likely to be augmented significantly in the next several decades through development of unconventional sources of supply. Although some forms of weather modification, particularly winter cloud seeding, appear technologically and economically promising, institutional obstacles are apt to inhibit its widespread adoption. Cost factors associated in part with their high energy intensity suggest that water importation and desalinization of sea water will not be profitable for use in irrigation. And a combination of cost, technical, and institutional uncertainties make icebergs an unlikely source of western water for the foreseeable future.

Institutional Factors

Western water law and management institutions were developed when water was plentiful in relation to demand. Important objectives of early water law and policy were to give investors clear and unambiguous title to water rights, to encourage the development of water resources, and to minimize uncertainty and conflict among users.

Today, the West faces a situation where water is scarce in relation to demand and the costs of developing new supplies are high in relation to its value in irrigation. Urban, industrial, recreational, and wildlife needs for fresh water are becoming increasingly competitive with irrigation. Yet, there has not been a corresponding adjustment in the laws and institutions that control and manage the resource. All too often the laws and institutions governing water use limit rather than facilitate the transfer of water to higher-valued uses and stifle rather than encourage conservation measures. Such deficiencies are common with most state water institutions, but they are especially severe in the case of federal projects which provide irrigators enormous subsidies but little to no opportunity or incentive to benefit from conservation.

Groundwater users do not have the security of long-term access to low cost water enjoyed by the owners of senior surface water rights. Groundwater supplies often are depletable resources threatened by the addition of new wells, and the costs of pumping are closely linked to energy costs. Individually, pumpers have improved the efficiency of their water use; collectively, they have sought government help in limiting depletion and curbing water cost increases. Many states have enacted or are considering legislation to limit pumping in order to extend the life of the aquifers. In terms of achieving a long-term efficient use of the resource, one problem with the current groundwater situation is that farmers' costs do not include the loss to neighboring farmers and future users of depleting an aquifer. Theoretically, taxes on pumping could internalize these costs, but, practically, it would be difficult to approximate the ideal level for such a tax, and any tax would be strongly resisted by pumpers.

Economic Factors

In general, groundwater irrigators pay the most for their water and are the most susceptible to further cost increases stemming from both rising energy costs and declining water levels. Groundwater costs vary widely depending on the pumping depth and the type and cost of the fuel. For a typical farmer pumping from 200 feet with electricity, water at the wellhead costs about $24 per acre-foot; distributing this water through a center-pivot system adds another $20 to $30 per acre-foot to irrigation costs (assuming 1980 energy prices and deflating all costs to 1977 constant dollars). A doubling of electricity prices would add another $32 to the costs of irrigation if no adjustments were made to the higher energy costs. Such cost levels would make it difficult to irrigate profitably grains, cotton, and many other crops in the absence of significant increases in crop prices. Farmers confronted with even higher pumping depths and declining aquifers will be even harder pressed to compete. Unless crop price increases compensate for rising water costs, many farmers will be forced to reduce or terminate their irrigation or radically alter their irrigation techniques over the next several decades. An increase in corn prices of roughly 25 percent would be required to offset the cost increases resulting from a doubling of electricity prices.[1]

Surface water costs also vary widely depending on the distance and height the water must be transported to arrive at the farm, the availability of subsidies, and the need for onfarm pumping to get it to the field. Surface water costs, however, tend to be considerably lower than groundwater costs and not as subject to change. Farmers with senior rights to neighboring surface waters which can be distributed through gravity have the lowest costs and are the least susceptible to future changes. For these fortunate farmers, water is virtually a free resource, and it is probably treated as such unless the farmer has an opportunity to sell or put to alternative uses any water saving. Another fortunate group of irrigators comprises the farmers receiving water from federal water projects. This highly subsidized water is used on nearly 20 percent of the West's irrigated acreage.

The opportunities for expanding irrigation with low-cost surface water are virtually nonexistent within the West's principal irrigated areas and very limited in other areas of the West. For the past several decades groundwater has been the basis of changes in western irrigation and it is likely to remain so for the foreseeable future.

---

1. For a farmer producing 105 bushels per acre, receiving $2.70 per bushel, pumping 2.5 acre-feet per acre a height of 200 feet, and using a center-pivot system, a 28.5 percent increase in corn prices would be required to compensate for a doubling of electricity prices (based on assumptions in tables 5-2 and 5-8).

The direction of future change will depend in large part on the ability of these farmers to adapt to rising water and energy costs.

Total water costs, of course, depend both on the unit cost of water and on the quantity of water applied. Farmers in arid zones who depend on irrigation to supply virtually all the crop water requirements are more affected by a rise in water costs than are those who rely on irrigation as a supplement to precipitation during the growing season. Most irrigators, however, have a wide range of opportunities for responding to high energy and water costs short of abandoning irrigation. Measures such as improving pump efficiency, tailwater reuse systems, and irrigation scheduling already are profitable under a variety of conditions. Future innovations undoubtedly will provide further opportunities for increasing the yields per unit of irrigation water and reducing the cost of water. Nevertheless, these innovations are not likely to alter the adverse impacts that rising energy costs and water scarcity are having on the profitability of irrigated relative to dryland farming since dryland farmers can also be expected to benefit from future technological developments. On the other hand, if real crop prices rise as some analysts predict, irrigators with their higher than average yields will tend to benefit more than dryland farmers.

Environmental Factors

A variety of environmental problems are associated with irrigation, but the only ones likely to have any significant effect on the role of irrigation are low streamflows, groundwater depletion, and salinity. Current water requirements, defined to include instream uses, already exceed average streamflows in the most favorable areas for irrigation. If irrigation water use were curtailed to the levels that will "ensure maintenance of streamflow for optimum fish and wildlife habitat and other environmental values," irrigated acreage would have to be reduced by 22 percent in comparison to the moderate export run for 1985 without environmental restrictions according to analysis undertaken by the U.S. Department of Agriculture as part of the Agricultural Resource Assessment Systems.[2] And, of course, in those areas where the aquifers are being mined, withdrawals eventually must be reduced.

An estimated 25 to 35 percent of the West's irrigated lands have salinity problems. But the lands where salinity is likely to significantly curtail production comprise a much smaller percentage. The productivity of several million acres, primarily in the lower Colorado River Basin and California's San Joaquin Valley, are threatened by high salt levels. The annual damages to agricultural plus municipal and industrial users of the salt-laden waters already probably exceed $100 million, and damages will rise unless preventive measures are taken. Improved basinwide and onfarm water management have great potential for reducing salinity levels and mitigating the damages from high salt levels. However, institutional obstacles to adopting improved basinwide management schemes and the high costs of some of the structural measures that might achieve the same result suggest an increasing number of farmers will be confronted with serious salt problems. Nevertheless, although the impacts will be serious within the affected areas, the overall impact on the productive potential of western irrigation is not likely to exceed 2 to 3 percent over the next several decades.

Another environmental problem that could affect the growth of irrigation over the next several decades is groundwater pollution from the infiltration of agricultural chemicals. Agricultural chemicals, especially nitrogen, are readily leached into the groundwater of the Nebraska Sandhills, which is the most likely area to experience a significant expansion of irrigation. Good onfarm water management can keep nitrate levels within tolerable levels, but failure to adopt such practices could lead to state intervention to enforce better management practices, possibly limiting the growth of irrigation in the area.

---

2. Paul Fuglestad, Robert Niehaus, and Paul Rosenberry, Agricultural Resource Assessment System: Alternative Future Analysis, vol. II (Washington, D.C., U.S. Department of Agriculture, 1978) pp. 68-89.

Projections of Irrigated Acreage

National-Interregional Agricultural Projections System

One of the two major models of U.S. agricultural production providing medium and long-term projections of irrigation is the National-
Interregional Agricultural Projections (NIRAP) system developed by the
Economics and Statistics Service of the U.S. Department of Agriculture
(USDA). NIRAP is a simulation model capable of providing considerable
subsector and regional detail of the agricultural sector. The model's
irrigation figures start from census of agriculture data and rely
largely on trends, adjusted to reflect the comments of local experts,
to project future levels.

Under the baseline (Series II) assumptions, NIRAP projects irrigated acreage in the seventeen western states at 39.7 million in 1985,
41.3 million in 1990, and 44.5 millon in 2000.[3] All these figures are
well below the 50.2 million acres the NRI estimates were irrigated as
of 1977. The low NIRAP projections do not stem from a conclusion that
irrigated acreage will decline over the next two decades. Rather the
low projections largely reflect the fact that the model uncritically
accepts the census data as a starting point. This feature together
with the partial reliance on trends to determine future changes in
irrigation suggest the NIRAP system has little value as an indicator of
future irrigated acreage.

The Iowa State Model

The other major model which projects irrigated acreage and production is a linear programming model developed at Iowa State's Center for
Agricultural and Rural Development (CARD) under the leadership of Earl

---

3. The Series II (moderate increase) assumptions include population
levels of 242 million by 1990 and 260 million by 2000, a 3 percent per
annum increase in GNP, a 2.2 percent per annum increase in disposable
income, and a moderate growth of agricultural exports. The NIRAP
results were provided by the Economics and Statistics Service of USDA.

Heady. The objective function of this model is to derive the least-cost means of producing exogenously determined demand levels subject to the restraints built into the model as to the availability of land, water, and other factors. The model divides the nation into 105 producing areas, each of which has restraints for land availability (broken down into nine dry and irrigated land classes), the level of production of eight crops, and a minimum irrigated acreage.[4] The Iowa State model and its variations have been used for several major studies designed to assess long-term agricultural developments. Among these studies are the Agricultural Resource Assessment System (ARAS) and the work mandated by the Soil and Water Resources Conservation Act (Public Law 95-192) which are considered briefly below.

The Department of Agriculture was assigned the task of developing the agricultural and related water use projections for the Second National Water Assessment. In response, the department linked up with Iowa State's CARD to develop the Agricultural Resource Assessment System. The Iowa State linear programming model, which was substantially revised for the purpose, was used for the ARAS projections. Alternative scenarios involving variations in factors such as the demand for U.S. agricultural products, land and water conservation standards, and energy development were examined. Among the outputs from the model are projections of irrigated acreage.

The ARAS projections of irrigated acreage under the "modified" central choice" (which is considered the most likely situation), the high demand for U.S. agricultural products, as well as all other scenarios considered are well below the 1977 levels estimated by the National Resources Inventory. The modified central choice scenario projects western irrigation at 38.4 million acres in 1985 and 40.0 million acres in 2000. The high export scenario increases the acreages

---

4. The model is described in Anton D. Meister and Kenneth J. Nicol, A Documentation of the National Water Assessment Model of Regional Agricultural Production, Land and Water Use, and Environmental Interaction (Ames, Iowa, The Center for Agricultural and Rural Development, Iowa State University, December 1975).

by only 0.7 million acres in 1985 and 0.3 million in 2000. A land and water conservation scenario which constrains cropping patterns and conservation practices to maintain long-run productivity actually reduces irrigated acreage to 39.2 million in 2000.[5]

Since the Iowa State model provides a least-cost solution, one interpretation of the ARAS results is that any other outcome would entail higher production costs Within the assumptions of the model, this interpretation, of course, is correct. But since the projected irrigation levels are so low in comparison to actual levels, the results raise some question about how irrigation is treated in the model. The economics of irrigating differ considerably depending on the availability of the infrastructure required to get water to the field. For example, if the well and canals are already in place, their costs are incurred whether or not the farmer actually irrigates. Thus, the initial level of irrigation and the availability of the required infrastructure are likely to be key determinants of the level of irrigation deemed profitable by the model. The ARAS base year levels are from the 1967 CNI updated to 1973 for irrigation; allowance is also made for Bureau of Reclamation projects expected to be in place as of 1985 and 2000. The comparatively high level of irrigation in the 1977 NRI raises questions as to whether these assumptions accurately reflect the economic situations facing farmers. On the other hand, the analysis of water institutions, water supply conditions, and economic factors presented in earlier chapters suggest that most irrigators are not paying the full costs of water. Thus, the conclusion that a more socially efficient producton would have a lot fewer acres under irrigation than are actually irrigated may well be correct. Nevertheless, as it is currently used, the Iowa State model is a poor vehicle for projecting irrigated acreage. Indeed, although the ARAS system was undertaken to

---

5. Marlin Hanson, Paul Fuglestad, and Roger Strohbehn, Agricultural Resource Assessment System: Benchmark Analysis and Modified Central Case, vol. I and app. A; and Fuglestad and coauthors, Alternative Futures Analysis, vol. II and app. A.

provide projections for the Second National Water Assessment, the Water Resources Council (WRC) concluded that the model was not capable of describing accurately the agricultural resource situation; alternative projections (presented below) were made for the Assessment.

More recently, the Iowa State Model has been used by the USDA in assessing the nation's long-term soil and water needs as mandated by the Soil and Water Resources Conservation Act (RCA). The land base data used in the model were updated for the RCA process to incorporate the results of the 1977 NRI. Yet, the RCA projections of irrigated acreage still remain well below the NRI's estimated level for 1977. Irrigation as of 2000 is projected at 33.9 million acres for the medium demand case and at 40.1 million acres for the high-demand case.[6]

The Iowa State Model also was used to complement the Resources for the Future (RFF) study of the resource and environmental impacts of agricultural growth. The two model runs done for the RFF study assume demand for U.S. farm output is high in comparison to the RCA moderate scenario The focus of the model runs for RFF was to examine the adoption of conservation tillage practices and erosion levels under alternative assumptions. Irrigated acreage for 2010 was projected at 45.6 million under the scenario with no restrictions on the model's allocation of tillage practices and at 43.7 million when the land placed in conservation tillage was restricted.

Second National Water Assessment

As noted above, the ARAS was initiated to provide estimates of irrigated acreage and associated water use for the Second National Water Assessment, but the results of this analysis were not incorporated into the Assessment. Instead, two separate estimates of

---

6. The assumptions of high- and medium-demand cases differ by more than the demand levels. Assumptions used in the RCA linear program are described in U.S. Department of Agriculture, 1980 Appraisal, Review Draft Part II (Washington, D.C., 1980) chapter 2. RCA data were provided by David Post, U.S. Department of Agriculture, Soil Conservation Service.

irrigated acreage are presented in the Assessment--the National Futures (NF) estimate which was developed by group consensus of representatives from the federal agencies involved in the Assessment and the State and Regional Futures (SRF) developed by the committees established by the WRC in each region. These committees were composed of local river basin, U.S. Geological Survey, and Soil Conservation Service officials and others.

Both the 1975 base-year levels and the 1985 and 2000 irrigation projections of the two groups differ significantly. Not only are the SRF base year estimates higher than the NF (46.3 versus 40.5 million acres), the rates of expansion of the SRF projections also are much higher. The NF projects a 7 percent increase in irrigated acreage by 1985 to 43.4 million acres and a further increase of only 1.2 million acres by 2000. In comparison, the SRF projects a 16 percent rise to 53.6 million acres in 1985 and an additional 14 percent rise to 61.0 million acres by 2000. By the turn of the century the SRF projections show 37 percent more acres irrigated than do the NF projections. The Assessment does not provide justification for either set of irrigation projections.

Projections From This Study

Over the next several decades changes in total irrigated acreage will depend in large part on what happens to agricultural prices. Indeed, the relation between crop price levels and the expansion of irrigation will be much stronger than in the past. Past expansion was primarily a function of technological developments, water projects, and a learning process as farmers followed what their more progressive neighbors had proved successful. Future expansion will be influenced by very different cost and resource conditions which make past trends of limited use for making projections and the profitability of irrigated relative to dryland farming in many areas dependent on higher crop prices.

Although irrigation in many areas of the West is constrained by physical and institutional limits on developing new water supplies, there are additional lands with access to water for irrigation. Within these areas, the important constraints on irrigation are economic. Significant increases in product prices would offset the negative impacts of high energy prices and increasing pumping depths; the development of new irrigated lands would be stimulated, and the decline in irrigated farming in areas with significant groundwater mining would be slowed.

Table 7-1 summarizes what should be viewed as very rough projections of irrigated acreage by farm production region during the decade from 2000 to 2010 under alternative assumptions of no change and a 25 percent increase in real crop prices.[7] These projections are impressionistic estimates drawing on the analysis of recent trends, water supplies, and institutional, economic, and environmental factors examined in chapters 2 through 6 of this study.

Even in the absence of any significant change in crop prices, some net expansion of western irrigation seems likely. Most of the expansion will be in the Northern Plains states, and more specifically within the Nebraska Sandhills. This area has considerable potential for expansion, and based on recent investments in wells and center pivots, irrigation investment in the area is profitable at current price levels. Modest increases in irrigation within the Dakotas is also

---

7. A range of 2000 to 2010 for the projection period is used to indicate the very rough nature of the projections as well as to reflect a suspicion that total irrigated acreage in the West will peak during this decade in the absence of major institutional changes providing the owners of surface water rights with strong incentives to adopt water conservation practices. In 1977 constant dollars, the average prices received by farmers in the United States from 1975 to 1980 was $2.21 per bushel of corn, $3.01 per bushel of wheat, $3.69 per hundred weight of sorghum, and $0.56 per pound of cotton lint. Inflating these prices by 36 percent would convert them to 1980 prices. These price levels are based on 1980 preliminary prices from U.S. Department of Agriculture, Agricultural Outlook (Washington, D.C., March 1981) p. 27 and 1975 to 1979 prices from U.S. Department of Agriculture, Agricultural Prices Annual Summary 1979 (Washington, D.C., June 1980).

Table 7-1. Projections of Irrigated Acreage by Farm Production Region
Under Alternative Crop Price Scenarios

(millions of acres)

| | | Projections for 2000 to 2010 | |
| | | No change in | 25 percent rise in real |
Region	1977 NRI Estimates[a]	real crop prices	crop prices
Northern Plains	10.7	15.0	16.5
Southern Plains	9.0	7.0	8.0
Mountain	17.2	16.5	17.5
Pacific	13.3	15.0	16.0
17 Western states	50.2	53.5	58.0

[a]From table 2-1.

likely, although irrigation will remain relatively unimportant in these states. The increases within the Northern Plains will be partly offset by some reduction in irrigation in the Kansas and Nebraska High Plains.

The impacts of high energy costs and declining groundwater tables will force a significant decline in irrigation by the turn of the century within the High Plains of Texas and Oklahoma. Increases in irrigated acreage within the eastern areas of these states will be modest in comparison to the declines in the western areas. Thus, with no change in crop prices, a 2 million acre decline in irrigation is projected for the Southern Plains.

The Mountain region will experience little net change in irrigated acreage but within this large, heterogeneous area comprising eight states, significant changes in the location of irrigation are likely. The southern areas and eastern Colorado, where current levels of irrigation are dependent on nonrenewable water sources, will experience some decline in irrigated acreage. In the absence of high crop prices, these declines will be offset only in part by some modest increases in irrigation within the rest of the Mountain region.

In the Pacific region a modest overall expansion of irrigation is likely even with no increase in crop prices. A 1974 California water plan by the Department of Water Resources projected their state's irrigation would reach 9.5 to 10.6 million acres by 1990 and 9.8 to 12.1 million by 2010.[8] These levels compare to the NRI's estimate of 8.9 million acres in 1977 and the state's estimate of 9.3 to 9.6 million as of 1980.[9] The increases implied by the higher projections of the plan are improbable in view of the other demands being made on the state's water, the high cost of developing new supplies, groundwater mining in some regions stemming from current water use patterns, the prospective loss of nearly 1 million acre-feet per year of Colorado River water once the Central Arizona Project is completed, and the salinity problems threatening a million acres in the San Joaquin Valley. Indeed, the 1974 water plan did not even consider water as a constraint on expanding irrigation. Correcting for this oversight makes the high projections of the 1974 plan appear much too optimistic. Overall, California's irrigated acreage is not likely to rise significantly above 10 million acres by 2000. While the Pacific Northwest is the area least affected by water shortages, the region's water is becoming increasingly valuable for use in hydropower production and preserving the wildlife and amenities of the area. Furthermore, very inexpensive electricity is no longer available for expanding pumping. Consequently, additions to irrigated acreage in the Northwest over the next several decades are not likely to push the totals for Washington and Oregon much beyond 5 million acres without significant crop price increases.

---

8. State of California, The Resources Agency, Department of Water Resources, The California Water Plan: Outlook in 1974, Summary Report, Department of Water Resources Bulletin No. 160-74 (Sacramento, Calif., 1974) pp. 34-35.

9. Based on Agricultural Commissioner reports for each county and the Resources Agency's land use surveys, Warren Cole estimates there were 9.3 million acres with full irrigation and 0.3 million with low water applications as of 1980. Personal communication February 28, 1980 with Warren Cole, supervising engineer of the California Department of Water Resources.

A 25 percent increase in real farm prices might add another 4.5 million irrigated acres in the West, more than doubling the growth of irrigated acreage over the next two to three decades. Yet, even assuming such a substantial increase in crop prices, irrigation is projected to rise only 15.5 percent over two to three decades. In comparison, western irrigation doubled over the previous twenty-five years, rising 21 percent from 1967 to 1977. The long-term elasticity of irrigation with respect to crop prices implied in the projections of table 7-1 is only about 0.3 (that is, a 25 percent increase in crop prices increases irrigated acreage by about 8 percent.) This relative insensitivity to real price levels is primarily a reflection of two factors--the fact that no foreseeable crop price levels will make irrigation competitive with most municipal and industrial water uses and the importance of institutional and resource factors in determining the level of irrigation. Few areas have the water to support a major expansion of irrigation under any realistic projections of crop prices. Groundwater is often the only water available for expansion, but many western aquifers are already being mined at significant rates. Major expansion of surface water irrigation outside of the areas that have other significant handicaps to high-productivity farming requires institutional changes which will provide irrigators with incentives to conserve water. Conservation would enable the available supplies to be spread over more acres. In the absence of such changes, groundwater will remain the primary water source for new irrigation. While high crop prices will encourage greater pumping, the impacts of increased pumping on total irrigated acreage may be relatively short-lived in view of the nonrenewable nature of much of the groundwater.

Qualitative Changes in Western Irrigation

The nature as well as the rate of growth of irrigation will be very different from the past when irrigated farming was stimulated by the availability of inexpensive water and energy. Water withdrawals will be reduced as it becomes more profitable both to make water-saving investments and to reduce the water delivered to plant even if it means some reduction in crop yields. While total irrigated acreage may not peak until the first decade of the next century, total withdrawals for irrigation probably will peak much sooner, perhaps within the next decade. Improved yields to water inputs and shifts to higher-value crops will enable the value of production from irrigated farms to rise even after the quantities of land and water in irrigation have peaked and started to decline. Thus, both water withdrawals and acreage are likely to become increasingly poor indicators of changes in the contribution of irrigated output to national agricultural production.

As is evident from a recent report of an interagency task force group which assessed the potential for improving the efficiency of irrigation water use and management in the United States, most water conservation opportunities actually imply a substitution between water and other inputs such as capital, labor, and improved water and agronomic management. There are, of course, limits on the substitutions which are profitable, and these limits depend importantly on the cost of water. The task force group concluded that in addition to "ongoing programs, public and private investments of up to five billion dollars should be made over the next three decades to implement needed water conservation measures."[10] These investments could "result in decreasing gross annual diversions by 15 to 20 million acre-feet and making two to five million acre-feet of water available for new uses."[11]

The conclusions of the task force study draw on the results of Soil Conservation Service (SCS) field estimates of the measures required to achieve a "reasonable level of irrigation water management" in the seventeen western states. The major means of reducing conveyance losses is lining canals or piping to reduce seepage losses. Further reductions in conveyance losses could be made through consolidation realignment, or enlargement of canals and control structures.

---

10. U.S. Department of Interior, U.S. Department of Agriculture, Environmental Protection Agency, Irrigation Water Use and Management: An InterAgency Task Force Report (Washington, D.C., GPO, June 1979) p. ix.

11. Ibid.

In total, an estimated 3.1 million acre-feet of water per year could be saved through off-farm investments of $6.2 billion.

Onfarm water losses can be reduced through lining or piping of field distribution systems, land leveling, water control or measuring structures, automation, tailwater recovery systems, and changing to sprinkler or drip irrigation. The SCS survey concluded that "about one-fourth of the irrigated land in surface systems requires land leveling, over one-third could use tailwater recovery systems to reduce flows, and about 60 percent should use more effective ways to schedule and apply water to meet the needs of the crops and reduce deep percolation and excessive return flow."[12] In total, an estimated investment of $8.4 billion plus an annual cost of $142 million for irrigation water management could reduce onfarm water losses by 4.5 million acre-feet per year.

In addition to the reductions in irrecoverable or incidental water losses, other major changes in water management are implied by these infrastructure investments. For example, the proposed measures would result in a 38.6 million acre-feet reduction in water withdrawals, a 35.3 million acre-feet reduction in return flows, a 4.3 million acre-feet increase in crop water consumption (which helps increase farm output by $500 million per year), and a $109 million reduction in energy requirements.[13]

Future federal water projects likely will focus more on improving water use efficiency and preserving the productivity of existing irri-

---

12. Ibid., pp. 84-85.

13. Ibid., pp. 84-85, and tables 14, 15, and 18. California's Department of Water Resources has serious reservations about whether the water savings identified in the task force report actually refer to water that would otherwise be unusable. Gerald Meral, deputy director of the Department of Water Resources, suggests that the analysis for California did not differentiate savings subject to reuse from those that would otherwise be lost to the system. It is conservation of the latter type that can be viewed as an alternative to developing new supplies through construction of reservoirs or interbasin transfer facilities. (Meral's reservations were expressed in a December 4, 1980 letter to the author.)

gation rather than continuing the past concentration on developing new supplies. Numerous opportunities for reducing onfarm and off-farm water losses through structural means are noted in the task force study cited above, and major structural solutions for reducing salinity problems in the Colorado River Basin and the San Joaquin Valley are noted in chapter 6. Even if the economics of such projects are not more favorable, they have political advantages relative to supply-oriented projects. Well-organized and powerful environmental interests can be expected to oppose efforts to develop additional western streamflows for use in agriculture, but there is no established opposition to conservation or salinity control projects other than those concerned with the budgetary considerations of any major government project.

Nonstructural measures may prove to be even more important than the structural alternatives for improving the returns to water in irrigation. Improved irrigation scheduling, higher-value or less water-using crops, tillage practices designed to conserve soil moisture, and seed varieties offering higher returns to water will become increasingly attractive to farmers confronted with high water costs. Furthermore, the technologies available for responding to high water costs can be expected to expand significantly in the coming decades. For example, California's Department of Water Resources believes there is considerable potential for reducing evaporation from cropped areas and increasing the portion of transpiration directed to commercially desirable features of the plant. Three requests for proposals were issued by the department in the fall of 1980 for (1) preparing a report on cropping pattern changes to conserve water, (2) a study of the relationships between evaporation from soil and water surfaces and plant transpiration to identify means of reducing evaporation from irrigated lands and to evaluate the potential for water conservation savings by such means, and (3) a report on potential for saving water through the use of improved cultivars.[14]

---

14. Department of Water Resources, The Resources Agency, State of California, requests for proposals nos. 80 AG-CONS-2, 5, and 8.

The overall potential for increasing irrigated production through a combination of structural and nonstructural measures without increases in total water use is great. The extent to which this potential is realized depends in large part on the institutions and policies affecting water use. Before turning to the overall policy implications of the analysis, however, the environmental issues are reviewed since alternative policies should be evaluated for their environmental as well as for their production implications.

Environmental Implications of Anticipated Qualitative and Quantitative Changes in Western Irrigation

The changing character of the growth of irrigation is having some beneficial environmental effects. As is noted in chapter 6, the environmental problems of erosion, sedimentation, and water quality degradation which are associated with irrigation generally diminish as the application efficiency of water increases. Thus, the same investments and irrigation practices that are becoming attractive to irrigators as water costs rise also help reduce the environmental damages caused by overirrigation.

Adoption of improved water management practices, however, largely has been limited to farms with expensive water. Although water costs are generally rising, a large segment of surface water users remain insulated from the impacts of increasing water scarcity. Little improvement in the environmental impacts of their farming practices is likely to occur as long as these farmers pay little for their water and nothing for the environmental damages resulting from its use.

Understanding the environmental implications of irrigated agriculture requires looking beyond the impacts associated with the irrigation process itself. Irrigation is both a land-conserving technology and a means of expanding the land that can be used for cropping in arid and semiarid regions. Since irrigated yields tend to be much higher than the overall average, any ..ange in the number of irrigated acres affects the total number of cropped and pastured acres required to produce a given output. Consequently, an increase in irrigation reduces the pressures on other agriculural land resources, an outcome of increasing importance when the marginal lands that would be brought into production in the absence of irrigation are apt to be particularly susceptible to erosion. The anticipated reduction in the growth of irrigation suggests that future growth of agricultural output will place greater pressures on the land base.

Several studies suggest the environmental costs of substantially increasing the cropland base would be high. A study of the potential for and costs of converting woodland and pastureland to cropland in the Mississippi Delta region estimates that conversion would increase soil erosion by an average of 8.38 to 14.06 tons per acre per year depending on the number of acres and the soil groups converted and the crop rotations selected.[15] A similar study of the State of Iowa indicates that converting up to 2.5 million acres to cropland in Iowa would require using larger portions of highly erodable lands with steep slopes.[16] To some extent, these are environmental costs that have been avoided by the growth of western irrigation; assessing policies that will affect the future role of irrigation should take these impacts into account. For example, restricting water withdrawals to ensure streamflow for optimum fish and wildlife habitat (and, thereby decreasing irrigation water use by 22 percent) undoubtedly would hasten the conversion of highly erodable lands to crops. These conversions in turn would have adverse impacts on water quality in the affected areas.

15. Robert N. Shulstad, Ralph D. May, and Billy E. Herrington, Jr., "Cropland Conversion Study for the Mississippi Delta Region" (Fayetteville, University of Arkansas, a report prepared for Resources for the Future, April 30, 1979) pp. 139-142.

16. Orley M. Amos, Jr., "Supply of Potential Cropland in Iowa." Ph.D. dissertation, Iowa State University, preliminary draft, Feb. 7, 1979, p. 149.

Final Conclusions and Policy Implications

The West is not running out of water. It is running out of low-cost water, however, and no set of policies and programs will alter the fact that water is becoming increasingly valuable in the West.

As a resource becomes scarcer and more costly, development tends to move in directions that conserve on the use of that resource. These changes take two forms. For a given activity, it becomes increasingly profitable to substitute other inputs for the increasingly scarce factors of production. In addition, the mix of activities tends to shift toward those that produce higher values per unit of the scarce resource. The West is undergoing such a transition in response to the increasing value of its water. But this transition is proving unnecessarily costly and disruptive to the region's overall development because the laws, institutions, and policies governing the allocation and use of western water often preserve an illusion of cheap water for some users which increases the scarcity imposed on others.

Most of the legal and institutional arrangements that influence western water use evolved during and are most appropriate for conditions of relative water abundance. An important objective of the 1902 Reclamation Act was to stimulate settlement of the arid West, and the subsidies built into federal irrigation projects undoubtedly encouraged western rural settlement during the first five or six decades of this century. State water laws helped attract investment to the West by providing assurances of continued access to water, and these laws provided settlers some protection from unscrupulous developers by restricting the transfer of water rights. These water policies and programs which fostered western development in the first half of this century are having negative effects on the region under the water scarcity conditions prevalent in the 1980s. By insulating some water users from the increasing value of the resource, other users and potential users find it more difficult and costly to fulfill their needs. Administration of federal water projects as well as state water laws and policies not only allow an inefficient use of western water, they often ensure inefficiency by reducing or eliminating the incentives and opportunities for transferring water to higher-value uses.

Farmers have never had to pay for water rights, only for the cost of getting water from its source to the farm. Even these costs often have been subsidized. Charging farmers for only the costs of delivering water to their fields is an economically sound pricing policy under conditions of abundant water. When there is sufficient water in a stream to satisfy all users and no environmental costs are associated with a given use, there are no additional costs to withdrawing surface water. Likewise, as long as groundwater pumping does not exceed natural recharge or affect neighboring users, the farmer's pumping costs reflect the social costs of groundwater use. But these conditions no longer prevail in most of the West. Commonly, water requirements exceed streamflows and groundwater use exceeds recharge. Consequently, the water itself has a value which should be reflected in user's costs if water is to be used efficiently.

Improving the efficiency of western water use does not require forcing the owners of water rights to pay for what has been legally given to them. Indeed, any attempt to abrogate these rights would be futile and potentially damaging to the region since it would threaten the entire legal and institutional structure that has brought order to the allocation of western water. A more acceptable alternative for providing incentives to conserve water in areas where it is scarce is to allow and facilitate the sale of water that is not used by the owners of the water rights. Then, even if a farmer does not have to pay for the water, there would be an opportunity cost to putting the water to any particular use. Water laws vary among states, but in many western states, the principal changes in existing water laws required to implement water markets would be to classify water sales as a beneficial use and to eliminate provisions making water rights appurtenant to a given piece of land. Of course, farmers must have an opportunity as well as a right to transfer water if a more efficient allocation is to be achieved. Establishing effective water markets will require the creation or transformation of institutions to provide for the transfers of money and water.

Since irrigation is a relatively low-value user, a more market-oriented allocation system is likely to transfer water from irrigation to municipal, industrial, and other uses. However, these negative impacts on irrigation might be more than offset by the added incentive that would be provided to increase the returns to the water used in irrigation. Moreover, since irrigation is such a predominant user of western waters, a small improvement in the efficiency of irrigation might save enough water to satisfy nonagricultural water needs without significantly reducing irrigated acreage. Where irrigated acreage is reduced, market forces would focus the impacts on the lower-value uses such as forage and pasture. A reduction in the environmental damages from irrigation practices would be a further benefit of policies designed to make water costs more nearly reflect the scarcity value of the resource.

If the transition from water abundance to scracity allows for an efficient use of the resources over time, irrigation will contribute to agricultural production and growth for many more decades. Future potential lies primarily in increasing the returns to water, not in the development of new water supplies. Realization of this potential requires providing incentives to conserve water and encourage the development of more effective ways for farmers to respond to higher water and energy costs and salinity levels. The social returns to agricultural research have been very high in the past, and the benefits from research to develop improved irrigation practices, new crops and seed varieties requiring less water, improved understanding of the transpiration of plants, and a host of other promising areas for increasing the options for irrigated farming are likely to be very high in the future. These research efforts, which represent the real hope for the long-term contribution of western irrigation to agricultural production, should be encouraged. Nevertheless, innovations will be adopted in a timely way only if the institutions provide the correct incentives regarding use of the region's scarce resources.

Western irrigation is not likely to make the contribution to agricultural growth that it did when water was abundant and cheap even if the relevant research is encouraged and institutional reforms are made. The inevitable adjustments to declining groundwater supplies will bring hardship to some areas. Nevertheless, the socially most expensive response would be to provide subsidies to either enable farmers to pump to greater depths or to import water. An area where agriculture depends on declining groundwater supplies inevitably will become a higher-cost irrigated producer. Spreading the cost increases among the general public clearly helps farmers in the affected region. But it also ensures higher overall production costs due to inefficient use of society's resources. The serious problems will emerge if we attempt to keep water inexpensive when it is not. Such efforts will ensure its inefficient use and push the social costs of irrigated production to levels well above those of the dryland alternatives.[17]

The underlying resource conditions as well as the national interests in the use of western water have changed dramatically within the last several decades; there is now need for a corresponding adjustment in the laws and institutions that control and manage the resource. The potential beneficiaries of such reform surely outnumber the potential losers. Irrigators are not helped by existing policies that prevent them from selling water rights. To the contrary, most farmers would welcome the opportunity to sell their water for many times its value in agriculture. Nor are current policies justified as necessary protection of the nation's capacity to produce food and fiber. To the contrary, these policies may limit the long-term role of irrigation by discouraging farmers from adopting water conservation measures and by hastening the mining of nonrenewable supplies. Existing water laws and institutions, however, have proved useful to some groups as a vehicle for at least delaying developments that they consider undesirable. For instance, water rights issues have been used to stall energy projects by groups concerned primarily with impacts on the environment and lifestyles. The concerns of such groups may be legitimate and, indeed, might warrant major changes in the design or even

---

17. Even now society may be paying more for farm output produced on its irrigated lands. Certainly, irrigated production would not be as great as it is if farmers paid the full cost of getting water to their farms. Moreover, as noted earlier, results of the national agricultural model developed at Iowa State University suggest that our nation's agricultural output could be produced at lower cost with fewer irrigated acres.

cancellation of a project. But there are environmental laws and regulations which enable the airing of such concerns, and these should be
strengthened if society believes they provide inadequate protection.
Such concerns do not justify retention of outmoded and inefficient
water institutions.

INDEX